NEW PROCLAMATION

New Proclamation
Year A 2011

Advent through Holy Week
November 28, 2010—April 24, 2011

Mary Lin Hudson

Robert P. Hoch

Susan Marie Smith

Craig A. Satterlee

David B. Lott, Editor

Fortress Press

Minneapolis

NEW PROCLAMATION
Year A 2011
Advent through Holy Week
November 28, 2010—April 24, 2011

Unless otherwise noted, scripture quotations are the author's own translation or from
the New Revised Standard Version Bible, copyright © 1989 by the Division of Christian
Education of the National Council of Churches of Christ in the USA, and are used with
permission.

Illustrations: Joel Nickel, Peggy Adams Parker, Robyn Sand Anderson, Meg Bussey, and
Paula Wiggins, © 2010 Augsburg Fortress.
Cover design: Laurie Ingram
Book design: Sharon Martin

Library of Congress Cataloging-in-Publication Data
The Library of Congress has catalogued this series as follows.
New Proclamation: Year A, 2010–2011 Advent through Holy Week.
      p. cm.
    Includes bibliographical references.
    ISBN 978-0-8066-9631-7
        1. Church year. I. Moloney, Francis J.
    BV30 .N48 2001
    2511.6dc21 2001023746

Library of Congress Cataloging-in-Publication Data
ISBN 978-0-8066-9631-7

Manufactured in the U.S.A.
13   12   11   10   1   2   3   4   5   6   7   8

Contents

Epiphany—Time after Epiphany / Ordinary Time
Robert P. Hoch

Lent
Susan Marie Smith

Holy Week
Craig A. Satterlee

Preface

For nearly four decades Fortress Press has offered an ecumenical preaching resource built around the three-year lectionary cycle, a tradition that this latest edition of *New Proclamation* continues. *New Proclamation* is grounded in the belief that a deeper understanding of the biblical pericopes in both their historical and liturgical contexts is the best means to inform and inspire preachers to deliver engaging and effective sermons. For this reason, the most capable North American biblical scholars and homileticians are invited to contribute to *New Proclamation*.

New Proclamation has always distinguished itself from most other lectionary resources by offering brand-new editions each year, each dated according to the church year in which it will first be used, and featuring a fresh set of authors. Yet each edition is planned as a timeless resource that preachers will want to keep on their bookshelves for future reference for years to come. In addition, *New Proclamation,* true to its ecumenical scope, has traditionally offered commentary on all of the major lectionary traditions. Now, reflecting changes in practices among the mainline Protestant denominations, those number just two: the *Revised Common Lectionary* (RCL) and the Roman Catholic *Lectionary for Mass* (LFM).[1]

New Proclamation is published in two volumes per year. This first volume covers all the Sunday lections and major festivals from Advent through Easter Vigil. The second volume, which will be published later this year, begins with new commentary on the Easter Vigil and covers the remaining Sunday lections and major festivals through Christ the King Sunday. For those churches that celebrate minor feast days and solemnities, including saints' days, denominational days such as Body and Blood of Christ (Corpus Christi) or Reformation Day, and national days and topical celebrations, a separate volume covering the texts for those days is available: *New Proclamation Commentary on Feasts, Holy Days, and Other Celebrations* (ed. David B. Lott; Fortress Press, 2007).

Longtime users of *New Proclamation* will note that this latest edition adopts a fresh look, which ties the series in visually with Augsburg Fortress's popular worship resource *Sundays and Seasons*. We hope that this change not only makes the text more readable and accessible, but also encourages readers to use these fine resources in tandem with each other. We also invite you to visit and consider a subscription to this volume's companion Web site, www.NewProclamation.com, which offers access not only to this book's contents, but also commentary from earlier editions, up-to-the-minute thoughts on the connection between texts and current events, user forums, and other resources to help you develop your sermons and enhance your preaching.

What has not changed with this edition is the high quality of the content that *New Proclamation* provides to preachers and those interested in studying the lectionary texts. Each writer offers an introduction to her or his commentary that provides insights into the background and spiritual significance of that season (or portion thereof), as well as ideas for planning one's preaching during that time. In addition, the application of biblical texts to contemporary situations is an important concern of each contributor. Exegetical work is concise, and thoughts on how the texts address today's world, congregational issues, and personal situations have a prominent role.

The writers in this volume all have in common that they hold seminary teaching positions in which they straddle the interconnected worlds of preaching and worship, yet readers will appreciate how each one approaches the texts with his or her unique voice. Mary Lin Hudson, Robert Hoch, and Susan Marie Smith make their Fortress Press debuts with this volume; Craig Satterlee has previously contributed to the *New Proclamation Commentary on Feasts, Holy Days, and Other Celebrations* as well as to numerous Augsburg Fortress worship publications. All four breathe new life into the lectionary texts and will help preachers do the same as they proclaim the gospel within the congregations they serve. We are grateful to each of these contributors for their insights and their commitment to effective Christian preaching, and are confident that you will find in this volume ideas, stimulation, and encouragement for your ministry of proclamation.

David B. Lott

Note

1. Some denominations generally follow the RCL, but occasionally deviate from its assigned texts with their own variations. Such variations, except in a few isolated cases, are not treated in *New Proclamation*.

Advent

Mary Lin Hudson

In the theology of the early church, the resurrection of Jesus marked the dawning of the "age to come," in which the fullness of God's power was revealed. By the fourth century, Western Christians had calculated that God's work of salvation in the "Word made flesh," the incarnation of Christ, theoretically had its conception on the same date as the resurrection, March 25, the date of the Passover and the vernal equinox. Nine months from that date is December 25, the birthday of Jesus Christ. From that date, days were set aside for fasting and penance prior to Christmas Day that had the same purpose as the season of Lent before Easter. The season of Advent marked the preparation for receiving the gift of God's salvation in the "Word made flesh."

This time of watchful wondering foreshadows the story of the human birth of Jesus. It is a time for standing with the prophets who preach in the future tense about the sudden justification of all things under the leadership of God's appointed agent. We imagine what a new earth looks like under fresh leadership. We learn hope from people who had little else. We plan a party for the coming of salvation.

The lectionary texts for the season of Advent are centered in the Gospel of Matthew and the prophecy of Isaiah. In most cases, the messages within these two sources are linked through Paul's theological arguments in the letter to the Romans. Isaiah envisions a world at peace through God's just and right governance of all nations. His proclamation inspires confidence in a family of people who have been threatened, defeated, and enslaved by aggressive empires around them. Paul writes to a blended congregation of Gentile and Jewish Christians learning to live in radically unconventional ways, even in the midst of Roman persecution and oppression. Matthew's gospel focuses on the radically prophetic work of John the Baptist and his undeterred faith in the promise of God. Matthew's version of the birth narrative also centers on the faith of Joseph who humbly accepted God's instruction. Joseph devoted himself to the work of assisting God in the birth of a savior, and he protected Mary and the child from the violence of society.

This "waiting time" of Advent evokes in the listeners a longing for life to be more just, more merciful, and more peaceful than it is. A friend of mine noted that for the past few years, the business of warfare and violence has often stepped to the forefront during Advent to dominate the consciousness of people in the United States. For instance, public conversations about war in Iraq and Afghanistan have escalated during Advent times, casting a dark shadow over the church's sense of expectancy. Somehow, the contrast between the policies of nations and the vision of the peaceable kingdom stands in sharper relief because of the themes of the Advent season. When these lectionary texts are read and preached during worship, we sense the revolutionary nature of our expectancy as Christians. We anticipate that God will see to it that the earth is judged, turned right-side up, and governed by truth and compassion.

Preaching during this season should cause people to stop and think about something other than holiday shopping, baking, and partying. It raises the question of whether we have so overinvested in the security of earthly "empires" that we have lost sight of a God whose intentions for creation exceed our limited vision of a "new earth." Preaching calls into question the amount of control that we have over the principalities and powers around us, and it helps us admit our doubt in the unseen power of the Divine Life in our midst. Good Advent preaching expresses the deeper longings of the troubled communities and cities where we serve until faith emerges in people who risk stepping into the unknown for the sake of God's future.

The life of a prophet is not an easy one. True prophets have never lived in mansions or been the pastor of affluent churches (at least not for very long). John the Baptist moved his ministry to the outskirts of town and finally ended up confined to a jail cell. But what a preacher he was!

Preaching prophetic sermons can be difficult. A prophetic sermon should tell the truth, exposing deception and revealing injustice. The prophet also points the way to hope by bringing the words of the page to life in the present. Hope is real when the preacher has caught the vision and can see it in the world. But be careful not to mistake anger for passion. Anger can sound like passion, but it serves only the emotional needs of the preacher. Passion, on the other hand, enthusiastically surrenders to the compelling claims of the gospel. Passion seeks to draw others into the reality of God so that they can be shaken, renewed, and embraced by the work of God in saving the world.

Advent is a time of watchful waiting. More than waiting for a day to arrive on a date designated for a celebration, Advent is a time of waiting for the truth of the story to take root in our hearts and lives. While Advent offers time for us to wait on God, God is waiting on us—waiting for our faith to catch up with the power of the story that lives forever in our memory.

November 28, 2010
First Sunday of Advent

Revised Common Lectionary (RCL)
Isaiah 2:1-5
Psalm 122
Romans 13:11-14
Matthew 24:36-44

Lectionary for Mass (LFM)
Isaiah 2:1-5
Psalm 122:1-2, 3-4a, 4b-5, 6-7, 8-9
Romans 13:11-14
Matthew 24:37-44

First Reading
Isaiah 2:1-5 (RCL, LFM)

The liturgical year begins with a strange vision of a high mountain. Like Mt. Everest, which rises 29,029 feet high, above all the mountains of the world, so this mountain towers above all others. High above the clouds, it stands clearly as the premier pinnacle on earth. It is awesome, mysterious, and inviting. In the deep valleys below, massive groups of people (nations, corporations, special-interest groups, disenfranchised) are streaming in all directions toward the mountain. People—black, bronze, red, yellow, and white—can be seen approaching. Young and old, male and female, wealthy and poor, healthy and ill are gathering to undertake this demanding climb, not just for the adventure or the challenge of conquering such a peak, but because of the glorious presence that awaits them there. Truth abides there. Like the Tibetan monks who make their home at the foot of the highest mountain in Asia, so people will move in mass to live in the presence of the Divine Creator of the universe, seeking enlightenment and transformation. There they will discover anew the kind of power that exercises wisdom and justice, settling disputes between sworn enemies, and bringing fairness and restoration to the poor and needy. What a nice dream, the kind from which you'd just as soon not wake up!

Therefore, let the text guide you into more dreams. No one will need to go to war or attack each other with knives and guns to get their way. God's government will establish peace. And what's that they're singing? Sounds like, "Gonna lay down my burden [something most folks would need to do to prepare to climb a high mountain] down by the riverside … I ain't gonna study war no more!" You can hear the guitars playing, the feet marching, and the hands clapping in time as the voices join in perfect harmony.

And what will people do instead of stockpiling weapons, training for combat, and mapping military strategies? Folks will lay down their weapons and start beating them into something completely different. Like artisans who melt down solid metal in the hottest fire in order to pound it into a new shape, people under God's rule will place their weapons under the "fire" of God's instruction in order to shape them into instruments of cultivation for the sustaining of life. Listen to the rhythmic pounding of metal on metal. Feel the sweat pouring from the bodies as they engage in difficult and demanding work. See the metal flatten and bend and sharpen into tools for a new economy. This is a different kind of worship. Under the wisdom of the One who rules all things, human action contributes to the well-being of the world through nourishment, healing, and restoration—the truest form of worship.

So why are we shown this vision on the Christian equivalent of New Year's Day? This text serves a purpose similar to it original intention, which is to renew faith in divine wisdom and rekindle hope that peace can come among us on the earth. The vision challenges us to believe in One whose purposes seem far higher than our grasp and to act consistently with those purposes. In a world that spends much time studying the ways of war, haven't we learned that violence fails to put an end to violence? Rather, it perpetuates it. Can we, in good faith, make the commitment to study ways to end violence in our own daily lives? If we see a different way to be at peace in the world, let's change direction and live that way, letting God draw us into a future of wholeness and peace.

Psalmody
Psalm 122 (RCL)
Psalm 122:1-2, 3-4a, 4b-5, 6-7, 8-9 (LFM)

By the time I was five years old, I could recite the first verse of this psalm. In my innocence, coming into the church house (God's house) was something done with gladness and good cheer. In God's house, people were nice and kind and said "thank you" to God for all that God had done for them. As I look at this text now, however, I tremble ever so slightly at the importance of these words. Sung by pilgrims on their way to visit the temple of God, this psalm celebrates that place as a sacred magnet of sorts; drawing together kinfolk from every tribe and distant place to renew the covenant between God and God's people. The welfare of the human race depends on people gathering around a common appreciation for the Source of Life that creates, sustains, and renews earthly existence.

At first glance, "Pray for the peace of Jerusalem" (v. 6) looks like a slogan for Zionist causes and some people interpret it that way. For generations, since the establishment of a centralized domain for Israel under the Davidic rule, faithful Jews had looked to the success of Jerusalem and the protection of its temple as the evidence of God's favor. References to the throne of David reminded them that their well-being was uniquely tied to the right leadership who, like the ruler David, would draw power from his or her deep respect and love for God. This is the song of a people who returned to the same place, year after year, to renew their covenant with the One who gave them their identity and unity. The words are sung out of love and devotion to God who has allowed them to establish a central place where the "holy" can be found again and again. Perhaps at one time it was the theme song of "nationalist" causes, but not so much for the listeners in today's congregations. These words renew hope in a Holy God who promises to meet us wherever we are, year after year, in order to assure us of God's concern for our welfare.

To claim a place as "sacred" takes a lot of faith in an age when space is thought to be a valuable possession to be bought, sold, traded, or fought for according to its value and importance rather than a place that belongs to a Holy Creator. We could take lessons from people who sense holiness in the beauty and wonder of the earth and therefore preserve it for the benefit of all people rather than trying to possess and control it for themselves.

Recently documentarian Ken Burns produced a series of films chronicling the preservation of awesome places of natural beauty and wonder in the U.S. National Park system. Through the efforts of dedicated citizens, these U.S. lands remain preserved and available to all kinds of people to come and renew their souls as they experience the wonders of the natural world. From the rocky shores of Acadia National Park to the waterfalls of Yosemite, from the mysterious geysers of Yellowstone to the sculpted hoodoos of Bryce Canyon, visitors may stand in awe and humility before a creation that virtually shouts out the glory of the Creator. In these places many of us are moved to a higher level of consciousness and gratitude than we normally experience. Some of us might be inclined to say, "I was glad when they said to me, 'Let us go visit the Grand Canyon.'" These special places that renew our souls have become sacred spaces that beckon persons to return again and again to renew their love for the Divine Creator of all things.

Praying for the peace of a place comes from knowing at a deep level that our own security is tied to its well-being. Any place where a sense of the holiness of God dwells can be considered worthy of our prayers. In a sacred space, God reminds us that were it not for the gift of life, each human being would be a pile of ashes, and God assures us that God's justice, truth, mercy, and grace will seek out and make a way for human community as long as people seek God. Let us be glad, then, to return once again to God's house. The future of the planet and its world depends upon it.

Second Reading
Romans 13:11-14 (RCL, LFM)

"Wake up!" The pounding on the door at predawn startles the deep sleeper into semiconsciousness. "What time is it?" she responds. "It's time to get up and get ready," her elderly father replies. "My doctor's appointment is scheduled for 10:30 this morning!" The urgency of the announcement in Paul's letter to the Romans seems as overdrawn as this unexpected wake-up call. "You know what time it is," writes Paul. "The night is almost gone, the day is almost here." Written to a community living under the shadow of the Roman Empire, this word announces boldly that the "day of the Lord" is, indeed, standing on their doorstep pounding to get their attention.

In earliest times, people hoped that God would come and take control of every nation. This hope remained alive in Jesus' day. Then came Jesus, whose preaching about the kingdom of God was punctuated by his execution and subsequent resurrection. Jesus gave the spirit of life to a new community following his own example. While they lived a different, marginal kind of existence, they hoped for Jesus' return. These early Christians dodged daily threats from Rome's imperial guard. Dressed in heavy armor and bearing sharp swords, Roman soldiers sometimes left bloody victims in their wake as they obediently silenced opposition and implemented the so-called *Pax Romana*. Christians hoped that Jesus would hurry up and show up soon to crush the tyrants and strip them of their arrogant and brutal power![1]

Close to home, internal violence hurt people, too. This violence did not come from swords and spears, but from words and actions among members of the church. Instead of living out the plain truth that was revealed in Jesus, people got distracted by other things and slumped back into old practices of quarreling, envying each other and engaging in permissive sexual activities that mimicked the hated Romans. Paul challenges them to change their ways. "Wake up! Day is dawning, and you don't want to miss it," I can hear him saying. "So like soldiers, but unlike those who persecute you, put on the armor that is uniquely yours—the armor of light."

The actions that hurt other people in community must be left behind, like last night's dreaming. Christians have an ethical responsibility to translate future hopes into present actions. As days turn to years with no vindication in sight, it is easy to forget that we are already living under the reign of God. The rest of the world simply has not caught up with us yet.

Today, people are still bombarded with predictions of "end times" and cataclysmic events destined to destroy our planet. Environmental groups call us to "wake up." Economists call us to "wake up." Social workers call us to "wake up." Artists and dreamers are calling us to "wake up" to the need for change in policies, in priorities, in purchases, and in personal practices before it is too late. Have we lost sight of God's justice and righteousness that refuses to abandon God's good creation? Are we actively engaged in the ways of God working for the well-being of the earth and all who live in it? In many ways it is much easier to sit back and wait for some cataclysmic event to intervene. If we do, though, we are the ones who lose the joy of salvation to a life of fear. "Wake up, people!" Now is the time to act with honor, compassion, and faith so that God's intended purposes for all creation may be revealed in our world today.

Gospel
Matthew 24:36-44 (RCL)
Matthew 24:37-44 (LFM)

Memphis is home to the Center for Earthquake Research and Information, sponsored by the University of Memphis. The center tracks seismic activity all over the country and the world, but it takes a special interest in the fault line that runs through the boot heel of Missouri and the area near the heart of Memphis. In an effort to predict the time that an earthquake is likely to occur, scientists and their apprentices keep watch over the rumbles beneath the surface. Every few years they sound a warning to the citizens of Memphis to get ready for an earthquake. That means that persons should keep a wrench in a place easily accessible to the gas main, stock up on water and food, purchase new batteries, pack the first-aid kit, and make a plan for where to meet in case families get separated from each other in the area. For a time, most residents make some kind of preparation for an emergency. After a while, however, the fear subsides, preparedness is forgotten, and life returns to normal.

At the time of the writing of Matthew's gospel, Christians had just survived a bloody battle that devastated Jerusalem more than any earthquake. The Roman emperor had destroyed the Temple and defeated Jewish resistance to Roman rule. In his wake, the emperor had set up statues to honor the victory of Rome and produced coins that depicted Jewish defeat and humiliation at Roman hands.[2] Christians in Antioch suffered along with Jewish communities the oppression of Roman rule. The hope that God would intervene and overthrow the tyranny of Rome seemed crushed by the weight of such military rule in their cities and region.

Written in this time of dejection and despair, Matthew's gospel reminds the audience not to give up hope. God's judgment is not predictable and may take everyone by surprise. They are admonished to "be ready," because no one can predict what a completely free and all-powerful God will do.

We may be living centuries after this message was written, but we know all too well what it means. People go about their normal routines of working, shopping, or partying and then something unexpected happens that very few saw coming. Families break apart, banks fail, or floods overflow the banks of a river. A tornado rips through a community and people marvel at how one home may be completely demolished while the one next to it remains upright and secure. One life is radically reversed while the other life stays just the same.

It is easy for people to let the routine of their lives blind them to the judgment that inevitably will come to all. The Divine Presence, with wise and righteous ways, dwells within the structure of all creation. Most of us lack an awareness of the power and presence of God until the plans of our lives crumble into pieces before our eyes. In those moments, we realize that we are judged by the wisdom and righteousness of God. Does the act of destruction destroy us because we lose all that we have ever trusted to be true? Or are we saved by what is taken away, because we abide in the presence of God whom we trust day to day? Belief anticipates a future before it ever happens. Living under the reign of God's justice and mercy now, we can be ready for anything, even bank failures and planetary changes. Be ready, for you never know when something drastic and far reaching will happen!

Will It Preach?

The expectancy of Advent begins with a renewal of faith in divine authority to bring new life to a world that so desperately suffers within the old one. The four texts work together well to develop the primary theme of "waiting for God." The good news of these texts is that God, who is just and righteous, keeps covenant with people from generation to generation, bringing judgment that establishes peace and wholeness in the world. We just need to "wake up" to be able to see it. The imperative to "wake up" and "be ready" is not too difficult for congregations to grasp. They hear it on television and radio advertisements trying to get people to stores early to be the first to purchase special bargains for Christmas. It is more challenging for them to understand what they should "be ready" for in this day and age. Is the "black Friday" after Thanksgiving their ultimate Advent expectation, or should they look for something else?

Another challenge for preaching could be to counter popular culture's apocalyptic views so that the focus of the congregation is not hijacked by concerns over an ultimate cosmic conflict between good and evil, like in a *Star Wars* movie. Fortunately, we got past the turn of the millennium without major glitches, so we are haunted by fewer predictions of doom right now. Preaching, however, still needs to help congregations grasp the power of resurrection that subverts the dead-end practices of the contemporary world, and help them see its projection into a peaceful future.

In a secular, but somewhat spiritual, world, preaching will need to help persons decide if they really believe in a God who is just and merciful. Can you help them identify their longing for God to transform the world from warfare into peace? Motivating people to "wake up" and embrace life-affirming practices may be easier than evoking a real faith in an illusive God who is never fully present and fully known. As a preacher, you may need to contemplate this in your own life. Ask yourself what changes might take place if you and your community really responded to this message and believed!

Notes

1.   Warren Carter, *Matthew and the Margins: A Sociopolitical and Religious Reading* (Maryknoll, N.Y.: Orbis, 2000), 36-40.
2.   Neil Elliott, *The Arrogance of Nations: Reading Romans in the Shadow of the Empire* (Minneapolis: Fortress Press, 2008), 142.

December 5, 2010
Second Sunday of Advent

Revised Common Lectionary (RCL)

Isaiah 11:1-10

Psalm 72:1-7, 18-19

Romans 15:4-13

Matthew 3:1-12

Lectionary for Mass (LFM)

Isaiah 11:1-10

Psalm 72:1-2, 7-8, 12-13, 17

Romans 15:4-9

Matthew 3:1-12

First Reading
Isaiah 11:1-10 (RCL, LFM)

The old redbud in my parents' yard had to be cut down. I can remember when it came up one summer, unprotected and vulnerable. It bloomed brilliantly each spring as an adult tree, but as the years passed, the branches twisted out to the side in different directions. With old age, the redbud had lost much of its ability to bloom. Then one summer day, an intense thunderstorm stripped down one of its gnarled branches. Split in two, its heart lay exposed to the elements. We knew the tree had to come down. After the ax was finished, all that was left was a stump about fourteen inches in diameter and only seven inches high. The winter came and went. The spring arrived but there were no more branches, no more blooms to greet it. Its life was cut off. Just a dead stump remained in the place of a beautiful tree. But then, one warm summer day, I noticed a tiny green shoot inching its way up from the roots below the ground. Nature surprised us. The stump that appeared to be dead and decaying still had the power to produce life.

This text from Isaiah offers two compelling images that are worthy of our hope. The first image depicts a strong and noble leader devoted to justice for the world, especially for the disenfranchised. Different spiritual gifts enable him to rule this way: wisdom and understanding, counsel and might, knowledge and fear of the Lord. His physical attributes symbolize his deeper authority. The sound of his words jolts the planet and a moving wind of his spirit sweeps clean the world around him. This leader has integrity. It springs from his authenticity in his relationship to the Divine. His power to uphold life in its fullness comes from his authentic trust in God's own love for the world.

I remember the live footage on my television screen of tears streaming down faces of people whose hopes were being realized. People from all races, genders, ages, and backgrounds gathered in Chicago's Grant Park to witness a moment of great joy. A man from African and American background, who had worked for the rights of ordinary people through community organizing, who had served his state in the U.S. Senate, now stood with his wife and two daughters before the crowd. Could history be coming full circle to correct the racial wrongs of the past? Could a new person with a different perspective offer fresh opportunities for a country that kept turning its back on the poor and the meek? No one could know the answers for sure, but one thing was certain: hope for change was alive that night in a visible display that the world had not witnessed before from the United States.

The second image in Isaiah's vision has captured the imagination of artists and spiritual giants for generations. One of the most famous expressions may be Edward Hicks's *Peaceable Kingdom*, the best-known version of which currently resides in the National Gallery of Art in Washington, D.C.[1] In his painting, the vision of Isaiah is depicted as wild beasts sitting together with children under the shade of a large tree. In the foreground, an ox with horns that form a perfect circle over his head sits beside a lion whose face is punctuated by wide green eyes taking in the view. A bear and cow are curled in a sleeping pose side by side. A sheep and goat lie safe beneath the paws of a pointy-eared fox, and a swift pronghorn reclines along side a couple of leopards. In their midst are children: one innocently hugging a tiger, another tweaking the nose of a wild beast. All are safe and without fear among these animals of the natural world. What a wonderful picture! But Hicks does not stop there. In the distant background of the painting, barely visible, stand eight statesmen of his day signing a treaty with eight Indian tribesmen. This vision of political accord in the midst of a wild and undeveloped frontier seems as if it is attempting to reach the peaceable kingdom, but stops short of the goal. The irony is not lost on contemporary viewers; what symbolized political peace in nineteenth-century America came at the expense of Native peoples who eventually became refugees in their own country. Human efforts to achieve God's purposes are always marred by a lurking self-interest. The partial good that we do can only be completed by the power of God who restores all creation with a merciful justice. When that happens, God will get the attention of everyone in the world!

Psalmody
Psalm 72:1-7, 18-19 (RCL)
Psalm 72:1-2, 7-8, 12-13, 17 (LFM)

This psalm echoes the expectation sparked by Isaiah's vision. It is probable that this psalm was sung at the coronation of rulers as they assumed the throne.[2] After all, new leadership revives the hopes of a people. Through a fresh beginning, the expectations of a nation and its surrounding peoples surface once again in the hope for new justice and prosperity. The hopes expressed in this psalm are no exception.

Because of this long-held tradition of hoping for a ruler who would execute the justice and righteousness of God, people of a later time had trouble recognizing in Jesus the attributes of a Messiah who would challenge the injustices of their troubled lives under Roman rule. The prophetic voice of John the Baptist announced the approaching reign of God in Jesus of Nazareth. Those who listened to his voice and turned to look at Jesus had difficulty seeing how a Palestinian Jew could manifest the authority of God against an emperor's reign.

In current times, with its political turmoil and economic disparity, this reiteration of Isaiah's vision seems lost on the wider world screen. Human hopes have been dashed too many times. In a world dominated by powerful political regimes and global corporations, it is hard to hope that a righteous leader will arise to make a sweeping difference in the quality of ordinary lives in this global village. But what if people of faith and doubt would allow that ancient vision to project onto themselves? Are we any more willing than the world to allow God's kingdom ideal to shape our relationships and our economy? Perhaps the unseen, unexpected remnant that we are waiting for is really alive in us and waiting for us to believe. When we act with unswerving integrity as a community in the face of pressure from special-interest groups to conform to their agendas, then we live without fear. When we ignore the mandate of powerful corporate giants to "buy, buy, buy" and choose instead to "share, share, share," then hope for the world need not die. When the poor are treated justly and the outcasts welcomed into community, God is showing up to reorder the world.

It isn't easy to trust in the day when God's purposes for creation will be realized on earth. It is hard to believe in something that we have never fully viewed. History does, however, remind us that political systems, like ancient empires, will come and go. Economies will collapse and be reborn. In the meantime, God remains at the heart of existence, bringing life out of death. Justice is not a dream. It is woven into the fabric of the universe. Why not wrap ourselves in its cloth and join God's future now?

Second Reading
Romans 15:4-13 (RCL)
Romans 15:4-9 (LFM)

It isn't hard to recognize that this epistle reading was chosen because of the author's use of the words of Isaiah 11. In his letter to the Christians in Rome, Paul's refers to verses 1 and 10 of Isaiah in an effort to demonstrate that past hopes for the coming of God's righteousness on earth have been fulfilled in Jesus. The Jews in the congregation could be hopeful when they heard this because God's ancient promises had come true! The Gentiles in the congregation could be glad that God's promises were for the whole wide world, not just for the descendants of Jacob. As Paul uses the words from Isaiah in his letter, he wants to inspire hope and goodwill in the followers of Jesus.

So what difference did it make for the congregation in Rome to believe that God's promises were fulfilled in Jesus? It made a big difference! From their perspective, after the death and resurrection of Jesus, Christians could look back and see that God could be trusted to keep promises. If God fulfilled this promise entrusted to the prophet Isaiah, God would finish what was started at that time in the gift of Jesus. Waiting for Jesus' imminent return, their community could anticipate Isaiah's vision of peace breaking in at any minute.[3]

It was not easy to demonstrate this hope when Christians lived under the shadow of the Roman Empire. After being evicted from the capital city by the decree of one emperor, many Jews had later returned after the edict was lifted, but without property and status. The Jews who believed in Jesus as the Messiah joined newly converted Gentiles who had not experienced the harsh persecution of imperial tyrants in the same way. So when Paul pushes this community to "live in harmony with one another" and "welcome one another as Christ has welcomed you," he's not talking in broad generalities; he's talking specifically and personally about the Gentiles welcoming back the Jewish Christians from exile. If this congregation in Rome actually hopes that Christ will return to establish God's just rule on earth, then they need to start acting like it. Dreaming is always easier than doing, especially if doing requires you to open your home to strangers, feed the hungry who gather at your table, clothe people who show up with only the tunics on their backs, and share whatever scarce resources you may have scraped up to live on because you do not belong to the wealthy elite. On top of that, it is easier to welcome people like yourself, from your own culture and class, rather than welcoming people who have thought for centuries that they are superior to you. Only a few years ago these same people had refused to eat with Gentiles, let alone receive help from one of them. Now Paul is telling these Christians to live together as family. When Gentile Christians welcome Jewish Christians, they imitate Christ who came to serve the Jewish people by fulfilling God's promises, and in doing so, opened the way for Gentiles to be included in God's extravagant new creation.[4]

Not only does this argument clarify for the folks in Rome the ethical obligation of Christian community, but it also seems to support Paul's ongoing mission to the Gentiles. In practical terms, this meant that Jewish Christians should set aside prejudices that would prevent the full inclusion of Gentiles. At the same time, it encouraged Gentiles to embrace openly the people who were suspicious of them. The community would be sustained by these choices during difficult times. These radical and far-reaching practices were not simply useful, however; they got folks ready for the coming realm of God.

Gospel
Matthew 3:1-12 (RCL, LFM)

He dresses like Elijah. He eats crunchy insects dipped in fresh honey. He uses colorful language and shows little respect for the powerful. He announces a new world order. Surely this man is a genuine prophet! Listen to him!

The gospel reading for the day interrupts the holiday cheer that reverberates through households, airwaves, and city streets. Listeners follow a detour into a most unlikely place. Far beyond the lights of the city lies the wilderness, inhabited by wild things, where John the Baptist lives. The wilderness is a place outside the purview of the powerful leaders, a place where humans are tested and tried. If people want to "repent," to turn away from old ways of life, then they must go out, get away from home and all that controls them. There they meet the prophet, confess sins, and are baptized. The Advent season demands the same of us. If we want to return to a state of expectancy in our faith, we must travel outside of holiday sounds, sights, and social events to the place in our lives where "wild things" live in order for something new to be born.

Remarkably, in this text, lots of people made that journey to be baptized by John the Baptist! That tells us that folks were desperate for change. Turning back to God seemed the right thing to do, especially when the preacher was announcing that God's realm was just around the corner and, in fact, would arrive any day. The climate seemed to be charged with a renewed judgment of the way of life that held them captive.

John's message was about political and social change; he was quick to point out the wickedness of unbridled power and wealth. His message went beyond the realm of politics, however. He preached against religious abuse and hypocrisy. When Pharisees and Sadducees came out to the wilderness for baptism, John went ballistic! John got up in their faces and confronted them in front of all those crowds who had come out from Jerusalem and all Judea. (Fear of conflict did not seem to be a part of John's character.) If these religious leaders thought they could make a public display of their righteousness by being baptized by a prophet, they didn't really know who John the Baptist was! So John preached a sermon that got their attention and challenged them to true repentance, which, in Matthew's gospel, never happens.[5]

We preachers should definitely be alarmed because we can identify both with John and the Jewish leaders. As we listen again to John's sermon we are reminded that the "word of the Lord" is powerful, and sometimes very painful.

"You brood of vipers!" This insulting image of poisonous snakes slaps down the arrogance of the religious leaders. He likens them to the snakes that killed the wandering Israelites in the desert under Moses' rule. He accuses them of being the "lowest of the low," those who deceive and destroy.

"Do not presume to say to yourselves, 'We have Abraham as our ancestor'" (v. 9a). John must have heard this line before. Their arrogance presumed that they were God's best friends and favorite sons. It was easy to forget that God had chosen Abraham and his descendants as God's own people, and God could choose Gentiles to join the family just as easily. In fact, John said that God could take a dead rock and make it a living heir of the promise, if that's what God wanted to do.

"Good fruit" seems to be what God is looking for from the tree that took root in Judea. The message is clear in John's sermon: ethics matters! How life is lived in relation to others is the truest measure of a person's character and identity. For the Pharisees and Sadducees, the proof of their repentance would be demonstrated by a radical embrace of humility, generosity, and acceptance of others, especially the poor, the outcasts, and those outside the Jewish community.

John's sermon ends with a prophecy that punctuates the message of the entire sermon. In essence, he is saying to the people that if they think his water baptism for repentance of sins is harsh, they just have to wait a little while. The Promised One will come after John, bringing a new righteousness and justice that will be as decisive as a razor-sharp ax. The image of the "winnowing fork" suggests that the judgments will be decisive and efficient in separating the good from the bad, in preserving the beneficial and destroying the wasteful elements of God's harvest. What parts of your life are worth saving and what parts are completely inconsequential? Through the life, death, and resurrection of Jesus, we are given a chance to find out for sure.

Will It Preach?

These texts interact through imagery and rhetoric to evoke some striking theological themes for preaching. The readings begin with a stump and end with an ax posed to create another stump. A wild and woolly prophet stands face to face with brightly clad Pharisees and Sadducees. There are dead rocks and slippery snakes on the ground, but lambs and lions also graze in peace. Rod and wind from the mouth of God blend with fire of judgment and water of repentance coming from Jesus, the Messiah. The preacher must grapple with the double-edged sharpness of the theological meaning within these texts. Judgment and hope stand side by side. It would be tempting to preach this as a "judgment/mercy" sermon that leaves listeners wrapped in the security of grace. It might feel right to set up the problem as the social and moral deviance of society in contrast to Isaiah's vision and then offer the solution of social repentance and faith in Jesus. But each of these approaches misses the paradox that is exposed here: judgment and hope are always inextricably linked, woven together in one piece of cloth. The two should not be played against each other. Both are gifts of grace and mercy to a world in need of newness. The paradox should be preserved by laying aside our tendency to paint life in opposite dualities of good/evil, punishment/ reward, judgment/mercy. Let preaching embrace both judgment and grace as gifts of a God who is always near at hand, saving us from ourselves.

Notes

1. See http://www.nga.gov/fcgi-bin/tinfo_f?object=59908, accessed December 14, 2009.
2. John S. Kselman, "Psalms," in *The New Oxford Annotated Bible,* 3d ed. (New York: Oxford University Press, 2001), 836hb.
3. A. Katherine Grieb, *The Story of Romans: A Narrative Defense of God's Righteousness* (Louisville: Westminster John Knox, 2002), 129-33.
4. Neil Elliott, "Romans," in *The New Oxford Annotated Bible,* 242-43nt.
5. Warren Carter, *Matthew and the Margins: A Sociopolitical and Religious Reading* (Maryknoll, N.Y.: Orbis, 2000), 90-101.

December 12, 2010
Third Sunday of Advent

First Reading
Isaiah 35:1-10 (RCL)
Isaiah 35:1-6a, 10 (LFM)

In 2005, the areas of Nevada and California experienced above average rainfall during the winter months. The result was the blooming of wildflowers as far as the eye could see. So I took a trip during spring break to take a look for myself. Standing on the floor of Death Valley and looking toward the surrounding rim of the mountains, I witnessed a myriad of rare blooms blanketing the desert landscape. Seeds of plants that grew only in that harsh, dry region, hidden in the hard, dry soil for years, now sprang into being, exposing new and exotic life-forms. The variety alone was amazing. It was a resurrection of sorts—the response of a waiting earth to a rare gift of water from above.

This text from Isaiah depicts a neglected environment suddenly brimming with abundant life. A contrasting prophecy in the previous chapter predicts the destruction of Edom, a powerful conquering nation, into a wasteland unfit for habitation by anything but predatory creatures. In chapter 35, however, God's people witness a vision of restoration, a radical transformation of the struggling homeland into a location of vitality, health, and peace for plants, animals, and humans alike. It becomes a place of joy and singing, and people marvel at God's ability to bring forth a site of such magnificent beauty and goodness. God's presence produces the new life of salvation within this living organism we call earth that will host the regathering of God's people.

The text specifically speaks about the renewal of people who are not "valid" (invalid) in society. The blind shall see. The deaf shall hear. Those defined by their impairments shall be fully restored. The renewal goes beyond ordinary restoration, however. The lame will not simply walk, but jump with the grace of a deer. The speechless will not simply speak again, but sing out their joy for the world to hear. The earth will not simply come back to life, but will be fed by springs and rivers to form sanctuaries for waterfowl and other creatures like never before. Abundance and wholeness take residence in creation.

Running down the middle of this lush, green landscape is a major thoroughfare called the "Holy Way." This special road provides the way for God's people to come home. In contrast to the typical dangers from wild animals, robbers, and sworn enemies encountered on the ancient roads through the wilderness, this highway will be safe and secure for those entering Zion. The sound of joyful singing shall mark the entrance of God's people as they walk along this highway into their home in God's salvation.

These words of Isaiah brought hope to a people who were exhausted by a succession of weak rulers who could not protect them from invading opponents. Later, these same words gave hope to captives who had been led into exile by their conquering neighbors. Surely these words accompanied God's people as they returned to their homeland to rebuild their identity as a nation. This vision of possibility holds great potential to sustain and motivate people in the midst of desperate circumstances.

What would the prophet say to us today? Instead of dwelling on the way things are, perhaps the prophetic voice would lead us to look at what could one day be. Instead of complaining about violence on the streets, lethargy inside the public schools, corruption of government officials, damage to the planet, or the breakdown in society, we could strain to see the new thing God intends. People who critique the problems of our world tend to measure the failures by a gilded portrait of the past. People of hope and faith, however, look into a world unbalanced by forceful and volatile changes and see the possibility of something new occurring. Perhaps today we need to focus, not on the restoration of old patterns, but on the advent of the new: new cities, new schools, newly ordered ways of life, new care for this planet, new kinds of families and workplaces and churches. Glance backward to the prophet in order to look forward to a new future. Hope in God who makes all things new!

Psalmody
Psalm 146:5-10 (RCL)
Psalm 146:6-7, 8-9a, 9b-10 (LFM)

The response to Isaiah's prophecy of renewal is praise! The Creator who is still at work in the renewal of the earth and its people can be trusted. This psalm expands the list of those who are receiving the attention of God to include the oppressed, the hungry, the prisoners, the blind, the bowed down, the orphan, and the widow. God makes provision for the dignity and renewal of all these lives and has called God's people to do the same. Their well-being is the evidence of God's reign. This will always be true for generations to come.

When a congregation responds with this psalm, I wonder if they see the real faces of people who are being helped by God. Many times we focus on our "good doing" as Christians, rather than on the "God doing." We fail to attend to the actual change that takes place in the people who are being helped. Hungry people are fed and feel fresh energy return to their weakened bodies. For a moment their lives are no longer defined by what they lack. The bent-over one straightens up and suddenly looks others directly in another's eyes as an equal. Miracles often disguise themselves in tiny moments that many of us take for granted. God loves those who live right by following ethical standards for justice and mercy. God's glory, however, is revealed in the faces and bodies and lives of those people who receive the help and are saved, even if only for a moment, from hunger or imprisonment or abandonment. Sure, they may come back again smelly, hungry, tired, sick, or in trouble and in need of God's help, but so do we. Don't look at what hasn't happened for all of us, but focus on what already has. Look to them and see the kingdom of God draw near.

Luke 1:46b-55 (RCL ALT.)

An alternative response to Isaiah's prophecy is the song of Mary, the mother of Jesus. This canticle reflects Mary's own gratitude and praise to God at the confirmation from Elizabeth that her pregnancy is truly a blessing from God. Elizabeth commends her for having the kind of faith that believes that God can be trusted to do what is promised.

The song is sung from the perspective of one who has been honored and helped by God. Like Hannah's song (1 Sam. 2:1-10), the *Magnificat* offers extravagant praise to God who chose a young peasant woman to carry out God's intended purposes for the world. The God of Israel reached beyond the boundaries of the established order of things to bring about the renewal of the world.

God begins changing the order of things by destabilizing the lives of those who respond in faith to God (people of royalty trade places with the peasants, the proud experience humiliation, the rich become poor, and the poor receive good things), and it isn't always a joyride of sustained spiritual bliss. We are asked to do things that draw us into controversy, persecution, and sometimes even death. At a young age, Mary was suddenly thrown into chaos with the scandal of personal impropriety accompanied by responsibility for a dependent child. In addition, her body was taken over by a baby for nine months! Mary can testify to God's power because she knows it at a physical level. She doesn't just think that change in the world is possible; she embodies change in her body and in her spirit. Her cells are alive with anticipation of new birth and her heart beats in rhythm with the Expected One inside of her. The presence of God is carried in human flesh. Mary knows God as all-powerful, yet One who leads her into a future she cannot fathom for herself. It is amazing that in the midst of being thrown into such unsettling circumstances, Mary chooses to sing of the mystery and grace of a God who changes everything!

Second Reading
James 5:7-10 (RCL, LFM)

A childhood friend of mine recently became a grandmother for the second time. Her oldest daughter was giving birth for the first time to a little girl that she and her husband had already named Sophie. Sophie was due to arrive on November 17. When the day came, Sophie's rather petite mother was more than ready for her baby to disembark, but there were no signs that Sophie was ready for her big adventure. The doctors, however, thought they knew better than the baby. (Patience is not a great virtue for people who think they have to be in control of life.) They stood by ready to take matters into their own hands in case the birth process did not unfold as planned. They recommended the use of drugs to induce labor. A surgeon stood ready to take the baby by C-section, if needed. In good time, though, the waiting paid off, and at 10:30 P.M., on the evening of the seventeenth, Sophie entered the world. She nestled into the arms of the woman who had patiently carried her for nine long months. Her father embraced her as a personal miracle. Sophie's arrival changed forever the life of her family and world.

Birth is a process that requires patience. Farming involves patience, too. In the epistle of James, we read of the farmer waiting for crops to grow and mature before the harvest. The metaphor reveals a lot about "waiting." Farmers don't control crops, they assist them. When humans try to control the growth and maturation of crops with chemicals, the results have sometimes proven toxic and deadly. The plant has its own internal clock, assisted by environmental factors such as sun, rain, climate, insects, and soil. The farmer is only one of many factors in the growth of a crop, but the farmer enjoys the benefits of the produce in time.

All analogies break down at some level, but some truth remains. Believing people must be patient people. We're not in control of the birth of justice, although we sometimes think we ought to be. We can't force the movement and maturity of a newly ordered world when God is not ready for it to happen. It will come in its own time whether we're ready or not.

This doesn't mean that we can sit back passively and do nothing, however. In our waiting, we can prepare for justice to be served. In our watching, we can assist and nurture the fruit of righteousness and peace. But we can't control it any more than we can control the wind.

The letter of James gives very straightforward advice to Christians on how to live in response to God's purpose made known in Jesus. If we want to understand how to be patient, we should look at the example of the prophets. The prophets preached

God's deliverance and God's judgment as the Spirit directed them, but most of them never saw radical change happen in their own lifetimes. Still they preached and labored on God's behalf, experiencing persecution and even death for the power of their truth. The prophets never gave up on God even as they waited and waited and waited for God to do something.

Churches always seem to have a problem with "patience." We end up getting on each others nerves because of it! The sounds of grumbling fill the hallways and parking lots just after the shouts of excitement in worship have quieted down. We want successful fulfillment of our expectations, and we want it now! The writer of James seemed to know this well. His argument for conflict resolution goes something like this: if you are expecting the "day of the Lord" to arrive at any time, then you must realize that the ultimate Judge is walking right up to your doorstep about now. If you are waiting for that Judge to pass judgment on the whole world, then you no longer need to pass judgment yourselves and damage your relationship with one another. Suspend judgment and wait for God!

When I was a small child I had a book entitled *If Jesus Came to My House*. I must have had my parents read it to me a zillion times. It made the coming of Jesus very concrete and literal for me at that age. The book was full of examples of work to be done for my house and myself to be ready for company to come. It demonstrated the way to exercise proper hospitality to friends who came to visit. Finally, it ended with the front door opening and Jesus walking into the living room with plans to stay for dinner. The book made Jesus' coming very real and very exciting for me. The model is not lost on me today, for the visual myth brings to life spiritual truth at both a personal and a cosmic level. We learn to abandon the illusion of being personally responsible for the fate of the world, but we must be ready to welcome the One who is responsible. Aware that God comes in God's own time to us and is, in fact, beyond our conscious control, we learn to wait expectantly. Faith requires patience for ourselves and one another as we wait for God to stop by.

Gospel
Matthew 11:2-11 (RCL, LFM)

This text begins with the prophet's important question: "Are you the one, or should we wait for another?" Most prophets lived their lives in anticipation of a world yet to come. John the Baptist was no different, except that from prison he heard the news that another great teacher had taken up the urgent message and was attracting crowds of followers. The message of this teacher was the same, the time was right, and John's own expectation of "one coming after me that is greater than I" seemed to be fulfilled in Jesus. Could it be that the waiting was over? Could he dare believe that divine intervention had started to happen in his own lifetime? His question was practical, because he could advise his followers to join Jesus' work while he was imprisoned. It was personal, because he needed assurance that his own impending death was not the end of his hope. It was cosmic, because the answer had the potential to change the course of human life as it was known, and the long generations of prophets would stand vindicated before those who had persecuted and killed them in defiance of God.

The response of Jesus does not disappoint John. Jesus gives evidence of his identity in the renewal of life that followed him. His actions are consistent with the intentions of God as envisioned by Isaiah, with two additions: lepers are cleansed and the dead are raised. The cleansing of the leper Naaman occurred during the time of Elisha (2 Kings 5). Now it is happening during Jesus' ministry. The book of Daniel anticipates the resurrection of the dead in relation to the coming of the Son of Man to institute God's reign on the earth (Dan. 12:2) Now, people are being raised from death with the coming of Jesus. Jesus' response to John, therefore, seems laden with clues that Jesus is the One John has been looking for. John should know from Jesus' answer that he is anointed by God to usher in God's realm on earth, he is greater than Elisha, and he carries the authority of the Son of Man to bring the dead to life.

After identifying himself to John the Baptist, Jesus turns and identifies John the Baptist to the people. He poses a series of six questions as a strategy to clarify not only John's role as a prophet, but also John's role as a messenger preparing the way for God's work in Jesus. "What did you go out to see?" Jesus asks. Hope for change can motivate people to seek out a prophetic voice at the margins of the normal discourse of their world. When the syndicated voices of the airwaves offer no new perspectives but only more of the same tiresome rhetoric, do you have faith to turn them off and look elsewhere for answers? If so, do you go looking for someone to criticize harshly the social agenda of the day by exposing its corruption and greed? Or do you prefer to consult a well-respected entrepreneur who will offer you the secret knowledge of how to achieve a life of luxury, wealth, and status? Or do you seek out a prophet who knows the unseen world of God and is not afraid to speak about a future transformed by God's power and mercy? Jesus' questioned the crowd so that they would affirm John the Baptist as a true prophet of God.

But wait; there's more! Jesus proclaims the prophet John the Baptist to be the messenger—the one who prepares the way for God's saving work in Jesus. By quoting a line from Malachi 3:1, Jesus compares the preaching ministry of John the Baptist to Elijah as the messenger of God's judgment. John is even more important than Elijah. John the Baptist worked as an advance man of sorts, getting the crowds ready to see God's salvation already begun in Jesus. John the Baptist's ministry was essential to Jesus' own, and John worked with an awareness of the importance and urgency of his task.

This passage ends with a startling twist. John the Baptist is declared by Jesus to be the greatest human being that ever lived, but immediately Jesus turns the tables on the crowd to proclaim that the least in the realm of God is even greater than God's greatest prophet! Perhaps this statement is meant to be paradoxical, rather than polemic. The listener is thrown off balance by the pronouncement because it forces the imagination to consider something it knows nothing about. While the audience may understand the importance of prophecy or even grasp the ultimate importance of one who prepares the way for Jesus, the audience still has not grasped fully the human embodiment of God's presence in their midst. Only Jesus could understand that fully.

When the fullness of God enters completely into the life of the world, participants will become more than messengers about God or advocates on God's behalf; they will embody the harmony of the universe. That is essentially the difference between John the Baptist and Jesus. John could only talk about the coming reign of God; Jesus lived it. Talking about God is always secondary to experiencing the presence of God.[6]

Will It Preach?

"Wake up, a new day is dawning!" The day will carry within it a judgment and hope for the people of the earth. So how, then, will we know that it is here when the day finally comes? The Third Sunday in Advent builds on the theological themes of the First and Second Sundays. What in the world should we expect from God when God is promising to bring forth life that is totally new?

In contemporary American culture, Christmas is the most anticipated day of the year. Why? The traditions of Christmas are strong. Stories of Christmas (especially the old ones) are told; old songs are sung; holiday food is prepared; symbols are hung in streets, shops, homes, and offices; and festivities mark the approaching day. The airwaves are filled with reminders to "shop, shop, shop" in order to make everyone's dreams come true. After all, a visit from Santa is worth the wait if he brings the presents we've wished for the most. We believe in the vision of trees trimmed with ornaments, tots with glowing faces, and torn paper surrounding an abundance of shiny new toys. Most of us are willing to do whatever it takes to serve that ultimate ideal.

Waiting for "Christmas" spurs consumer spending to fuel a free-market economy. It serves the system that drives the contemporary world. If you asked an average person if they would like to live on an earth where every day is "Christmas" all year long, year after year, however, I wonder how they would respond. Perhaps, at first, they might think that the idea would be delightful with its singing and joyous surprises. If you asked them to continue living as they have been in anticipation of making a way for it to happen day after day, perhaps their answer would be quite different. The current celebration of Christmas doesn't seem to fulfill the needs of our world or our souls. Is Christmas as we know it really the ultimate human expectation, or should we expect something else?

It is surprising to discover that society currently is full of apocalyptic images in culture and art. Artists and writers have responded to the strange restlessness of the human psyche brought on by this rapidly changing world. Films depict catastrophic events that rip apart the planet's crust and make way for the birth of new social and political powers on the earth. Through television, we imagine the visitation of aliens from space, the survival of a plane crash on a mysterious tropical island as we wait to be rescued, or the interruption of an entire planet for only a few seconds by a mysterious vision of the future. Apocalyptic themes reach out to human uncertainty brought on by political, economic, technological, and social changes that, while beyond our immediate control, affect all of our lives. They invite us to examine our fear and find the will inside us to follow with courage a vision of a new future. These art forms appeal to a society wanting authentic experiences of life, but questioning who to believe. It may be the perfect time for the church to talk again about "waiting on the coming of God."

The problem is that the old roadmaps of future hope have been stored on the dusty shelves of social consciousness. Today's culture has forgotten what ancient prophets once envisioned for a future under God's government. The text from Isaiah may be more familiar to your average listener than most of the passages from that book, but they have not studied it and internalized it as a contemporary myth that will lead them to recognize God's reign. So we preach it to a changing world, not as an old standard accompanied by strains of Handel's *Messiah*, but as a completely new vision coming to a prophet standing in the midst of a desert wilderness when hope seemed distant at best. We preach with a contemporary voice that asks hard questions and startles listeners to make a new way for the arrival of the realm of God. We open the door for the visionaries, poets, and dreamers to help us see what no one else can see. We bring into focus the story of Jesus as the one who "shook up" the systems of his day. Maybe the vision will come alive and we will learn to live as if a whole new domain is waiting on the doorstep of our world. If so, then we can do everything in our power to make a way for it to happen as we wait with an expectation more gripping than a child's anticipation of Christmas Day.

In order to preach this way, however, the preacher must first ask herself or himself: Are my expectations too small? Am I shaped by the same culture that markets Christmas as the most important day of the year? Can I admit my own limitations and ask for help from people who see differently than I? Do I have the courage to look into the mysterious unknown and ask to see a vision of an earth transformed by God's reign? What would it take for me to believe like John the Baptist did, if only for one Sunday of the year?

December 19, 2010
Fourth Sunday of Advent

First Reading
Isaiah 7:10-16 (RCL)
Isaiah 7:10-14 (LFM)

The prophet's message to King Ahaz of Judah is this: "If you do not stand firm in faith, you shall not stand at all" (7:9b). This king had been shaken by a recent attack from his closest neighbors, the Northern Kingdom of Israel and Damascus. When he refused to form an alliance with them in opposition to Assyria, they attacked him and set up their own ruler of Judah in order to bring them into compliance with their plan. As the rightful heir to the throne of Judah, Ahaz needed to regain control of his kingdom and reestablish his authority. The prophet Isaiah advised him against forming alliances with foreign powers. Like the great kings before him, he clearly needed to remain true to Judah's covenant with God instead. Isaiah urged Ahaz to trust God's promises to protect and deliver Judah because God cared about Judah and wanted the people to survive and flourish.

Sensing the lurking doubt and fear in Ahaz, Isaiah offered assurances to convince the king of God's ability to save Judah. He invited Ahaz to ask God for a sign, and not just any sign. He was to ask for something so amazing that he might be convinced that he should trust God above everyone else. But the king refused. It is not clear why Ahaz refused. Perhaps he felt betrayed when the leaders of the Northern Kingdom of Israel attacked their own relatives to the south. They worshiped the God of Jacob, too, so maybe God had taken their side against him. Perhaps Ahaz was weak in his own faith, and thought earthly measures were more reliable in solving earthly problems. Maybe he was angry with God because God had allowed this shame of defeat to fall on him. For whatever reason, Ahaz rejected God's invitation and failed to believe in the sign that Isaiah predicted would come true.

So God provided a sign anyway. Announced by Isaiah, it did not seem huge and far reaching. Instead, it was personal, human, intimate, and disclosive of new hope in the face of fear. "Look!" begins Isaiah (an interesting suggestion given the message he is commissioned to proclaim in 6:10). Open your eyes to see a pregnant young woman (the language of "virgin" came later in the Greek translation of the Hebrew word). When she gives birth (presumably within nine months from that time), she will name her child Immanuel, meaning "God with us." (The chapter earlier introduced the practice of symbolic naming of children to carry a message through them.) Before the time he can make choices for himself, the child will eat food that has been available in Judah only in prosperous times. This is because the kings of Israel and Damascus will already have withdrawn from Judah and its rightful authority will have been restored. In other words, the prophecy signals a change in the near future that will put things right. Instead of making rash decisions and dangerous alliances, Ahaz should wait on God to take care of the situation.[1]

The historical record shows that Ahaz decided to keep his eyes closed, ignore Isaiah's prophetic sign, and form an alliance with the Assyrian Empire, thus forfeiting Judah's independence in exchange for protection. In essence, Ahaz's fear moved him to sell his country into a form of bondage to Assyria in exchange for greater security. By taking matters into his own hands, instead of trusting God, Ahaz led Judah down a path that, for years, left them searching for a way out.

The signs of "God with us" in very unlikely places should strengthen our faith in the not-yet-fully-revealed power of God who longs to save the world from its own destruction. Left to our own devices, we tend to react to perceived threats out of fear, turning toward the power of other people, institutions, wealth, or achievement for our security. Taking a risk on the salvation of God, however, may bring more freedom than we could ever imagine.

Psalmody
Psalm 80:1-7, 17-19 (RCL)

The accuracy of the prophecy of Isaiah is confirmed by this response. The words of this psalm refer to the predicted defeat of the Northern Kingdom. The prayer seeks God's help in restoring that kingdom's place among the nations. The psalm depicts the grief and humiliation of a conquered people. They weep over the destruction of their homeland while enemies laugh at their shame. The song is punctuated by the refrain: "Restore us, O [LORD] God [of hosts]; let your face shine, that we may be saved" (vv. 3, 7, 19).

The language of the refrain refers back to the Aaronic benediction (Num. 6:24-26), which served to bless the nation at major assemblies and feasts. The appeal is made to a God of great strength who has the ability to win in battle over enemies. The image of a shining face may refer to a smiling face, one that discloses God's affection and good will toward God's people. The metaphor also seems to imply that God's face has been turned away from the nation in anger. Israel is asking for God's full attention to their plight. Just as the light of the sun brings clarity, warmth, and life to hidden seeds, so God's shining face is extending an ever-renewing grace and mercy to the people. The prayer asks for the revelation of God's presence in a way that is visible and effective. It is a way of invoking God as Immanuel to be with us once more.[2]

In an age when words like "holiness" and "glory" have lost their meaning and the only faces that shine have spotlights pointed at them, it is difficult to reclaim the power of the words in this refrain. Asking God's full attention to turn toward the world is bigger than most of us understand. It is much like asking someone for a light and getting a laser that penetrates the cancer in an inoperable part of the brain. All we thought we needed was enough light to read the latest edition of *O* magazine, not the full force of the sun. Asking God's face to shine is not just asking for attention, it is asking for presence—"God with us"—within every aspect of life on earth. It is the prayer of a people who have gotten into such a mess that they cannot possibly save themselves. It looks in faith to One who has the power, not just to restore them, but to recreate the whole world around them. This refrain allows us once again to invoke the presence of God to "come to us, abide with us, our Lord, Emmanuel" in the hope that, even today, we may be saved.

Psalm 24:1-2, 3-4, 5-6 (LFM)

When the first reading ends with verse 14 rather than continuing to 16, the giving of a "sign" becomes the theological focus of the reading, rather than the historical drama behind the prophecy. When translated into Greek, the Hebrew word for "young woman" becomes "virgin." The sign is this: "A virgin shall be with child and bear a son, and shall name him Immanuel."

Psalm 24 is an ancient entrance rite that was to be sung by those entering the sanctuary of the Temple, the dwelling place of God. It acknowledges God's power as Creator of the world. It outlines the required purity of those who dare to enter into God's holy presence. Their reward is God's blessing and vindication.[3]

Purity is required of those who are destined to receive "Emmanuel," God with us. With purity of heart and body, the virgin Mary became the dwelling place of God with us. With purity of heart, Joseph believed the messenger of God, took Mary to be his wife, and named her son "Jesus," which means "God saves." Both received God's promised favor and blessing.

The use of this psalm as a response to the prophetic word of Isaiah assures people that the "sign" of God's promise can be trusted. The one we "go up" to worship has "come down" as "God with us." The Holy One who requires us to be true and holy in life provides all the holiness we need by becoming one of us. In Jesus, God's face "shines" with gracious good will on all who seek God's face.

Second Reading
Romans 1:1-7 (RCL, LFM)

How do you preach a run-on sentence? You have to take hold of it and make it stop so everyone can catch their breath! The text from Romans gives you that feeling when you read it. Paul's letter to the members of the Christian community in Rome begins with this lengthy salutation. It introduces Paul himself, Jesus Christ, and the Jewish-Gentile audience in significant theological terms that set the stage for the reading of the entire letter.

This type of salutation was common in ancient letters. Imagine listening to it being read in the company of other Christians in Rome. Paul's self-understanding is clear: he is in slavery to Christ, not bound to any other obligation or under the patronage of any group; he is being called as an apostle of Jesus Christ, not having any authority of his own but only the authority of Christ; and he is set apart for the gospel of God, not claiming special status because of his own personal holiness, but because of the holiness of the gospel. (How's that for a run-on sentence?)

What is Paul sent to proclaim? The ancient gospel is known uniquely in Jesus. God put the spirit of holiness in a human being so that the relations of the world could be reordered and redefined by God's peace and goodwill. Paul writes to both Gentile Christians and Jewish Christians in Rome, addressing them as "God's beloved." They are "called," just as Paul is "called," to be "holy ones." The language of this message conjures up images of people who are so much into self-denial that they have nothing left to share with the world. Jesus' holiness, however, was more about self-giving than self-denial, and he was sent to do all that God intended so that both Jews and Gentiles could receive the gift of salvation.

The salutation ends with the expression of goodwill through a blessing. Grace and peace are the evidence of God's favor made known in Jesus. They are offered through the love and mercy of a God who keeps faith with God's people, and through Jesus Christ, the One to whom all are bound by his own gracious action toward the world.[4]

How do you preach a salutation? The same way you do every time you address a word to a congregation or group. You answer the question of who you are, what gives you the ability to say something meaningful to your audience, and what gives the audience a reason to listen to you. If, like Paul, we can begin to understand a little of what it means to be bound, called, and set apart as servants of a gospel much larger than ourselves, then perhaps we'll be given something important to say.

Gospel
Matthew 1:18-25 (RCL)
Matthew 1:18-24 (LFM)

Joseph was a man of true faith. According to his ancestry, Joseph carried the bloodline of the royal family of David, the family through whom God had promised to restore the fortunes of Judah. In his own right, Joseph's own progeny could have qualified as persons who could carry out God's work of salvation, just like Joseph was qualified. But Joseph was not yet married, and his fiancée had gotten pregnant without Joseph's approval or assistance.

Even today it is considered a disgrace to be in a relationship with a woman who is carrying someone else's baby. Imagine how scandalous it was back then. Joseph could lie about the baby's paternity and marry his fiancée quickly and quietly, but he would always bear the wound of knowing that his firstborn child was a result of Mary's unfaithfulness to him. He would have to bear that disgrace until he died. On the other hand, Joseph could protect his reputation by exposing Mary to public condemnation and allow her to bear the scar of shame for the rest of her life, unless she was publicly stoned first. The story tells us, however, that Joseph is a righteous man. He doesn't lie. He doesn't shame publicly the woman he had vowed would be his wife. Joseph keeps thinking about his decision until he figures out the right thing for everyone. He could let her go quietly to have her child somewhere away from her hometown where she would be safe from the gossip and scorn of neighbors. He would privately dissolve their relationship.

After finally reaching this difficult decision, Joseph went to bed satisfied that he was doing the right thing. During sleep, however, he dreamed that an angel stood before him and addressed him saying, "Joseph, son of David, do not be afraid to take Mary as your wife, for the child conceived in her is from the Holy Spirit. She will bear a son, and you are to name him Jesus, for he will save his people from their sins" (vv. 20-21). Whoa! What a dream! It was like the angel knew everything he had been thinking, and more! The messenger knew he was a descendant of David, so he knew about the whole bloodline issue. The angel knew about his betrothal to Mary and the option of getting married immediately. The most startling news, though, was that Mary wasn't bearing an "illegitimate" child. Mary was bearing a son who would save God's people from their sins. The child was a holy gift of God, rather than a source of humiliation and disgrace. Mary's child was quite "legitimate" after all.

As the story goes, Joseph woke up, immediately obeyed the angel in his dream, and married Mary. He refused to have sex with her until the child was born. The faith of Joseph is amazing. He does not hesitate or doubt that he is doing the right thing. He acts on unquestioning faith. Once he realizes that the child is a gift of God, he musters a character that is purer than his ancestor David's, defends and protects Mary his wife as she embodies the sign of God's promise as spoken through Isaiah, and assists in the birth of hope for the salvation of the world. He is truly a righteous man of God.

Once Mary gives birth to a son, Joseph names him Jesus. This is also a moment of deep faith for a man like Joseph. By naming Jesus, Joseph claims him as his own child, an heir to his own lineage. By naming him Jesus, Joseph commissions him for the mission God intends for him. Joseph believes the sign of God's promise as deeply as he cares for the infant in his arms.

What an interesting and delightful story! The Son of God, Immanuel, is born in an extraordinary way. His mother is an unlikely young woman, not yet married, whose innocence is protected and preserved until the birth of this holy child. He is holy because his mother is holy. His real father is the Spirit of God that brought him into being. He is holy because he is the child of God. His bloodline is traced back to the greatest king in his nation's memory because a righteous man, Joseph, adopted him as his own son and made him an heir in the family who traces its lineage to David. The promise of God is fulfilled, not in customary, conventional means, but in unlikely and wonderful ways. Jesus comes to life because Joseph risked responding in faith instead of reacting in fear.

Will It Preach?

A primary theme in all the readings for this Sunday is "faith." Isaiah's prophetic words, Paul's apostolic claims, and Joseph's righteous response all demonstrate faith that relies solely on a God who extends salvation when and where it is least expected. The faith we see in Scripture seems straightforward and simple at first. God speaks; humans are to act in faith. In reality, it is not simple at all! The lives in the text are full of complicated dilemmas and pitfalls that challenge the quick fixes of Sunday school theology or contemporary self-help sermons. People's worlds get messy and difficult, full of heartache and disenchantment, not because they've created all this chaos for themselves but because they responded to God's calling on their lives. All of a sudden they're faced with the most difficult choices of their lives.

In our world today, the problem of teen pregnancy is trumped by the birth of infants with birth defects, HIV, or an addiction to crack cocaine. Families live in tenements, automobiles, and shelters, unsure that they will be able to feed their children the next day. Children are abandoned, abused, molested, and often killed before they can reach their second birthday. It seems like the problems of our contemporary world are too complicated for the faith that we claim to believe. How do we respond?

Preaching these texts requires that we explore the stories in Scripture by unpacking the controversial situations that called forth the response of radical faith. They aren't fairy tales, they are messages about God's ability to evoke in human beings the will to risk everything for something greater than themselves. It allows us to imagine ourselves acting courageously even when we are cowards, trusting in God's claim on us and hoping for a future that will put the present to shame. Faith is not a formula. Faith is not even logical. Faith doesn't make everything lovely and civilized. Instead, faith takes a risk with no guarantees and trusts God with the rest. Climbing out on a limb on a windy day doesn't seem like an intelligent thing to do, but sometimes you have to do it to rescue a helpless creature. Believe the signs as best you can, listen carefully and trust God's voice, step out in faith toward a future that you can't even see, and maybe you'll become the agent of change in a troubled world.

Notes

1. Joseph Blenkinsopp, "Isaiah," in *The New Oxford Annotated Bible,* 3d ed. (New York: Oxford University Press, 2001), 988hb.
2. John S. Kselman, "Psalms," in *The New Oxford Annotated Bible,* 846hb.
3. Ibid, 794hb.
4. A. Katherine Grieb, *The Story of Romans: A Narrative Defense of God's Righteousness* (Louisville: Westminster John Knox, 2002), 2-4, 8.

Christmas

Mary Lin Hudson

The uproar over the substitution of the greeting "Happy Holidays!" for "Merry Christmas!" during the season of lights seems destined to remain alive for years to come. When Christianity is asked to share its holiday with other cultural celebrations, people are tilted out of the comfort of their conventional belief systems. In an effort to protect the honor of their long-held traditions, Christians assume a defensive and hostile posture against change.

In reality, however, Christmas is all about change. Christians did not begin celebrating Christmas until well into the fourth century C.E. The date was chosen for the celebration based on its proximity to Easter, which fell near the dating of the vernal equinox. At the time, it found itself in competition with a preexisting pagan festival known as *dies natalis Solis Invicti* (day of the Invincible Sun) instituted by the Emperor Marcus Aurelius in 274 C.E. This observance of the lengthening of days fell after the winter solstice and was celebrated with feasting, decoration of homes with green boughs and lights, family gathering (including the remembrance of the dead), and gift giving. Christians adapted the celebration to their own purposes by designating the anniversary of Jesus' birth as the "birthday of the Sun of Righteousness." It was the work of the preacher to aid the congregation in making the unlikely connections between the old and the new.[1]

The proclamation of the triumph of God over injustice and oppression turns quickly into Christian triumphalism unless preachers realize that God's realm of justice and righteousness levels out the inequalities among different people and groups. God does not measure faith according to levels of superiority or inferiority, but in terms of the full acceptance and inclusion of all people that is possible only in the receiving of God's own gift of grace.

During the Christmas cycle, prophetic texts ring with joy over the coming of a Savior to liberate and renew the world from the forces of domination and oppression. The generosity of this divine gift sets the world to singing and dancing out of sheer gratitude and elation that change has come. The epistles emphasize the grace revealed in Jesus who leads people into humble words and actions for the sake of harmonious community living. The gospel readings provide anything but a triumphant view of the incarnation of the Word in human flesh and blood. Nothing in these texts suggests that Christians should line up and defend the honor of their God against differing cultural influences. Instead, the opposite is true. The message of the gospel stirs us to lay down weapons and join hands with the rest of the world in a celebration of the gift of peace. Let us embody that same humility in the proclamation of salvation for the whole wide world.

Note

1.   Frank Senn, *Christian Liturgy: Catholic and Evangelical* (Minneapolis: Fortress Press, 1997), 159-61.

December 24 & 25, 2010
Nativity of Our Lord I (RCL)
Christmas: Mass at Midnight (LFM)

Revised Common Lectionary (RCL)

Isaiah 9:2-7
Psalm 96
Titus 2:11-14
Luke 2:1-14 (15-20)

Lectionary for Mass (LFM)

Mass at Midnight
Isaiah 9:1-6
Psalm 96:1-2a, 2b-3, 11-12, 13
Titus 2:11-14
Luke 2:1-14
At the Vigil Mass
Isaiah 62:1-5
Psalm 89:4-5, 16-17, 27, 29
Acts 13:16-17, 22-25
Matthew 1:1-25 or 1:18-25

First Reading
Isaiah 9:2-7 (RCL)
Isaiah 9:1-6 (LFM)

The opening of this text describes the restoration of Israel from Assyrian rule. All the regions named here were separated from Judah and established as part of the Assyrian Empire in 733 B.C.E. Joy shall return to the people of these regions because God's ruler will make things just and right again. This restoration will bring a return to the unity of a long-divided people. This sense of completion will bring joy.[1]

Who wouldn't be overjoyed to have military rule lifted? The images of yoke, bar, rod, and boot refer to the harsh and violent oppression that maintained control of the people from those provinces on behalf of the Assyrian king. Living under intimidation and the threat and punishment of imprisonment, enslavement, and heavy taxation drained the hope out of the imaginations of the people. Suddenly, their darkness has turned to light.

The dawning light of hope radiates from a child who is born as a gift to the world. He carries many names that describe him as a deity: Wonderful Counselor,

Mighty God, Everlasting Father, and Prince of Peace. These names identify him as the Messiah, the One sent by God to bring righteousness and judgment to the earth. The power given to him at birth will only increase with time and he will bring peace to those who live under his reign.

Psalmody
Psalm 96 (RCL)
Psalm 96:1-2a, 2b-3, 11-12, 13 (LFM)

This psalm of gladness responds to the good news of the dawning of justice and righteousness throughout the world. The news sets people to singing a new song in celebration of the newness of life around them. Not only do people sing, but the earth sings as well. All creation tells of the news of God's greatness and glorifies God through its worship. All is renewed by what God has done.

Second Reading
Titus 2:11-14 (RCL, LFM)

Christmas is a time of remembering and retelling the story of Jesus. God is worshiped for sending Jesus to save the world. In the midst of such joy, however, we hear this text from Titus telling us to pause a minute and think about the implications of this news for the living our daily lives. Although we are living in the "present age," our lives are being formed by the work of Jesus in bringing salvation to all. It isn't time yet for God's new creation to be completed. Until that time comes, people should live as if they already belong to the new creation, living according to God's justice and mercy, rather than reacting to things emotionally or without regard for others. The warmth and goodwill of Christmas Eve demonstrates the kind of life that is possible every day of the year. Let us take time to be quiet and allow the peace deep within us to emerge that comes from knowing that God is saving the world through Jesus.

Gospel
Luke 2:1-14 (LFM)
Luke 2:1-14 (RCL)

This ancient story evokes memories of the heart so deep that most of us can recite every word of this text. It is a classic story that deserves to be told with great love and respect for the power that it holds over us.

The story begins with a mighty emperor, self-proclaimed Son of God, exercising full authority over the region where Jesus himself, the true Son of God, would come to reign. His proposed census would measure how many people could be recruited for military service and also be taxed in support of the empire. Emperor Augustus had his appointed governor of Syria enforce his edict. This meant that Joseph, a descendant of David, went to Bethlehem to be registered according to his tribal roots. He had to make the long journey from the safety of his hometown with his new bride, Mary, to a place that was crowded and a bit dangerous in its proximity to Jerusalem.

Being "great with child" is probably a better description of Mary than the term *pregnant*! Can you imagine how uncomfortable this woman must have been trying to walk or ride the way to Bethlehem? It must have been bumpy, because as soon as she got there, she went into labor and delivered her child.

The setting is surprising in the story. A barn is a place where human beings rarely sleep. Instead, it is a place for creatures to be protected and stabled. In humility beyond measure, Mary and Joseph make a place for the child in a manger on the hay that was used to feed the creatures. God's own Son enters into the dwelling of God's earthly creatures, set apart from palaces, houses, or even guestrooms where humans normally abide. Jesus comes to the whole unredeemed creation, not just to a few select people. The curtain falls on this first act as Mary curls up near the child exhausted and messy from the labor of human birth. Joseph is also worn out by the ordeal, but still stands guard over the two entrusted to his care.

When the curtain rises on Act II, the stage is dark with only the light of the stars and a sliver of moon overhead. Shepherds sit listening for predators that might attack, scatter, and devour their flock of sheep. Without warning, a messenger appears from nowhere and a radiating light surrounds where they are resting. The shepherds' hearts pump wildly and they try to protect themselves from harm. The stranger speaks calmly, however, and comforts them with news: "Look—a Savior is born today in Bethlehem. He is the Messiah of God. This is the sign given by which you will recognize him: a child, wrapped in bands of cloth, will be lying in a manger." Even before they can ask questions, the messenger is joined by an army of angels who sing more convincingly than a gifted church choir, "Glory to God in the highest heaven, and on earth peace among God's favored ones." The sound fills the earth and the heavens, transforming the hillside into a pavilion of praise. And then it is all over. The grazing ground around them is dark, except for the light of the stars and the sliver of moon overhead. The only sound they can hear is the whisper of a breeze and the baaing of sheep. The curtain falls as the shepherds look at each other in amazement and head for the lights of Bethlehem.

Act III begins with breathless shepherds finding their way into the humble stable beside a quiet inn. They are startled to see exactly what they were told that they would find. Mary and Joseph sit in a makeshift shelter of hay with a child beside them lying in a feeding trough. The shepherds don't linger too long with the exhausted family, but instead head back through the streets of Bethlehem, sharing their amazing story to every person they see along the way. As they head out the gate of the city, they find themselves singing the tune that had just been sung to them by the angels: "Glory to God in the highest heaven, and peace to God's people on earth!"

At the Vigil Mass (LFM)

First Reading: Isaiah 62:1-5. The metaphor of marriage provides a description of the transformation that occurs when a woman's circumstances are reversed by a romantic, joyous marriage to the man of her dreams. In the movie *Pretty Woman*, the hooker is swept off her feet by a wealthy tycoon who falls deeply in love with her. The language of Isaiah carries a similar sentiment. God will vindicate the dishonor of Israel after the destruction of the Temple by its captors. The vindication will be so glorious that all who see it will have new awe and respect for the nation. With beauty and power like a bride at her wedding, Israel will be the envy of everyone. The one whom God sends will be like the bridegroom, swept off his feet by love, who is overjoyed because he has married the bride of his dreams. Such is the true joy that the earth will feel when God provides a savior for God's people.

Psalm 89:4-5, 16-17, 27, 29. This is an interesting selection in relation to the dominant theme of Isaiah 62. It is a psalm that laments the death of a ruler and the collapse of a dynasty, but it begins with a hymn of praise. The Creator keeps faith with a vast and glorious creation. Such faithfulness deserves a celebration to honor God's involving those who believe in the promise of love and righteousness. God promises to establish a ruler who is greater than all other rulers. He will govern the earth with the support of God, not just until he dies, but "as long as the heavens endure."

The chosen verses of this reading highlight promises made by God to a people who were longing for a strong Messiah to redeem them. Within the context of Christmas Eve, the call to celebration is recognition of a God who fulfilled these promises in the birth of Jesus. God's promises to the world are themselves something to celebrate! Surely God deserves our highest form of praise!

Acts 13:16-17, 22-25. Paul is preaching in the synagogue. His sermon on salvation history moves from the exodus to the settlement of Canaan, through the period of the judges to the establishment of the nation under David's rule. The traditional version of Israel's history takes a new turn, however, as Paul introduces the coming of Jesus, preceded by John the Baptist, as the new Savior of Israel who will set free God's people from sins and bring forth a new creation. The sermon brings good news to an expectant people.

Matthew 1:1-25 or 1:18-25. Matthew's gospel begins with the genealogy of Jesus as traced from Abraham through Joseph, the husband of Mary. The genealogy is notably different from others because its patriarchal structure is interrupted by the mention of four women: Tamar (Genesis 38), Rahab (Joshua 2), Ruth, and Bathsheba, the wife of Uriah (2 Samuel 11-12).[2] These women played important roles in perpetuating the family line, yet each of them behaved in ways that were outside of cultural norms. They cracked open the rigid, patriarchal model of identity and allowed people to glimpse a different model of faith that merits God's favor. Mary's pregnancy placed her in a similar situation of scandal and qualifies her as a bona fide member of the family tree.

The other odd thing about this particular genealogy is that it presents the ancestors in sets of fourteen, which leaves out a few of Jesus' less remarkable relatives. The first fourteen represent those who established the identity of God's people, and the second fourteen represent the generations that lived from the time of the Davidic dynasty until the deportation of God's people into Babylon. The third group of fourteen lived from the time of exile to the moment of deliverance through the birth of Jesus the Messiah. The consonants in the name "David" correspond to the number fourteen, which further serves to validate Jesus' identity as a descendant of David.

The genealogy of Jesus does more than simply bestow a royal pedigree on the Christ child; it demonstrates that God has been working continuously through all kinds of people to bring about the fulfillment of the promise made to Abraham, David, and now Joseph. God has always worked through unlikely people in complicated circumstances to keep alive God's future plans for the entire world. The coming of Jesus through this family line confirms that Jesus is a child of God's promise to save the world.

When the birth narrative is linked to the genealogy, it carries within it the overtones of God's agency through people of a previous era. Joseph, the husband of Mary, is a dreamer just like his ancestor Joseph. Joseph's action in marrying Mary gives her and her baby protection from scandal, persecution, and starvation, just as his ancestor Joseph's obedience saved his own family from destruction. With Joseph as the principal actor in Matthew's birth narrative, the listener is encouraged to see the correlation between this drama of salvation and the story of God's liberating triumph that set the people free from the bondage of slavery in Egypt. It is as if we view the birth narrative as a snapshot with a double exposure: the story of the exodus superimposed on the story of the life of Jesus so that you can't view Jesus without seeing the image of liberation covering his face.

(See the Fourth Sunday of Advent for another commentary on Matt. 1:18-24.)

Will It Preach?

The spirit of Christmas can warm the human heart with a desire to hear the good news proclaimed once again. The preacher usually has a small window of opportunity to preach good news because the message is usually packaged in the traditional words and music that congregations have been waiting to hear since the beginning of Advent. In this setting, preaching needs to be poetic and concise, evoking faith through fresh language that awakens a new awareness of an old story. With the sheer joy of a wedding dance, but with the wonder of a starry night, the sermon will remind the listener that the gospel is still good news in the present day. The Christmas Eve sermon is the preacher's gift to a waiting congregation.

Notes

1. J. Andrew Overman, "Matthew," in *The New Oxford Annotated Bible,* 3d ed. (New York: Oxford University Press, 2001), 9nt.

2. Warren Carter, *Matthew and the Margins: A Sociopolitical and Religious Reading* (Maryknoll, N.Y.: Orbis, 2000), 53-66.

December 25, 2010
Nativity of Our Lord II (RCL)
Christmas: Mass at Dawn (LFM)

Revised Common Lectionary (RCL)	Lectionary for Mass (LFM)
Isaiah 62:6-12	Isaiah 62:11-12
Psalm 97	Psalm 97:1, 6, 11-12
Titus 3:4-7	Titus 3:4-7
Luke 2:(1-7) 8-20	Luke 2:15-20

First Reading
Isaiah 62:6-12 (RCL)
Isaiah 62:11-12 (LFM)

"Look! They're coming! They're coming!" The word of the prophet announces the arrival of a processional. In the midst of the parade is the Promised One who is accompanied by joyous people coming from the ends of the earth. He brings salvation to God's people, redeeming them from enslavement to their enemies. He returns to bring glory to Zion with the return of God's beloved people.

This text joins together the longing for fulfillment and the joy of triumph as salvation comes to pass. As such, it clearly reflects the circumstances of the contemporary worshiper who both celebrates the event of the birth of a Savior but still longs for a time when life will be better. The people who gather to celebrate the story of God's salvation bring with them hopes that the full meaning of God's gift will be revealed in the world in new ways. Prayers are offered to God for help with mortgage payments, medical treatments, marriage vows, and drug addictions, to name a few. Some may have children or parents deployed to dangerous war zones in the name of peace. A few may be so gripped by depression that the prospect of another tomorrow may be more than they can bear. The pastor prays on behalf of a people in need of new changes to their lives. At the same time, the choir sings with joy at the coming of salvation. Longing is embraced by promised fulfillment. The two have a moment of joyous delight for the two are meeting once again in the birth of Jesus, Emmanuel.

Psalmody
Psalm 97 (RCL)
Psalm 97:1, 6, 11-12 (LFM)

This song of celebration praises a God who is so mysteriously all-powerful and glorious that the earth is overwhelmed by the intensity of God's influence. The lesser gods are put to shame while Judah rejoices in their God. God's salvation is like the dawn rising out of darkness. Those who see it are filled with gratitude and praise.

Second Reading
Titus 3:4-7 (RCL, LFM)

The spirit of gift giving accompanies the celebration of Jesus' birth. Family members and friends work to find a gift that will delight the one who receives it because it fulfills a need or a wish in their lives. With changes in the economic climate, many Christians are simplifying their gift giving in order to make Christmas less about extravagant spending and more about personal expressions of love and peace. Still, the acts of giving and receiving gifts inherently model the challenge and the joy of the meaning of Christmas.

The gospel is spelled out plainly by the author of this letter. The coming of the Savior is a gift to the world. It is God's merciful way of bringing new birth to people who long to enter into God's new eternal creation. Jesus Christ poured onto humanity the Spirit of Holiness, not as a reward for our fine achievements, but because of his kindness and goodness. We receive it as grace.

Gospel
Luke 2:(1-7) 8-20 (RCL)
Luke 2:15-20 (LFM)

See the gospel for Nativity of the Lord I, p.36.

Will It Preach?

Any sermon for a Mass at Dawn will be simple and concise. There's joyful good news about the birth of a baby who is sent by God to save the world. Yet, the news comes in the dark of night to peasants on a hillside protecting a herd of animals. They have no protection from the forces of the empire or from the poor nutrition and lack of basic resources that threaten their daily existence. When they go to see if the good news of the angels is true, they find a young couple, no more affluent than they, sheltering a newborn in an animal shed filled with hay. Even so, the shepherds believed the good news. Everything was different, yet everything was still the same. Only the eyes of faith could receive the good news and sing for joy in recognition of God's gift to the world.

December 25, 2010
Nativity of Our Lord III (RCL)
Christmas: Mass During the Day (LFM)

Revised Common Lectionary (RCL)
Isaiah 52:7-10
Psalm 98
Hebrews 1:1-4 (5-12)
John 1:1-14

Lectionary for Mass (LFM)
Isaiah 52:7-10
Psalm 98:1, 2-3a, 3b-4, 5-6
Hebrews 1:1-6
John 1:1-18 or 1:1-5, 9-14

First Reading
Isaiah 52:7-10 (RCL, LFM)

The runner is out of breath as he approaches the city gate, but as soon as the gate opens he shouts with the strength of an opera singer, "Your God reigns!" And as you listen, the prophets standing watch atop the walls of the city join in a rousing chorus of the news: "Our God reigns! Salvation is ours!" The city residents rush about, wildly hugging and dancing and singing with joy, "Our God reigns! We are saved! Hallelujah!" Isaiah employs the metaphor of a triumphant leader approaching his kingdom with the assurance of peace for his people. The response of the city is the unbridled expression of joy and gladness at the sight of their king.

The infant Jesus, the newborn king, comes again into our world through story, music, and ritual on Christmas Day. We who have waited watchfully during Advent can recognize the signs of salvation coming to us. They remind us that God does act decisively in the world, although God's saving work comes to us in unconventional ways. Today we sing at the top of our lungs because we glimpse our hope fulfilled in Jesus, God's agent of salvation for the world.

Wouldn't it be marvelous to imitate this text within the service of worship? Using the spirit of the good news alive in this text, let the preacher, cantor, or another individual begin by entering the sanctuary shouting or singing a simple announcement of good news, let singers pick up the same refrain one at a time until the entire choir has joined the chorus, followed by the congregation singing in full voice to the accompaniment of instruments of every kind! An experience of this text may mean far more than a mere reading of it.

Psalmody
Psalm 98 (RCL)
Psalm 98:1, 2-3a, 3b-4, 5-6 (LFM)

Can there be any better response to the first reading than singing? Psalm 98 is full of singing! The psalmist calls for a new song especially appropriate for a triumphant God. The song is accompanied by all manner of musical instruments, giving resonance and support to the great chorus of voices. The whole earth reverberates with the joyous sound. Oceans, hills, and all the rest of creation join the hymn to God. Celebrate the justice and mercy of a loving God who is revealed to us in Jesus, the Savior!

If the first reading is not sung, then the responsive reading should be. Again, the imitation of the intent of the psalm could accompany the reading, or follow it. Something festive and strong that can be felt as well as heard will express the psalm's intention.

Second Reading
Hebrews 1:1-4 (5-12) (RCL)
Hebrews 1:1-6 (LFM)

How appropriate that the second reading from the letter of Hebrews begins with a hymn![1] The language contains echoes of the hymn in Philippians 2:6-11 and also reflects the meaning of John 1. The Christology reflected in this text seems to relate strongly to the Jewish theological understanding of Wisdom as found in the apocryphal writings of the intertestamental period.[2]

This prologue to Hebrews supports the gospel reading for the day by explaining how Jesus embodies the Word of promise spoken by God to the ancestors and, in a more focused way, through the prophets. The incarnation of the Word of God has participated fully in God's creation and sustenance of the world. Now the Word has come to purify and reorder all things. Jesus is to be worshiped as nothing less than the offspring of the Eternal Source of Life.

The concept of the divinity of Christ introduced here provides a way for Christians to understand the interconnectedness of all things. The exaltation of Jesus as "Son of God" allows persons to move past the dualism that separates heavenly and earthly perspectives. It gives hope to people who have known the promise and those who are coming to believe the proclamation of the gospel even today. The Word creates, sustains, purifies, and reconciles all things. Let's let the Word come into the world and do its work for us and through us today.

Gospel
John 1:1-14 (RCL)
John 1:1-18 or 1:1-5, 9-14 (LFM)

One cloudy afternoon I was called into an office of a doctor who had been treating my mother for the past few years. "I need to talk to you," she said in a matter-of-fact way. "Around the time of Thanksgiving, a surgeon removed half of my liver during what was supposed to be a routine gall bladder procedure. They discovered a malignant tumor, a rare form of cancer, growing in my liver. The prognosis is not so good." I took a deep breath and waited for her to continue. "Fortunately my daughter in Minnesota has graciously agreed to take me in. I will be moving in with her family so that I can be just around the corner from the Mayo Clinic. In two days, I will close my practice of over thirty years and will relocate to the north where there's a snowman in every yard." She paused. "It isn't easy, but I believe that God is in all of this. With every obstacle, a way has opened up to provide what I have needed through this entire ordeal. God keeps amazing me!" Turning for a brief moment to look out the window, she added, "Sometimes I get a little weary of being amazed by God."

Christmas comes, whether we are ready or not, in the middle of time and space inhabited by embodied people facing their own mortality. The Gospel of John tells us that there is some symmetry to God's own life with Word and with Spirit. Word and Spirit are in the beginning with God. We anticipate God's finally victory at the end of all things when Christ and Spirit come to govern the universe. But in the between times, God's Word becomes embodied in the middle of time and space and moves into a fragile, uncertain human world of mortality.

On Christmas Day people of faith gather to celebrate that mystery once more. "And the Word became flesh and lived among us," the gospel tells us, "and we have seen his glory … full of grace and truth." The life, light, and power of God animating the physical life of the universe comes to reside in the blood, bone, and tissue of a Jewish body living in a harsh world. A flesh-and-blood God is hard to accept, especially when you take seriously the nature of the bodies with which human beings are born.

Bodies are amazing in their efficiency and resiliency. Water, air, and food fuel our living cells. Excess waste and toxins are eliminated while nutrients are incorporated. Passion and pleasure drive the process that perpetuates the race. Alien creatures invade and attack, but bodies resist and fight, winning battle after battle. Bodies break down, lose their chemical balance, age, and finally die. Bodies feel pain when violated. Bodies are strong, yet fragile and weak. Bodies disappoint and amaze us. Bodies matter.

Bodies matter, not because of how they look or how well they work. Bodies matter because we live in them in the midst of God's creation. The life that is in us is a gift from God. It took God becoming one of us to reveal and redeem the entirety of human experience that dynamically flows in and through us.

The Word in human life amazes us. It offers us a clear vision of the world through the eyes of God. It surprises us with an abundance of life-gifts in very human packages! The Word is embodied in the extraordinary care that opens a home to a broken body in need. The Word is embodied in the extravagant feeding of people who can no longer cook warm meals for themselves. The Word becomes flesh when it embraces with love the stranger who has come home. The Word is incarnate in the eyes of an innocent child just fresh from the womb who takes in the world for the first time.

On this day, we worship because God amazes us with truth and grace. In the weariness of the difficult embodied lives we lead, let us be amazed that God's love fills flesh and blood with life and leads us through darkness into the light of grace.

Will It Preach?

Christmas is more than a historical event or a collection of beautiful stories and songs. Christmas is an experience of God's grace. The more that our preaching can move people to experience the meaning of the gospel in the imaginations of the heart, the more it reflects the physical embodiment of the divine life in our midst. The first reading and response can be experienced in the unfolding liturgy of the day. Preaching on the gospel reading, however, needs to put people in touch with the physicality of the gospel. The spiritual and the physical have been joined in the incarnation of the Word. The message of salvation must be proclaimed to both the spiritual and physical aspects of the life of the world, or it will not have grasped fully the amazing message of grace and truth that Christmas brings.

Notes

1. Cynthia Briggs Kittredge, "Hebrews," in *The New Oxford Annotated Bible*, 3d ed. (New York: Oxford University Press, 2001), 370nt.
2. Ibid. See Prov. 8:22-31; Wis. 7:26, 9:9; Sir. 24:8; Bar. 3:37; 1 Enoch 42:1-2.

December 26, 2010
First Sunday of Christmas (RCL)

Revised Common Lectionary (RCL)

Isaiah 63:7-9
Psalm 148
Hebrews 2:10-18
Matthew 2:13-23

First Reading
Isaiah 63:7-9

The sharing of common memories is the glue that binds together families, good friends, and other social groups. Especially on significant occasions like birthdays, anniversaries, funeral gatherings, you can hear folks swapping their favorite stories about each other and times gone by. "Do you remember when … ?" the conversation begins. The people returning from exile sometime after 556 B.C.E. are listening to the words of the prophet that sound much like an old story recounted at a family reunion. "Do you remember when … ?" the prophet begins. "Then let me tell the story once more, so you will remember with me."

The story is about a great Sovereign who looked upon a struggling nation and decided to help them because he was generous and merciful. He thought that they, like he, would be honest and faithful in their dealings. And so instead of sending a messenger or an ambassador to take care of their needs, he came himself. His presence secured the life and good fortune of this nation, and his favor redeemed them from debts to their enemies. He kept them close to him and took care of their needs for a long, long time.

It is a great story that serves many purposes. First, it evokes admiration for one who is both strong and compassionate. It reminds people of a God who once acted on their behalf and will act again. Second, it sets up a high ethical standard that people should be prepared to meet if they are to maintain their relationship with this benevolent Lord. God enters into covenant because God has faith that this particular group of people can actually be honest with God and faithful in their relationship. It sets up the expectation that the beneficiaries of God's salvation would not disappoint God. Third, it reminds them that God is a "hands-on" kind of savior. "God with us" is a dynamic presence in the world that enters into the affairs of state and redirects them because God cares about folks like us who have trouble staying out of trouble. God's compassion steps in and raises an entire nation of people from despair to life.

Remembering stories like this are important for people who are often misdirected by the trends in their cultural context. Like the people returning after exile, we need to hear the story again and remember that long ago God became present in the world in order to save it. The desire for that same unmediated presence should prompt us to tell the story and watch for God's presence to accompany us today into the fullness of life.

Psalmody
Psalm 148

The greatest threat to the planet today is ... people! Of course, humans have been the enemy of the earth for a long, long time. As soon as human beings stopped honoring the earth and its creatures as sacred partners in creation, the plants, trees, mammals, birds, soil, and air have suffered at the hands of human "progress."

In an interview with Bill Moyers, Joseph Campbell talked about how the Native peoples in the United States had rituals to honor animals like the buffalo that they hunted and killed for food. Because the animal was sacred and life giving to the Indians, they ritualized the killing as they ate the meat and were careful to give special honor to the buffalo spirit, lest the herd be angered and leave them to starve. When European Americans discovered huge herds of buffalo on the plains, they killed hundreds of animals at a time just for the sport of it and left the carcasses rotting in their wake. Their strength was used to dominate and slaughter the life-forms that got in the way of their own sense of entitlement and control of the world.[1]

This psalm expresses the joy and wonder of a renewed earth turned toward God in praise. Heavenly beings, creatures of the galaxy, life forms of the deepest oceans, elements of the atmosphere, geological formations, animals, reptiles, and birds—all creation—takes part in this cosmic symphony to God. All the people of every class, race, gender, age, orientation—everybody—sings in the symphonic choir. The reason is that God has brought new life to a people who were as good as dead. God "has raised up a horn" or has renewed the generative, life-giving strength of those who belong to God.

If God's people could only realize the power that has been given to affirm the life around them and generate new life in their actions and words! The earth could be so different! No doubt, the earth would be the first to respond with glad praise to the Divine Wisdom that could turn people from predators into fruitful and creative partners in life. The whole cosmos would resound with the symphony of love and peace.

Second Reading
Hebrews 2:10-18

In the new age born of the development of communication and information technology, it is scary to experience the systematic dehumanizing of the world. Letters are now addressed to society in general, rather than persons in particular. The average person can do banking, pay bills, get the news, buy groceries and other necessities, all without being required to have a face-to-face conversation with another human being. People stand in checkout lines, carrying on intimate conversations on their cell phones, and never speak or acknowledge the ten other human beings within an arm's length of them. The popularity of the social networking Web site Facebook shows the preference of many people for virtual communities, rather than embodied gatherings in living rooms, classrooms, and even sanctuaries.

The text from Hebrews celebrates the rehumanizing of the world through the incarnation of God in a flesh-and-blood Jesus. "God with us" did not come in a box, a bottle, or a book with explicit instructions for life. God became a man—not a virtual being—and experienced human life full of suffering and death. God identified as a brother to each of us not through his goodness, but through his suffering.

After listening to someone struggle with being angry with God for placing her in a situation of great conflict, confusion, and loss, the friend responded, "If I've learned anything in the past sixty-odd years, it's that living involves suffering and loss. The character of a person is shaped by how they learn to deal with it."

Any baby born to Jewish parents in ancient Palestine under Roman rule was destined to suffer in some way. Jesus was no exception. It was how he lived in the midst of it that gives us a glimpse of the power and mercy of a God who identifies in every way with the lives we lead. No computer can do that, no matter how sophisticated the software. An embodied God is a compassionate God who comes to rehumanize a struggling world.

Gospel
Matthew 2:13-23

According to Matthew's gospel, Jesus was born into a region ruled by an egotistical tyrant. Jesus' father, Joseph, had little status and power except his link to his ancestor David, king of Israel. David died long ago and the Jews in Judea endured the harsh military rule of the Roman Empire under the leadership of Herod, an appointee of Emperor Augustus. With the birth of a child who was promised "to save his people," the stage was set for conflict between a king appointed by the emperor and the true king authorized by God.

After a visit from adoring Easterners who were warned to bypass Herod on their journey home, Joseph received his own warning about Herod. Joseph was a light sleeper like his ancestor Joseph before him in ancient Egypt. In a dream, similar to the one that convinced him to become husband and father to Mary and her son, Joseph is told to flee the country because the baby is in danger from Herod. In a drama cloaked in suspense and peril, Joseph and Mary leave during the dark of night and travel the long road to Egypt. Egypt was the very place that took in Jacob and his sons when the compassionate brother, Joseph, saved them from starvation. Now Jesus and his parents find themselves refugees, like their forebears, without a homeland, because of the violent madness of a fearful tyrant. Egypt would be their place of waiting, as it was long ago for their ancestors, for the time when God would lead them out of bondage and into freedom. The Savior of the world is saved by the wisdom of God in his father, Joseph, and taken in by strangers in order to preserve his future and the world's hope!

Millions of innocent people today have fled their homelands because of war, violence, and disasters that threaten them with death. Refugees can be found around the globe: children of parents lost to the atrocities of war, women dehumanized by mass rape and torture by soldiers of war, families displaced from their property by the explosive weapons of war. Thousands upon thousands have endured the poverty and squalor of temporary camps surrounded by wire and supplied with few resources. Even today in countries that border the ancient world which Jesus knew, refugees find life difficult without a country, a passport, and a home to go back to. Life, however, is still preferable to violence and death, and human spirits find ways to survive on little else than hope.

The story of Joseph's flight to Egypt carries with it an ethical demand for listeners. To the people of Antioch after the defeat of the Jewish uprising against Rome and the destruction of the Temple in 70 C.E., the story of struggling refugees was familiar. One of the ethical issues that faced them was how to accommodate the displaced brothers and sisters who had been forced to flee homes and communities in fear of their lives. To contemporary listeners who are aware of the plight of refugees in the world, perhaps this story awakens compassion for those stuck on foreign soil with no place to go. We must support efforts to provide for their needs while working urgently for resolutions to conflicts that lead to the devastation and horror of war.

The land of Egypt took in a family of foreigners fleeing a king so politically and personally insecure that he killed innocent babies to guarantee the future power of his office. The family stayed until Joseph heard from another angel in a dream who told him to take Mary and Jesus and return to his homeland. Obedient to every command from God, Joseph took his family and returned to Judea. When he arrived, he found that the threat to his family's safety was not buried with Herod. It lived on in Herod's son, Archelaus. Once again, the man of dreams received direction from a messenger of God and obeyed, moving his family to Nazareth in Galilee, far enough away from Judea that he could live his life in relative peace, away from the scrutiny of the king.

There is no coincidence that Matthew's gospel links the story of Jesus to the familiar story of Genesis, where Abraham's fledgling descendants were dramatically saved through the hand of God and God's servant, Joseph. The rest of the story told by Matthew's gospel carries within it the whispered memory of the exodus from Egypt that liberated God's people from slavery and set them on a journey of faith as God's own "light to the nations." The God of Abraham, the traveler; Jacob, the wrestler; and Joseph, the dreamer, is the same God of Jesus, son of Joseph, the refugee on the run from murder and mayhem. He came from a long line of wanderers, and, at an early age, he found himself becoming just like his ancestors, homeless for the sake of God.

Will It Preach?

Inherent within the readings of the day is an unsettling commentary about the contrast between the way things are and the way they could be. The texts expose the consequences of human violence on the lives of innocent people and creatures. Yet the readings also commend the celebration of redemption already at work in the unfolding purposes of God.

Preaching that falls after the climax of Christmas Day has a chance to address a church that is hanging on to the echoes of good news while getting back to the normalcy of daily routine. This is a time when the promised gift of salvation meets the corruption of the world without abandoning its work of redemption. What came as a warm gift on a cold winter's night now takes on the challenges of human existence with all its oppression and fragility. This is a time to discuss honestly with congregations that God's work does not bring limitless bliss and prosperity. A life of faith may mean losing our cherished security to advance God's future salvation of the earth. Yet as God saves us moment by moment, one redeeming act at a time, the suffering and loss of human experience is redefined in its relation to the larger view of the new creation emerging around us. Let the preaching of this day reflect an honest appraisal of the human situation and a realistic hope in the daily directions of God's presence in earthly life.

Note
1. A recording of Bill Moyer's interview of Joseph Campbell is available on the DVD entitled *Joseph Campbell and the Power of Myth* (Williston, Vt.: Mystic Fire Videos, 2001).

December 26, 2010
The Holy Family of Jesus, Mary, and Joseph (LFM)

Lectionary for Mass (LFM)
Sirach 3:2-6, 12-14
Psalm 128:1-2, 3, 4-5
Colossians 3:12-21 or 3:12-17
Matthew 2:13-15, 19-23

First Reading
Sirach 3:2-6, 12-14

The ideal family has often been portrayed as a white, middle-class, clean-cut unit of two adults and two cherubic children sitting happily at the dinner table sharing stories of their day. In reality, most families in the world are not white, not middle class, and not clothed in the latest styles bought off the department-store shelf. They do not sit down peacefully in the evenings to share stories of their days. Instead, many of them forage for food, stand in long lines for some form of relief from their hunger, or eat in shifts that honor the males of the household above the women and children. Around the globe, notions about the family are widely divergent from the American ideal.

Even when the happiest, most well-adjusted families embody this ideal, it is merely a fleeting snapshot in the ever-changing lives they lead. Children are born, grow up, find partners, and move beyond the closed circle around the table. Parents procreate, work hard to provide for the household, encounter difficulties and losses, and often slip quietly into old age before they realize that mortality has captured them in its grasp. Children become parents and parents regress into children. The only constant in families is change in the living out of these relationships to one another.

I am one of the many middle-aged adults who find themselves caring for their elderly parents. As I write, my eighty-seven-year-old mother is in a wrestling match with dementia that is strangling the life out of her brain. Some days she's a winner, sometimes she loses badly. She remembers me as a happy child playing in the backyard, but she deals with me as her guardian who handles her money, her medical treatment, and her living arrangements. She is forced by illness and age to trust me as if I were a parent, even though I am her child.

This text from Sirach instructs children to honor their parents, especially when they drift away into old age. Why? It isn't simply a matter of just setting a good example for the next generation by "doing unto them what you hope your children will do for you." Rather, it is a theological issue: God's care for creation is reflected in creation's care for its closest kin. The integrity of God's love for the world sets an example of human love for one another, especially through the changing relationships and roles that family members face.

It isn't always easy to honor a father who is stubborn and harsh in his old age, but you also have to remember that he is losing his distinctive identity and vocation as his mind and body fail. By honoring his dignity, you demonstrate honor in yourself as well. It isn't easy to meet a mother's expectations of her child when her needs outweigh the resources you possess, but you can still love her by caring for yourself so that you can be fully present with her when you are available.

Children leave the table of their parents and choose their own direction. Their actions in life may be self-destructive or hurtful toward others, or they can be life affirming and healing. Some may have lost their way, but found their way back home and into the arms of the next of kin. Eventually, children are challenged to return the care that was offered to them, honoring parents and siblings as gifts from God. Caring for families may not be easy, but it can be rewarding as we embrace the sacredness of life in one another.

Psalmody
Psalm 128:1-2, 3, 4-5

In a patriarchal society, a man was measured by two things: the quality and productivity of his work and the quality and productivity of his offspring. Both were considered blessings from God to a man who "feared the Lord." This psalm celebrates these aspects of a man's life. In all likelihood it was sung as a man went up to Jerusalem to take part in ceremonies to honor God, or it was sung by a man on a pilgrimage to a holy place in an effort to please God. As a man was engaging in rituals that demonstrated his "fear of the Lord," he would anticipate the peace of his family and the prosperity of his estate.

The patriarchal language of this psalm describes a culture in which the male is the head of the household and the women and children are merely reflections of the character of the man. In contemporary society, the lives of women and children are recognized as equally valuable and sacred before God. People living within differing models of family need ways to celebrate God's goodness and recognize the blessings and happiness that result from their faith and love of God. Otherwise, this psalm brings shame on those whose lives do not conform to the oppressive, patriarchal ideal of the past. As such, it is no longer a response of celebration, but a moral indictment of many modern family systems.

Imagine the joy of a congregational response to the words of Sirach if the language was changed to include all kinds of people in all kinds of family relationships: "Happy is everyone who fears God and walks in God's pathways. They shall eat the fruit of honest labor and be happy and content. A spouse within the household will enfold it with love, and a child will be seen as a blessing around the table. Thus shall everyone be blessed who fears God." This translation preserves the blessing of God that comes through honor and love between members of a family while not discrediting people who are single, childless, in same-sex relationships, or survivors of abusive relationships. The intent of the psalm may be somewhat altered from its original intent, but the message of God's blessing is made available to a modern audience who "fears God."

Second Reading
Colossians 3:12-21 OR 3:12-17

The general theological message of Colossians aims at encouraging Christians to realize that they have received new life through the resurrection of Christ and now live as members of an inclusive community made family to one another by Christ. As the creator of all persons and the "firstborn" of the new creation (1:15-20), Jesus Christ sets up this new family where "there is no longer Greek and Jew, circumcised and uncircumcised, barbarian, Scythian, slave and free" (3:11). Human relationships in this new family system are governed by "compassion, kindness, humility, meekness, and patience" (3:12). Forgiveness, love, and gratitude are the sources of harmony among the various members of the family.

Church conflicts can be painful and divisive. The rift between conservative and liberal factions is visible and visceral in the language and actions of U.S. politicians. It has taken up residence in churches today as well. In some church meetings a persons can walk into the room and feel the tension in the air. People engage each other in verbal combat. Clothed in their own brands of righteousness, they attempt to wrestle each other down, not to discover the truth, but to win the contest between right and wrong as they define it. They fight from a fear of losing the life they cherish, rather than celebrating the death of those ways in Christ. They have lost sight of the resurrection of all things through Christ, the "all in all." In the intimacy of families, human and divine, unity comes from letting go of the fear of losing while holding on to the joy and gratitude of what has been gained through the gift of this new creation. We are united as one, not because we are good, but because we are forgiven and cherished as the beloved of God.

Gospel
Matthew 2:13-15, 19-23

Within the context of the observance of the Holy Family of Jesus, Mary, and Joseph, this story of Joseph identifies an unusual family unit threatened by the volatility of a world ruled by intimidation and violence. Joseph is the person of faith in the story that responds to God's warnings with faith and action, thus preserving his family from harm.

Joseph was father of Jesus and husband of Mary in defiance of cultural norms. He took the risk of bringing dishonor on himself and his family of origin by marrying a woman already pregnant with a child that was not his. He adopts this child as his own by giving him the name "Jesus." Now, in Bethlehem, his family's hometown, Joseph receives foreign visitors who confirm the news of the angel messenger in his dream. Their presence in Bethlehem brings notoriety, not just to his own doorstep but to the entire town, along with imminent danger from the ruler of Judea.

Joseph is anxious about the security of his family, as well he should be. So he sleeps on it. In his dream, he learns what to do. Thus, he gets up and prepares to take his family in the cloak of night and flee to Egypt to save them. When he learns that Herod has died, he dreams again, and follows the direction of the messenger in a similar way. Getting back to Judea, he finds the situation unstable with Herod's son on the throne, and so he dreams again and heads for Galilee. He is a man who remains wakeful, even in his sleeping, to hear the voice of God. He is a man who trusts what he hears from God, and he acts in faith to protect his family.

When entrusted with the care of those in our immediate family, sometimes we are called on to do hard things. Tough love requires us to say "no" when we are inclined to say "yes" to the wishes of our families and friends. Danger in its many forms may require us to move beyond our comfort zone to protect those we love. Many times we are forced to make choices that alienate other people around us. Being a responsible partner in a family requires wakeful awareness, courage, and willingness to move beyond familiar lifestyles in order to embrace a hopeful future of salvation and peace.

Joseph, Mary, and Jesus survived as refugees in a foreign land until they could return home. Once at home, they had to choose to live far away from the seat of political power in relative anonymity so that Jesus could grow and flourish without drawing the attention of the king. Their choices were not based on what was easiest for them, but what was right for the future into which they were called.

In the patriarchal culture of ancient times, Mary and Jesus were at the mercy of the father's actions and decisions. Joseph was a merciful man, full of love and devotion to them and to the God who had placed them in his care. He acted responsibly for the good of all. Contemporary experience has moved us away from an inherent sense of belonging to something larger than ourselves. People are more socialized to think of themselves as isolated individuals who are in charge of their own safety and fulfillment. Persons seem to coexist side by side in partitioned cubicles rather than connect with the larger whole. In the present day, each of us can learn from Joseph about acting in faith for the benefit of all. Fathers and mothers, sisters and brothers, children and grandparents can examine their own commitment to be family to one another for the good of all.

Will It Preach?

The observance of the Holy Family of Jesus, Mary, and Joseph allows the church to pause and reflect on the nature of families and their role in the redemption of God's creation. Although some theologians have gone to great links to elevate the family of Jesus to a remote mystical status in the cosmic realm, the preaching of the lectionary texts for this day should do just the opposite. Preaching should take seriously the fact that although the elements of faith and commitment remain the same, families now come in all shapes and sizes. The struggles of ordinary people to accomplish extraordinary acts of mercy and love do not come easily to families where dirty laundry is piled high in plain view of all its members. Although it may be tempting, preachers should not burden with guilt those persons that do not fit the stereotype of an ancient patriarchal family. Preachers should not impose mandates for how families are supposed to behave in their various roles. Instead, the good news of the gospel offers preachers an opportunity to open the imagination of the listeners to a new vision of the sacredness of belonging to a family and invite people to explore the possibilities of discerning and acting together as family a life of faith in response to God's saving work in the world. Let preaching empower the people in families to stay compassionate and committed to each other in imitation of God's love for them.

January 1, 2011
Holy Name of Jesus (RCL)
Mary, the Mother of God (LFM)

Revised Common Lectionary (RCL)

Numbers 6:22-27

Psalm 8

Galatians 4:4-7 or Philippians 2:5-11

Luke 2:15-21

Lectionary for Mass (LFM)

Numbers 6:22-27

Psalm 67:2-3, 5, 6-8

Galatians 4:4-7

Luke 2:16-21

First Reading
Numbers 6:22-27 (RCL, LFM)

What does it mean to give someone a name? For my friends who just adopted a newborn baby, they have given themselves to this child as protectors, providers, and proud parents who delight in the life of this new person. Both friends are full of humor and goodwill in their own right, and have generously shared their lives with friends and with one another in love. Now they have given this little girl their name, the greatest gift they can offer her. In all probability she will never truly understand the depth of love they have given by giving her their name even after she grows up with the benefits of their protection and care.

In this text, God gives Moses the formula of blessing that God wishes to offer as a gift to the Israelites. God appoints Aaron and his descendants as the priests who will bless the people on God's behalf. The benediction that originally was entrusted to them has been passed on from generation to generation by those appointed for that same purpose. It confers God's name on the people as an act of God's favor.

Imagine Bill and Melinda Gates taking a personal interest in you. Sure, they have a foundation that serves the good of humankind through large grants for health care in foreign countries and money for major upgrades for public institutions that serve the needs of the poor. What if, however, the people behind the power actually learned about you and your congregation and decided that they would stop by to meet you, bringing with them a blank check and a basket of fine foods? They ask to become members of your congregation so that you would always have access to them whenever you needed something. They trust you completely as a friend and let you manage their gifts. It would be hard to imagine the kind of generosity and favor that they would show in order to make possible a fruitful and unlimited future with you and your ministry.

The generosity expressed through the Aaronic benediction carries this same kind of extravagance. Claimed by God and given the gift of God's favor, the people of God can feel hopeful and secure. They are named as God's own forever.

Psalmody
Psalm 8 (RCL)

This psalm gives praise and honor to the *name* of God. God is known by the intricacies of earth and space that reveal power, wisdom, and glory. God creates on a grand and superb scale. At the same time, God is known through vulnerability that is more powerful than any aggression which can harm and dominate. So why would human beings, mere mortals, be the object of God's kindness and compassion, especially when this favor comes from such an extravagant Creator? Why would God give these fragile, two-legged beings power far greater than that of all the other creatures around them? Good question! Obviously, human beings have the capacity to influence and control the world around them. Looking back, it is easy to see how the human race has often used that power for its own benefit and often to the detriment of the earth and its creatures. In light of their insignificance in the big scheme of things, however, mere mortals really don't deserve the kind of dignity and honor that has been conferred by a benevolent Creator.

The glory and beauty of the universe startles us into amazement at God's capacity to create and sustain the endless wonders of earth and space. It humbles us, then, to respond to this One who chooses freely to bless us with undivided attention. What else can we do but be still and breathe in the gift of life, so that we can, in turn, breathe out praise and joy to our Creator? Thank you, thank you, thank you, God!

Psalm 67:2-3, 5, 6-8 (LFM)

This response to the first reading echoes back the words of the Aaronic benediction. It begins by acknowledging the nature of God's blessing upon the people. The psalmist recognizes that God's blessing has consequences for *all* the people of the earth. It brings judgment and guidance that will convey prosperity and peace to the whole of creation. The natural response, then, is gladness, joy, and praise, praise, praise!

Second Reading
Galatians 4:4-7 (RCL, LFM)

A recent documentary film titled *Preacher's Sons*[1] showed at a local church. It tells the tale of a gay couple, one of whom was a clergyperson, who decided to care for hard-to-place children within the foster system. Their first child was born addicted to cocaine. A second had been abandoned in a hospital and then passed from family to family through the foster-care system. Two came as brothers, one with an outgoing personality and hyperactivity and both with a history of neglect and abuse. Their fifth child was an infant brother of the first foster child they took in, abandoned by the mother at the hospital. The fathers, Greg and Stillman, provided a place of safety, stability, and structure for these young children at a very high cost to themselves. They grew much attached to the boys as they learned the idiosyncrasies of each child and watched them grow more and more secure each month they were with them. Yet they knew that as long as the boys were only foster children, they could be snatched away from their home environment at any minute. They decided to adopt them all. It was one thing to care for children abandoned by families. It was another to adopt them legally and permanently into a family where they would not be abandoned or denied.

The letter to the Galatians uses the analogy of adoption to talk about God's power to extend full benefits of salvation to all people regardless of race, class, or gender. A son is free to call his father by the affectionate term, "Daddy." In a patriarchal society, however, he benefits greatly from his father's good name, place in society, and estate. Those who are "adopted" into God's family receive the same inheritance as "blood kin." The spirit of Christ in them provides access to God that is unlimited and complete.

Through Christian baptism, the church celebrates the mystery of adoption into the family of God. Through the work of the Holy Spirit, we are named as God's own. God claims us forever as sons and daughters who have complete and full access to God and who share in the benefits of membership in the family. The physical sign given in baptism assures us forever of God's faithfulness and love to us. We are not simply "foster children" who are wards of the state, but cared for by God until we reach legal age. We can be secure in knowing that no state system or workplace or institution can snatch us away from our rightful place as full members of the family who bears God's name.

The benediction is a similar sign, reminding the church that God's name is on us and we have God's full attention following us wherever we go. It is a free gift that God offers. We have only to receive it in faith and joy.

Philippians 2:5-11 (RCL ALT.)

This hymn of the early church celebrates the preeminent name that God imparts to Jesus because of his slave-like obedience to God. Humility turns into greatness. Obedience rises to rule with power. From death comes resurrection and glory. The hymn calls those who sing it to follow the example of Jesus, knowing that they will receive a similar honor in the kingdom of God.

Jesus respected God completely and gave himself over completely to God's objective to save the world, even though it cost him his life. God respected Jesus

59

completely and gave him complete authority over all things, even death, so that he might share in the glory that belongs to a merciful and wise Creator. In a world that has lost its confidence in all the world's institutions that once were sacred, can we regain a respect for God that moves us beyond self-interest and self-aggrandizement in our religious life? Let us contemplate the model of Jesus that this text offers, so that we might be humbled by God for the work that God has entrusted to our care.

Gospel
Luke 2:15-21 (RCL)
Luke 2:16-21 (LFM)

This beginning of this text will have been read at the dawn of Christmas Day. On the first day of the new calendar year, however, the focus of its message is on the naming of the child Jesus, the Savior, rather than on his birth. Jesus undergoes circumcision, the Jewish rite of initiation into the covenant family of God, in obedience to Jewish law. By this act, Jesus is recognized as a rightful heir of God's promise to Abraham and a member of the Jewish community. Mary and Joseph have already been told by a messenger that he belongs to God through the power and work of the Holy Spirit. As people of faith, they respect God's commands and mark him permanently as God's own child. They follow tradition, allowing the sign of circumcision to declare his ancestry and his relation to God.

At the time of circumcision, the child was named. The mother gave birth to the child, but the father named the child as a sign that the child belonged to him as an heir. Luke's gospel, however, reminds the listener that the child was given the name which the angel announced before his birth. This name was given by God to mark Jesus as God's own child. In humble obedience, Joseph honors God's plan by naming him Jesus, meaning "God has saved."

When I was lecturing in Japan some years ago, I was interested in the way Japanese people would introduce themselves to me. After telling me their name, they would explain its meaning, because the characters that represented their names also identified an object, emotion, or idea from life. They even told me that my middle name "Lin" means "forest" in Japanese. It was intriguing to hear the connection between the names of people and the blessing that their parents wished for them through the selection of their name.

Many of us bear the names of our ancestors. I was named for both my maternal and my paternal grandmothers, perpetuating their identities through my own life. Others bear the exact name of a parent or grandparent, so that the same legacy is carried generation after generation. Our names, whatever they happen to be, were given to us for some reason by someone. As such, they carry within them the intention and interest of the person who named us. We are marked by that name by someone and we carry the mark of that intention throughout life. Sometimes people are so haunted by their names that they are willing to go to drastic measures to rename themselves at a later time, but still the mark has been made and will be a part of them.

Children brought for baptism in the church are marked as Christ's own sister and brother forever. In baptism, the person is given the name of God and their own personal name before God and the world. He or she is inextricably linked to God's infinite grace and unending activity on behalf of creation, thus being linked to Jesus and the Holy Spirit at work in them. Yet each person is individually unique, having been made alive by the Eternal Creator and having been born into a relationship that is distinct from any other. In baptism, we learn our truest identity as children of grace who are infinitely loved and favored by the Creator who made us, and we join in the work of salvation that God has already begun in the world through Christ.

In my denomination, the liturgical rite of the Reaffirmation of Baptism allows Christians to renew their covenantal vows and reclaim their identity as God's people. The specific ritual of being touched again by water is accompanied by the words "Remember your baptism and be thankful." These rituals bring us back to the central meaning of our lives as we are reminded of the ethical implications of bearing God's name. At the same time, however, we are revisited by the assurance that the God who has claimed us will not abandon us, even in the most troubled times in our lives. We are heirs of God's promise. Let us remember and be thankful.

Will It Preach?

The theme for this day is unambiguously clear: the naming of Jesus. It is a time to explore what it means to be named, to be blessed, and to reflect that identity through one's actions. God, the One who is unnamed, reveals God's own identity through actions. Adoption into that name makes us recipients of God's actions, but, even more, identifies us as those who act on God's behalf.

Because all of the lectionary texts refer in some way to liturgical acts within faith communities, the message is better proclaimed through the ritual acts themselves than through a lengthy sermon. A sermon can inform the liturgy, but the language of the liturgy will convey the meaning itself. This would be a wonderful time for members of a congregation to reaffirm their baptism and give thanks.

Note

1. For more details visit http://www.preacherssons.com, accessed December 17, 2009.

January 2, 2011
Second Sunday of Christmas

First Lesson
Sirach 24:1-12 (RCL ALT.)
Sirach 24:1-4, 12-26 (LFM)

In celebration of God as Trinity, the Wisdom of God steps forward as the primary speaker in this text. Christ is the Word made flesh, the Promised One sent by God to save the world. On Christmas Day, the gospel reading focuses on this cosmic revelation of the eternal nature of Christ becoming very specific, contextual, and limited in human form. Today's first reading highlights the presence of Wisdom, personified as the female image of God, who was in the beginning of creation with the *logos* of God. The rhetoric of this text parallels in many ways the prologue in John's Gospel, demonstrating that the historical and concrete witness in Jesus Christ is not the only way that God has been at work to redeem the world.

Jeremiah 31:7-14 (RCL)

The fulfillment of God's promise to Israel is seen in the gathering together of the people who have been conquered by great empires and taken as prisoners to serve the empire in other places. The metaphor of the shepherd is used to describe God's compassion and responsible action in restoring the life of God's people. The prophecy ends with mourning turning into dancing and joyous merriment.

This image of salvation is good news for people who are alienated from their homeland. It speaks the restoration of community among those folks who had been separated from each other by the domination of the worldly powers. Coming back together, they rejoice at the experience of salvation that brings them home together.

Psalmody
Psalm 147:12-20 (RCL)
Psalm 147:12-13, 14-15, 19-20 (LFM)

The image of God in this psalm is generous, powerful, and faithful. God provides fine food to nourish God's people. God brings peace so that children may thrive in their environment, and the city enjoys security and protection from its enemies. The word of God's mouth is so strong that it melts ice and pours out water and wind to sweep through the earth. God's ways are known through God's word contained within the law.

Wisdom of Solomon 10:15-21 (RCL ALT.)

This response to the soliloquy of Wisdom in the first reading praises Wisdom for purifying and liberating the people from slavery in Egypt as she led them across the Red Sea and through the wilderness. She is attributed with giving people a voice with which to speak powerfully for God and to God.

Second Reading
Ephesians 1:3-14 (RCL)
Ephesians 1:3-6, 15-18 (LFM)

It is one thing to look at the wondrous ways that the Source of Creation shapes the minute details of this planet and the space beyond it. A life-force beyond our own conscious understanding conducts business beyond the confines of time and space. In this process of sustaining a dynamic and ever-changing being that we call home, we see the "hand" of God. In hospitals, on street corners, in refugee camps, and even in sanctuaries, we become aware that more is involved than merely human calculations in the negotiations that determine the world's future. An imperceptible presence inhabits the air we breathe and the sounds that are uttered. God has been intimately involved in the unfolding life of this world.

So what happens when this understanding of a powerful and amazing God is turned around to look at what God has chosen to do in human lives and communities? That same living Spirit has taken up residence in the midst of us, catching us up into the unfolding plan at the heart of God's activity. The power of God at work in Jesus is transforming us into God's own beloved community, forgiven and freed by grace. What God wants for the world has already taken root in us by the Holy Spirit who dwells in us. This gives us a sense of what life will be when God's own nature is fully revealed and recognized in the world.

When the gospel is heard and believed, we find ourselves claimed by that belief and set apart with new loyalties and loves. Our fundamental identity is made new. We are people of the realm that is not seen with the eye, but with the heart—the unseen realm of the Spirit. Feet planted squarely on earth, at home in bodies, and aware of the concrete needs of the world around us, we move according to the dynamic life coursing through our veins and animating the great cosmos. This power knows our individual selves as completely as it does the distant galaxy and it welcomes us to celebrate in the glory of God that is ours through Jesus, the glorious Word made flesh.

Gospel
John 1:1-18 (RCL)
John 1:1-18 or 1:1-5, 9-14 (LFM)

In concert with the text from Ephesians, the gospel speaks dramatically about the life of the created world and light illuminating a world that cannot see the plain truth which stands right in front of it. The Word at the heart of it all has been revealed to us in the coming of Jesus Christ. The power at work in him is available to all who accept him and believe in the truth and grace that he embodies.

The good news is that the glory of God is revealed in the mortal body and the human face. Believers do not have to imagine what heaven might be like, but they see with their hearts the divine life in the creation here and now. The power that will gather all things into wholeness and complete the work that has already begun to reconcile, restore, and renew the creation lives within the creation already. What was fully revealed in the life, death, and resurrection of Jesus is not yet fully revealed in us, the beneficiaries of this new creation.

(For more on John 1:1-18, see the gospel for the Nativity of Our Lord III, p. 48.)

Will It Preach?

The Second Sunday after Christmas is often celebrated as Epiphany. In this calendar year, however, the Second Sunday falls before January 6, so some churches may choose to use these lections instead. On this occasion the church is given an opportunity to explore the feminine expression of God in the personification of Wisdom. The parallels between the work of the masculine *logos* and the feminine Wisdom of God are clearly drawn through the readings. Preaching can imaginatively draw comparisons between the two in order to express the interrelationship of these various expressions in God's saving work in the world. What a rare opportunity to explore the role of Wisdom in the life of Christian community! What a wonderful chance to affirm the feminine side of God in all of us that works in concert with the traditionally masculine models of God's being!

Epiphany—Time after Epiphany / Ordinary Time

Robert P. Hoch

Epiphany chronicles God's appearing for a world buried in darkness—"deep darkness" according to Isaiah. As God's light, it not only illuminates, but it also transforms. Indeed, just as God's speaking in Genesis couples word and act, so also Epiphany narrates more than light shining on passive faces; God's appearing illuminates our darkness and transforms our realities. Epiphany not only *sheds* light, but it also chronicles the *increase* of light, or "more light," particularly through the prophetic imagination.

On the one hand, shedding light calls to mind the kind of social criticism that the judgment of God, apprehended through the law, should incite: the law, and particularly our departure from its commands, opens our eyes to the world that we are making or, as the case may be, the world we are *un*making. As interpreters pass through these texts they will probably see invitations to critical thinking about our place in society, as a nation in the world, as congregations, and as members of communities. But if social criticism is all we see then we have not seen very much or, at least, we have not seen much more than a good social critic might see. While prophets are social critics, that is not all they are: rather, they witness to something genuinely new.

This is perhaps the heart of the witness of Epiphany: in the increase of light, particularly uncreated light, we witness not merely what we are but who, by God's grace, we have become through God's promise. And what we have become shatters ordinary categories of being with prophetic imagining. In Christ, we see the embodiment or actuality of that yearning coming into radical being, namely an infant who reigns as the king while still in the manger. Augustine marvels at this paradox of kingly greatness and infant mildness: "Who is this king, so small, so great; not yet talking on earth, already promulgating edicts in the heavens?"[1] Likewise, what we have become, even God's own community, is not easily reducible to categories that creaturely light can reveal to us.

Rather, to the contrary, the increase of light shows us that we have become something profoundly new, so new that we no longer fit into the "old wineskins" of the old dispensation. Although the Gospel of John only makes one appearance among the assigned lections for this season, his announcement that "light has come into the world" suggests that God's light spills into creaturely darkness with a bewildering abandon, splashing into the darkness of the prison house, illuminating the way of those who are confused, stunning any who are prideful, and introducing the mystery of grace to a world whose end, in the light of reason, seems all too predictable. See, says Isaiah, God is about to do a new thing!

Conventional language gives way to superlative expressions and sometimes scandalous ones, as we search for the metaphor, the likeness that can begin to approximate what we see through illumination of the Spirit. Language attempts to probe the interior reaches of this epiphany, as in Matthew's account of the transfiguration, but our language is always crumbling before its task. But our yearning finds grateful interruption with the lections for this season, the Spirit interrupting our reaching words with God's startling insinuation (Matt. 17:5a; Acts 10:44).

A word about our two major lections, Matthew and Isaiah, is probably in order. Second Isaiah (Isaiah 40-55) comprises the majority of the first readings assigned in Year A, the exceptions being the Fourth, Sixth, Seventh, and Transfiguration Sundays. Of those days that include readings from Isaiah, all but two—the day of Epiphany (Isa. 60:1-6) and the Third Sunday (Isa. 9:1-4/Isa. 8:23b—9:3)—come from Second Isaiah. Most scholars believe, based on evidence from within the text, that Second Isaiah was written while the prophet was living with the exiles in Babylon. That tumultuous reality, with some seemingly profiting from exile while others mourned, adds layers of complexity to our reading of Isaiah.[2]

With this historical situation in mind, the tradition sometimes dubs Second Isaiah with more affective titles, like "The Prophet of the Exile" or the "Prophet of Consolation."[3] The former recalls the context and the latter underscores the purpose of these acts of communication. Dislocation, cultural disintegration, as well as cultural and religious assimilation were realities confronting Second Isaiah. Just as significant as the external context was the internal knowledge of national failure. Isaiah's witness to "the servant" seems to evolve from a more corporate understanding of Israel to end up taking shape as a person, which, in the Christian tradition, we hear as a witness to Jesus Christ. Even while the tradition of Christian interpretation views these texts through the prism of the New Testament, it would be a mistake to see the servant as bereft of its connection to Israel or reduced to an individualistic anthropology. The servant makes *new* the covenant and Israel, even as the servant constitutes the new community that, through his fulfilling work, brings this promise into reality.

This may be as good a segue as any into Matthew's readings, the bulk of which come from the Sermon on the Mount. Beginning with Jesus' baptism, the Matthew readings deliberately call to mind the history of Israel and Moses, and the giving of the law; but it would not be correct to call Jesus a "New Moses" because of the implied comparison. Instead, Matthew insists that Jesus brings something utterly new onto the face of the creation, even if it is historically linked to the history of Israel.[4] Indeed, the abundance of irony within Matthew's account (even allowing for anti-pharisaical polemic) creates a dramatic recasting of the "old dispensation" of the law with the "new dispensation" of the servant community. The "new dispensation" does not drop the covenant but multiplies it beyond anything we could either imagine or achieve. Only by receiving Christ who "teaches as one with authority" and to whom "all authority in heaven and on earth has been given" can we begin to actualize our new reality as the peaceable kingdom of God on earth.

Even so, the actualization is never really realized by our ascending to God but, rather, by God's condescension to us. That act is never simply an act of egalitarianism, but one that incites us to a different way of life, calling members of the community to the cruciform path of repentance and reconciliation. Like the Mosaic covenant that commands Israel to "walk in [the Lord's] statutes," the way of discipleship is not, to borrow a common expression, achieved by great acts of faith but by small acts done with great faith.

Of course, the discipling community walks a path, too, following Christ, who goes ahead of us, making a way where none existed before. Just as God in Christ takes a path we did not know, namely the path of the cross and tomb, so, too, we are called to pick up our cross and follow him.

Perhaps no other image captures the paradox of Epiphany better for me than an illustrated manuscript of the Rabbula Gospels, finished in the year 586. The illustration combines the image of Jesus the crucified (on the top half) and the empty tomb (on the bottom).[5] The top image shows the crucifixion, with the spears of Roman soldiers that pierced Jesus' sides being thrust at sharp angles from below. Beneath this image, the picture of the tomb visualizes the resurrection "as a veritable explosion of light bursting open the door of the tomb, overthrowing its three guards in the process."[6] The artist evokes the outburst of light as sharp beams, thrusting outward, bursting through the door of the tomb. But what strikes me as especially suggestive is what the two images do together: the artist positions the spears at the same angle he positions the light, intimating in this way that the spears that pierced God's side have been transformed into uncreated light.

Deep darkness, indeed.

And maybe even more light: "And they shall beat their swords into plowshares, and their spears into pruning hooks …"

Notes

1. Augustine, *The Works of Saint Augustine: Part III—Sermons*, vol. 6 (184-229Z), trans. Edmund Hill, ed. John E. Rotelle (New Rochelle, N.Y.: New City Press, 1993), 79-80.
2. Paul D. Hanson, *Isaiah 40-66,* Interpretation: A Bible Commentary for Teaching and Preaching (Louisville: John Knox, 1995), 2.
3. Ibid.
4. Douglas R. A. Hare, *Matthew*, Interpretation: A Bible Commentary for Teaching and Preaching (Louisville: John Knox, 1993), 34.
5. Richard Harries, *The Passion in Art* (Burlington, Vt.: Ashgate, 2004), 18-19. See http://www.beith-morounoye.org/gallery/rabbula-crucifixion.jpg, accessed December 22, 2009.
6. Ibid., 20.

January 6, 2011 / January 2, 2011
Epiphany of Our Lord / Epiphany Sunday

Revised Common Lectionary (RCL)	**Lectionary for Mass (LFM)**
Isaiah 60:1-6	Isaiah 60:1-6
Psalm 72:1-7, 10-14	Psalm 72:1-12, 10-11, 12-13
Ephesians 3:1-12	Ephesians 3:2-3a, 5-6
Matthew 2:1-12	Matthew 2:1-12

We woke our girls, two and four years of age, well before dawn, around 4:30 A.M., so we could catch our flight, which was scheduled for departure early that morning. We worried at first that they wouldn't respond to us, the hour being so early. But as soon as we stirred them, with morning rituals they recognized as familiar, they stepped into those early hours of darkness as if it were day. And yet, if they stepped confidently into the day the rituals announced, they were shrill in their reaction to what they saw outside the window of my parents' home: when they looked out the window, they saw "night" and cried, "Look!," startled by the incongruity of a morning rite taking place in the darkness of night.

The church may, at least initially, hear these texts as a familiar rite, announcing the "familiar story" of Christ's appearing. Like a sleepy-eyed toddler, we fit the text, even its reversals, into patterns we have learned to expect. It is morning, we say to ourselves. It is time to wake, the sun is rising. We are taken into the text's familiar closeness. We murmur the words, gold, frankincense, and myrrh, like warm milk in the morning, like every morning. But as we waken, we may be startled to see incongruities between the rite and the reality. Perhaps even more important, these texts lead communities of faith to apprehend their realities within God's uncreated light, prompting the church to enter a darkened world with eyes tutored and voice trained by the prophetic imagination.

First Reading
Isaiah 60:1-6 (RCL, LFM)

"Arise, shine!" The feeling of this chapter expresses the sudden the release of joy, the feeling of hearts "thrilling" that had not known thrill but only fear; now those who knew darkness, they abound in light, a light that has shone on God's beloved (vv. 3-4). The prophet sees and expresses wondrous hope, a sense of sheer relief carrying his words forward as praise; indeed, the words of the prophet seem to pant with praise, the words barely able to keep up with the thrilling event of a return out of exile.

Still, while the prophet announces the return of Israel's exiles (v. 4), Isaiah shows a picture of troubling darkness. Israel knew hardship, as is evidenced by the frequency with which the prophet returns to the theme of darkness (e.g., 9:2; 42:16).[1] Isaiah's language in verse 2 ("darkness shall cover the earth, and thick darkness the peoples") recalls Genesis, the creation account, "and darkness covered the face of the deep" (Gen. 1:2a). Clothing the creation story with the cadences and experiences of African American preaching, James Weldon Johnson hauntingly evokes the expansive darkness, moments before God spoke, as "Blacker than a hundred midnights/Down in a cypress swamp."[2] Likewise, the darkness of which Isaiah speaks is no ordinary darkness, one that will yield to the torches of reason. Isaiah's darkness is reminiscent of the moments before creation.

According to the Old Testament scholar Walter Brueggemann, Isaiah speaks in the context of a "resurgence of chaos,"[3] characterized by idolatry, dislocation, exile, and sociocultural disintegration, each condition belying the covenantal status bestowed on the people of Israel. Within the specific context of Second Isaiah, we hear the report of a second exodus that, in effect, eclipses the exodus out of Egypt. The nature of the prophet's speech in this context is "inescapably disputatious," cutting through this present darkness, announcing an even more real presence: "Arise, shine; for your light has come, and the glory of the LORD has risen upon you" (v. 1); "… but the LORD will arise upon you, and his glory will appear over you" (v. 2b). Amid deep darkness, the prophet stirs his audience into wakefulness with a promise: "Lift up your eyes and look around" (v. 4a). The prophet says, "Look with the new light that dawns against this present darkness, it is the light of my promised coming." Verse 5 suggests that when our eyes are filled with the radiant of light of God's promise, "Then you shall see and be radiant; your heart shall thrill and rejoice" (v. 5a).

It is actually quite difficult to comprehend Isaiah 60 without briefly considering the immediately preceding chapter, chapter 59, in which the prophet speaks of a society that uses law not to limit evil but, rather, to promote its power, twisting what was intended to be wholesome into that which hurts and destroys (e.g., 59:6). The darkness reported by Isaiah is not imagined but real. But the prophet shows a picture of God's mercy that cannot be contained by the limits of social criticism: "You shall suck the milk of nations, you shall suck the breasts of kings; and you shall know that I, the LORD am your Savior and your Redeemer, the Mighty One of Jacob" (60:16).

The light announced by Isaiah was not only a light that exposed darkness for what it is but also created a vision that could not be contained or held captive by historical experiences of shame, fear, or guilt.

Reflection

It was supposed to be a "service of reconciliation" between the Native community and the surrounding white population. Dawn Helton-Anishinaabeqwa, an Ojibwa elder and Methodist lay leader, was presiding at the service in northern Wisconsin, where Natives and Caucasians had gathered for prayers. Just as the service was about to begin, from the back of the church, a man yelled out, "We should have got rid of you [expletive] Indians when we had the chance!" If that startled the congregation with unfamiliar honesty, Helton-Anishinaabeqwa witnessed to the church with prophetic power: "Thank God! We have a prophet in our midst, someone who is willing to tell the truth!" What she named that day was the truth that despite all the pretty talk of reconciliation between races, it remains that U.S. laws and policies of assimilation continue the slow but grimly determined work of genocide against Native peoples. With her witness all who were present saw the darkness of a hundred midnights created by the U.S.-engineered decline of Native American cultures and identities.

We who are preachers are often loath to tell the truth, because the truth threatens us as well as everyone else with a resurgent chaos that would seem to have the power to devour us all. Unlike many of us, however, toddlers and prophets remain sensitive to the incongruity of light and darkness: a toddler, on expecting morning and seeing night, will say what a thing is, naming its incongruence with shrill-voiced perception. The prophet reminds us of this, raising her own "shrill" voice as an alarm, pulling away the mask of politeness by which we disguise our often mindless participation in fallen systems. At the same time, as Brueggemann reminds us, we are not merely social critics: "The poet/prophet is a voice that shatters settled reality and evokes new possibility in the listening assembly."[4]

Psalmody
Psalm 72:1-7 (RCL)
Psalm 72:1-2, 7-8, 10-11, 12-13 (LFM)

Psalm 72 is thought to be a "coronation psalm," perhaps recalling the royal coronation ceremonies that would have accompanied the likes of David or Solomon. It has the feeling of a prayer, perhaps much like a prayer of supplication offered on behalf of our public servants during the Lord's Day service. Unlike many of these prayers, however, which are quite general, asking that God be with our leaders for the general good, the psalmist offers an intercessory prayer, asking that the king "defend the cause of the poor, give deliverance to the needy, and crush the oppressor" (v. 4). Moreover, this king answers "the needy when they call, the poor and those who have no helper" (v.

12). Psalm 72 reminds us that God's sovereignty is not expressed by "the greater good" so much as it is expressed by responsiveness to the "least of these" or, in the tradition of the African American pulpit, our God hears the cries of the "the least, the last, and the lost." Prayers for our leaders are not intended to support nationalistic ambitions but, rather, as the prayers of God's people, to quicken us as church and society to hear the call to justice, mercy, and humility.

Second Reading
Ephesians 3:1-12 (RCL)
Ephesians 3:2-3a, 5-6 (LFM)

Paul's "mystery made known" (v. 3) may strike contemporary hearers as anachronistic since, for the most part, we do not live in a world of mysteries made known but of discoveries made. Our perspective comes from our agency in disclosing the inner workings of the natural world and, from looking at popular book titles, one gets the sense that those areas of human identity previously held to be hidden (personality, artistic insight, creativity, beauty, and so on) are now being "discovered" through neurological-scientific research. Nevertheless, the language of faith stresses not the elimination of mystery but speaks instead of the act and implication of receiving God's mysteries in the reconciling work of Jesus Christ.

This is what Paul is about in his letter to the church at Ephesus: receiving the mystery of Christ by participating in the mysteries revealed through the visible signs of grace in the life of the church. Paul, speaking of his call, says that he is compelled "to make everyone see [or *to bring to light*] what is the plan of the mystery hidden for ages in God who created all things, so that through the church the wisdom of God in its rich variety might now be made known to the rulers and authorities in heavenly places" (vv. 9-10). If the word proclaimed is heard, it is, in the tradition of worship, sealed by the visible sacraments of God's grace that we receive in faith. They are mysteries received by the inner illumination of the Spirit.

Gospel
Matthew 2:1-12 (RCL, LFM)

To supply some framework for the current text, we might note Matthew's careful construction of Jesus' genealogy, which would seem, at least initially, to "fit" into the tradition of Israel's kings. There are all the familiar names we would come to expect from a great king of Israel: Abraham, Isaac, Jacob, David, and so on. But an attentive reader will notice a bit of a wobble in the otherwise orderly development of the tradition, as Matthew names in this peculiar king's ancestry a Moabite, a prostitute, a murder victim and his wife, Bathsheba, and then last, "Joseph the *husband* of Mary, of whom Jesus was born, who is called the Messiah" (1:16). And then, as if nothing happened, Matthew closes his genealogy with the compact summary of verse 17, indicating to the reader that this account fits into the numerological habits of Jewish tradition.

This text might hit a reader the way an earthquake at the lower end of the Richter scale ripples through the living room of familiarity with an unsettling whisper, a slight shift, perceptible but just barely. It is the kind of earthquake that gives one pause, though not quite alarm. We ask, usually ourselves, "Did I just imagine that or did the world of the familiar just go bump?" Indeed, it is the kind of experience that will get people talking to each other, even perfect strangers, as they try to determine whether that shift was imagined or real.

Matthew means to show us that the "shift" is real and what we witness in chapter 2 is something of a growing shock wave passing through the entire gospel, radiating out from the intimately related centers of Jesus' birth and death. This insight finds particular expression through the significance of the gifts brought by the Magi. We might recall in this regard that Isaiah, speaking of the coming exaltation of Jerusalem, saw foreigners from all over the world coming with "gold and frankincense" proclaiming the "praise of the LORD" (Isa. 60:6b). To this mixture of worship (gold) and honor (frankincense), Matthew throws in myrrh, which Augustine points out is "a sign of his future burial."[5]

Our hearing of this particular detail is much diminished by familiarity and it is only by the startling analogy that we can refresh the sharp crack of change announced in this text. Perhaps one way to renew our hearing is to imagine the reaction of an expectant mother and gathered community were a guest to bring the "gift" of a funeral urn to a baby shower, to hold the ashes of the child, as if to welcome the child's death. One might well expect to be ushered out of that gathering, along with the so-called gift. But not so in Matthew's gospel. The symbol of death is received as a "gift" by the One who takes our death in order that we might be joined to his resurrection.

Reflection

It is not uncommon for contemporary interpreters to identify analogically with the rabbis and scribes of Matthew's gospel, especially since clergy are seen as responsible for preserving the received tradition. The image of scribes bent over ancient texts seem to be more "like" us than astrologers peering into night skies, trying to read the meanings of the celestial beings. But in these days of post-Christendom realities, it may make more sense to take the position of the magi. Shifting our analogical imagination from scribe to astrologer might lead to sermons that challenge the conventional allegiances that tie congregations to the status quo.

Striking in this regard is the way Matthew's account narrates the activities and allegiances of the magi, who at first seem to have a cooperative, and indeed naïve, relationship to Herod. In the first part of Matthew, they seek Herod's counsel and supply him with valuable information that we might characterize as contributing to "national security." Given their status as "aliens" they may well have felt the need to take precautions with the powers that be. On the other hand, the magi's apparent allegiance to Herod seems easy, more assumed than stated, as if there was no doubt about it to begin with. Perhaps indicating their subordinate spirit, Matthew notes that the magi only left after they "heard the king," as if they journeyed under the aegis of his authority. Once they offered their gifts and worship to the Christ, however, they would defy Herod, this time taking a path foreshadowing Christ's own cruciform path, leaving "for their own country by another road" (v. 12b).

The American historian Arthur M. Schlesinger tells the story of a 1962 meeting between a delegation of the World Council of Churches (WCC) and President John F. Kennedy. The delegation came to plead with Kennedy, making the case against the continued proliferation of nuclear weapons fueled by an arms race that was heating up between the two superpowers, the U.S.A. and the U.S.S.R. Kennedy responded to the delegation by making a persuasive case for the continued testing of nuclear weapons. Apparently, Kennedy was quite persuasive because, at the end of their meeting with the president, a member of the delegation asked how they, members of the WCC, could help him in this great cause of national security. Kennedy answered, saying only, "Perhaps you shouldn't."[6]

"… and they returned to their own country, by another road."

Notes

1. Paul D. Hanson, *Isaiah 40-66,* Interpretation: A Bible Commentary for Teaching and Preaching (Louisville: John Knox, 1995), 219.
2. James Weldon Johnson, *God's Trombones: Seven Negro Sermons in Verse* (New York: Penguin, 1927), 17.
3. Walter Brueggemann, *Theology of the Old Testament: Testimony, Dispute, Advocacy* (Minneapolis: Fortress Press, 1997), 549.
4. Walter Brueggemann, *Finally Comes the Poet: Daring Speech for Proclamation* (Minneapolis: Fortress Press, 1989), 4.
5. Augustine, *The Works of Saint Augustine: Part III—Sermons*, vol. 6, trans. Edmund Hill, ed. John E. Rotelle (New Rochelle, N.Y.: New City Press, 1993), 92.
6. Arthur M. Schlesinger, *The Cycles of American History* (Boston: Houghton Mifflin, 1986), 80.

January 9, 2011
Baptism of Our Lord
First Sunday after Epiphany
First Sunday in Ordinary Time

Revised Common Lectionary (RCL)
Isaiah 42:1-9
Psalm 29
Acts 10:34-43
Matthew 3:13-17

Lectionary for Mass (LFM)
Isaiah 42:1-4, 6-7
Psalm 29:1-2, 3-4, 3b + 9b-10
Acts 10:34-38
Matthew 3:13-17

Wow!' said Lilly. That was just about all she could say—'Wow.'" This is the near-speechless reaction of Lilly the Mouse to her teacher, Mr. Slinger, in Kevin Henkes's children's story, *Lilly's Purple Plastic Purse*. To Lilly's eyes, Mr. Slinger epitomizes wit, fashionable taste, intelligence, as well as undisputed coolness. A different color of tie for each day of the week, colorful suspenders, a bedazzled Lilly can only sigh, "Wow!"[1] Even if we chose a different word to express our wonderment before God, we could be forgiven for feeling like Lilly, overwhelmed by the sheer grandeur of the texts assigned for the Baptism of Our Lord / First Sunday after the Epiphany. Yet here is the irony of this series of lections: we are not left to admire God's appearing from a distance. Rather, when what is above submits to what is below, a relationship is born that requires response, and perhaps the response of discipleship in particular.

First Reading
Isaiah 42:1-9 (RCL)
Isaiah 42:1-4, 6-7 (LFM)

"Here," declares Isaiah, is the Lord's servant—in the immediately preceding verses, we hear the prophet despair as he looked for someone to bring good news: "But when I look there is no one; among these there is no counselor who, when I ask, gives an answer. No, they are all a delusion; their works are nothing; their images are empty wind" (41:28-29). But in the opening verses of the present chapter, the prophet shouts with recognition, "Here is my servant, whom I uphold, my chosen, in whom my soul delights" (42:1a). Without anticipating too much, the baptismal scene of Matthew is foreshadowed in the tradition of the church's reading of these texts. One could hear these opening verses as longed-for confirmation and consecration of the servant community, a community sent for the work of redemption: "Behold, this is my son, my beloved one."

The prophet distinguishes this servant from others on the basis of his character. As one who is chosen, the servant is distinguished by what he is not: "He will not cry or lift up his voice, or make it heard in the street; a bruised reed he will not break, a dimly burning wick he will not quench; he will faithfully bring forth justice. He will not grow faint or be crushed until he has established justice in the earth; and the coastlands wait for his teaching" (vv. 2-4).

To some ways of hearing Isaiah, this text might express an apolitical spirit in the servant of the Lord, particularly in the acquiescent spirituality that might be suggested in the language of one who will not "lift up his voice or make it heard in the street." Indeed, if "awe" belongs to these texts, one may anticipate a sense of relief that finally we can surrender our searching and perhaps even our work in the world. In particular, we could hear the determination not to "cry or lift up his voice or make it heard in the street" as characteristic of withdrawal from the world, a character trait not uncommon to the larger church. This view, however, is problematic, particularly as one reflects on what the "street" represents for the prophetic imagination.

For the prophet, the street is the place of the public economy, where business is conducted, transactions are made, and these are a constant concern for the prophet. The street is also connected to the "way of the LORD," but an utterly new way, "who makes a way in the sea, a path in the mighty waters, who brings out chariot and horse, army and warrior; they lie down, they cannot rise, they are extinguished, quenched like a wick" (43:16b-17). Amid the chaos of nihilistic and destructive powers the Lord God announces a new way in the place where the sounds of the streets clamor and collide within a rising cacophony of confusion.

The prophet is not surrendering the street to the gang violence of superpowers but, rather, he offers a vision for what the servant community will be about: a called community (it is not born of captive imagination but of the righteous God); it is a "kept" community; it is a community that is "given ... as a covenant to the people, a light to the nations" (42:6b). If the servant community is gathered by God, it is given as a covenant to the world, including its streets, making a way through the "mighty waters" by being a "light to the nations," opening eyes that are blind, bringing out prisoners from the dungeon, from the prison those who sit in darkness (43:7).

Reflection

Taking Isaiah seriously would entail a politics of the servant community, where resistance is born out of the particular character of the community itself. One contemporary expression of a community that interrupted the torture machine of Chile was known as the Sebastián Acevedo Movement against Torture, described by William Cavanaugh in his book *Torture and the Eucharist: Theology, Politics, and the Body of Christ.* Amid political repression, organizers of the Sebastián Acevedo Movement chose locations "for their symbolic importance: places of torture, the courts, government buildings, media headquarters."[2] At a prearranged time, members of the movement would seemingly materialize out of the crowd, out of nowhere, interrupting traffic, passing out leaflets, enacting with their bodies and voices liturgies like this one:

> They arrest Juan Antonio Aguirre—and the justice system is silent
> They lock him up in Precinct 26—and the justice system is silent
> They torture him—and the justice system is silent
> They make him disappear—and the justice system is silent …
> All Chile is a land of torture—and the justice system is silent.[3]

In a matter of minutes, after demonstrating through liturgy, the group disappeared into the crowd.

However brief the act, the embodied liturgy exposed otherwise characterless institutions and places as complicit in acts of oppression, thereby unmasking the disguise of civility with the anticipation of true community: "In an astonishing ritual of transformation, clandestine torture centers are revealed to the passerby for what they are, as if a veil covering the building were abruptly taken away.… . The entire torture system suddenly appears on a city street."[4] Perhaps even more significantly, the character of the servant community begins to make its determined appearance amid threats of annihilation. In the words of Fr. José Aldunte, "They can beat us or attack with water and gases, but there we are to anticipate this new society."[5] Through a liturgy of the body of Christ made visible, "the imagination of the state is supplanted by another imagination."[6]

Psalmody
Psalm 29 (RCL)
Psalm 29:1-2, 3-4, 3b + 9b-10 (LFM)

Psalm 29 has a significant liturgical history in the church, attributable in part to its dramatic imagery. Carroll Stuhlmueller believes that Psalm 29 may be the inspiration behind the imagery of the Pentecost in Acts 2:1-13, in part because the Talmud linked the psalm to the Feast of Weeks (Pentecost), a celebration commemorating the giving of the law to Moses on Mount Sinai in Exodus 19. The psalm, according to Stuhlmueller, "extends a bridge into the Canaanite world of Baal worship" through significant wordplay. But the bridge here is less conciliatory than comedic, since real power and royalty are exclusively attributed to the Lord.[7] Of course, if the psalm is vaguely taunting in its character, it nevertheless anticipates the intrusion of God into the mighty waters, bringing the *shalom* of the Lord to the watery chaos of principalities and powers.

Second Reading
Acts 10:34-43 (RCL)
Acts 10:34-38 (LFM)

Where the imagery of Psalm 29 dramatizes God's reign over the creation, Luke–Acts introduces Peter's sermon to the community associated with Cornelius. Peter's sermon underscores God's agency in opening the apostle's understanding to the implications of what is termed "the turn to the Gentiles," the new community foreshadowed by the story of Pentecost. According to Peter, God shows, sends, anoints, raises, appears, feasts, and forgives. Like the writer of Psalm 29, Luke-Acts attributes these verbs to God in Jesus Christ, who is "Lord of all," the economy of salvation being completed in him. Indeed, as if to demonstrate the priority of God's action, in verse 44, the Spirit bursts through the frailty of Peter's speaking: "While Peter was still speaking, the Holy Spirit fell upon all who heard the word." As preachers who "tell about God," we keep company with the likes of Peter, whose words find ultimate meaning only through God's holy interruption.

Gospel
Matthew 3:13-17 (RCL, LFM)

The church may blush when it contemplates Jesus' baptism by John the Baptist in the Jordan. After all, we, just as John the Baptist, know these waters to have been sullied by a sin-loving world. We also know, from what Matthew has already reported, that Jesus is the Living God. Matthew accentuates the intense sense of embarrassment occasioned by Jesus' baptism, using the contrast of one ordinary act (undoing the thong of a sandal) with an exponentially more significant and sacramental act (baptism), bringing into sharp relief the crisis confronting John and every other prophet who answered the Lord's call to be a messenger.

Comparing Matthew with Mark, the earliest of the synoptic gospels, adds additional insight. In Mark's gospel we get a straightforward (and brief) account of baptism: "In those days Jesus came from Nazareth of Galilee and was baptized by John in the Jordan" (1:9). By contrast, Matthew's account seems verbose, evasive, and perhaps apologetic: "Then [John] consented [to baptize Jesus]. And when Jesus *had been* baptized …" (vv. 15b-16a). In addition to Mark's brevity, Matthew only implies John the Baptist's agency in the act of baptism. Matthew carefully veils John's agency, implying his action but not focusing on that action.

Why the coy description? Why not a more direct account of Jesus' baptism by John? One possible answer is that Matthew suffers from the same embarrassment that he notes in John the Baptist: "Who are we to baptize you?" We could conclude that Matthew is engaging in a game of theological chicken: seeing Jesus' determination to do what he is going to do, Matthew blinks first, his "blink" coming in the form of the passive voice.

A more compelling view might be that Matthew employs the passive description not so much because of theological awkwardness but out of a sense of appropriate focus, shifting our gaze from John's trembling hand to God's benedicting voice. Matthew foregrounds the way in which the creation responds to Jesus' presence ("suddenly the heavens were opened to him …") and then describes the way he experiences God's appearing ("… and he saw the Spirit of God descending like a dove and alighting on him"). If in verse 14 we saw the hands of John trembling before baptism, in verse 17 Jesus and the reader both hear God offer the crown of benediction, saying, "This is my Son, the Beloved, with whom I am well pleased."

Reflection

On June 21, 2009, the city of Cleveland commemorated the fortieth anniversary of the day that the Cuyahoga River burst into flame, the slick of oil on its surface having been ignited by the sparks of a passing train. Although it was not an isolated event during this period, the image of the Cuyahoga River billowing with flame and smoke became symbolic of America's problem with industrial pollution. Cleveland earned the nickname "The Mistake by the Lake," recalling its role in the pollution of the river. For decades, Cleveland suffered with that moniker, a title given to it not so much because it was the only city in America that treated its rivers badly but because it was most visibly entangled with the legacy of environmental pollution.[8]

Not long ago, an evangelical magazine reported a study showing that a majority of non-Christians see church people as hypocrites, suggesting that, in the view of the larger public, our baptism into the church's life is an embarrassingly visible "mistake by the lake."

Hypocrisy may be an inescapable affliction of being associated too closely and too intentionally with God. Much less likely to attract the charge of hypocrite are those who claim to be "spiritual without being churchy," or those who have general ideas of God but not the sort of whose experience of God would entail either confusion or moral responsibility. It is the close association between knowledge of God and the sense of moral responsibility that flows from that knowledge which gets the church in trouble. Ellen Charry reflects on this topic, explaining our possible squeamishness: "The emotional liberation of the gospel brings responsibility in its wake."[9]

One may at first be relieved by the sense of awe that rushes into our awareness of God becoming flesh and then, in the next instant, we may (with John the Baptist) struggle with the complicated (maybe embarrassing) work of using our hands, bodies, and voices (unclean, all of them) to announce the new thing of God in Jesus Christ. However, we may discover through reflection on baptism that, to use Abraham Heschel's words, "[We] are better than our assertions, more intricate, more profound than our theories maintain."[10] One suspects that Peter, though fumbling with his words, was at first embarrassed but ultimately humbled by the Spirit who intruded as holy presence, deepening his words beyond any meaning either he or his listeners could assign on their own.

Perhaps this is one outcome of these texts taken together: our awe should never be reduced to our words, which either excuse or accuse, but, rather, our words, like our hearts, should yield to the One who leads us in a way that we did not know (Isa. 42:16b).

Notes

1. Kevin Henkes, *Lilly's Purple Plastic Purse* (New York: Greenwillow, 1996).
2. William T. Cavanaugh, *Torture and the Eucharist: Theology, Politics, and the Body of Christ* (Malden, Mass.: Blackwell, 1998), 274.
3. Ibid., 274-75.
4. Ibid., 275.
5. Ibid.
6. Ibid., 276.
7. Carroll Stuhlmueller, "Psalms," in *Harper's Bible Commentary*, ed. James L. Mays, et al. (San Francisco: Harper & Row, 1988), 446.
8. "Burning River Anniversary Event Sure to Be Hot Time in the City," *Akron Beacon Journal*, June 21, 2009, at http://www.ohio.com/news/48708322.html, accessed June 26, 2009.
9. Ellen Charry, ed., *Inquiring after God: Classic and Contemporary Readings* (Oxford: Blackwell, 2000), 232.
10. Abraham J. Heschel, *What Is Man* (Stanford: Stanford University Press, 1965), 114.

January 16, 2011
Second Sunday after Epiphany
Second Sunday in Ordinary Time

Revised Common Lectionary (RCL)	**Lectionary for Mass (LFM)**
Isaiah 49:1-7	Isaiah 49:3, 5-6
Psalm 40:1-11	Psalm 40:2, 4, 7-8, 8-9, 10
1 Corinthians 1:1-9	1 Corinthians 1:1-3
John 1:29-42	John 1:29-34

Adrian Moody (Nez Perce) stood naked in front of us (equally undressed) explaining the tradition of what he called a "spiritual sweat" in the Nez Perce Christian community. At the heart of this tradition, he said, was the act of "reentering the womb," symbolized by the sweat house, a simple structure of blankets covering a frame of willows bent into bows and tied together with twine at the joints. As we waited for the rocks to heat in the fire, he talked more about the spiritual sweat where, he said, we would become as we were before we were born: surrounded by the dark, wet heat of our Creator, particularly as she cleansed and then pushed us with her heat into the world, returning us to the world lathered with creation's sweat. In the context of this commentary, it seems to me that while the sweat-house experience may not be in the lexicon of most preachers, the sense of going through labor with a biblical text surely is: surrounded by the close, damp, and dark heat of the text, preachers often report something akin to what Luther describes as "sweating" with the labor of preaching.

As it turns out, the Reformer was no stranger to sweat. According to Martin Luther, we will either "sweat with our merits" and be in the darkness of our anxieties, or we will perspire with Paul who "sweats in *this* labor," that is with the word we have received, and be "led by the light of the Gospel to the right way."[1] For Luther, human beings will either sweat with the anxiety of their relative righteousness before God or they will sweat with the word that they have received, through no merit of their own. Perhaps we sense some of this in John's gospel, a gospel that seems to "pant and gasp" with the labor of the Word that was in the beginning and has become flesh so

that "we have seen his glory, the glory of the father's only son, full of grace an
(John 1:14). With these words, John asks the community to follow Jesus, his v
us almost like a midwife coaxing and wooing and encouraging and teaching a
deep pangs of labor sweep through the creation, telling us that we are being b
above (John 3:3).

First Reading
Isaiah 49:1-7 (RCL)
Isaiah 49:3, 5-6 (LFM)

"Listen to me, O coastlands, pay attention you peoples from far away!" (Isa. 49:1a). So
begins the prophet who addresses the nations as a servant who is sent on their behalf.
This marks a shift in tone from the address that speaks principally out of Israel's
experience. The present chapter moves from the seemingly fussy preoccupation with
Israel's history, to the breadth and depth of the messianic hope in which "the nations"
receive the covenant of God. Nevertheless, in keeping with the rest of Isaiah, this
chapter continues what Paul Hanson identifies as a basic pattern of thought in Second
Isaiah: "Israel is precious to God and the object of God's compassionate justice. But
Israel's responsibilities extend beyond its borders to reach out to the nations of the
earth."[2]

Some view texts like this one as "universalist" in their disposition. There is,
indeed, a sense of wideness in this text, the servant appearing to address the cosmos,
nations and creation alike, rather than only the tribes of Israel. As Martin Luther puts
it, the servant speaks differently here: "By a comprehensive and far-ranging way of
speaking He is addressing Himself to the whole world. He does not say, 'You, Jacob,'
but He calls all [peoples]."[3] For Luther, the obvious second interpretive step is not
universalist but christological in nature: "The following text compels to understand
these words as applying to Christ …"[4]

Some interpreters may be uncomfortable reading this text in a way that seems
too christocentric, believing instead that Isaiah has a more universalist objective,
the prophet seen here as wresting the covenant of God from the parochialism
of nationalism for the lofty heights of globalism. However, while contemporary
interpreters might detect a universalist bent in such texts, it is more likely, as Hanson
argues, that the prophet links God's redemptive work with God's creation.[5] This view
seems to bear up to scrutiny given the way the prophet frequently recalls the motif
of creation as he announces redemption, both in this address and others (e.g. 42:5, 9,
14; 43:1; 44:23; 45:7, 12, 18). For Isaiah, redemption is inseparable from the creation
itself and, hence, by extension, any story of redemption will be incomplete without
a restoration of the entire cosmos. Likewise, any story of creation without the story
of redemption is partial at best. In this respect, then, Luther's reading, stressing the
redemptive work of the servant vis-à-vis the creation, is probably the more consistent
reading, resonating with the internal logic operative in Isaiah and ancient Israel.

With this in mind, the text's next set of moves makes sense, shifting from the wide-angle view of the servant addressing the nations to the very moments preceding the creation, in which God's redemptive purpose was intimately connected with God's creative work: "The LORD called me before I was born, while I was in my mother's womb he named me" (v. 1b). The prophet witnesses to the story of redemption as one insinuated into the story of the creation. One can almost hear whispers of the new creation at work in the way the prophet speaks of the birth before birth, namely the servant's calling and commissioning even before a "natural birth" or his birth into our creaturely reality.

That the servant enters the creation with redemptive purpose becomes clear in verse 2: "He made my mouth like a sharp sword, in the shadow of his hand he hid me; he made me a polished arrow, in his quiver he hid me away." A trained tongue, says the prophet, is what you get. Not a strong hand, or an enormous budget, or a cache of sophisticated weapons, but a tongue that enters into the world of physical combat with prophetic power. If the work of redemption is couched in the creation, it is not a theoretical task, according to Hanson: "... [The] delivery of the divine word often brought the verbal 'swords and arrows' of the prophets into conflict with the metal swords and arrows of kings."[6]

After the vote of confidence in verses 1-3, one might be surprised by the sigh of futility that escapes the lips of the servant: "But I said, 'I have labored in vain, I have spent my strength for nothing and vanity'" (v. 4a). After this very personal sigh of surrender, the prophet turns to identify who it is that ultimately judges the worth of his efforts as well as one who supplies his strength: "... yet surely my cause is with the LORD, and my reward with my God" (v. 4b). If the servant has spent his strength, God "has become [the servant's] strength" (v. 5b). Verse 6 tips the balance decisively in the direction of God's activity through the servant, with God amplifying the calling of the servant: "It is too light a thing that you should be my servant... . I will give you as a light to the nations that my salvation may reach to the end of the earth" (v. 6b). If one hoped for an "adjustment of expectations," the God of Isaiah, a God of glory, only knows the language of doxology: more and more.

Reflection

She says, for her, preaching is like going through labor, it is exhausting. But what, she wanted to know, do I have to show for it? The congregation leaves, either praising the weather or thanking me for the sermon, but then it seems to pass into the distraction of days, and my efforts? Well, they seem forgotten, if not by me then by the congregation I serve.

Most pastors would readily identify with her frustration: the *act of preaching* is a harrowing journey of labor pangs but the *life of preaching* often seems futile. Those who experience this sort of frustration keep good company: "As for me,

Martin Luther, unless God had closed for me the eyes of reason, I would long ago have stopped preaching and have despaired. Now a boldness, or certainty, comes to my aid."[7] What I suppose we could take from these sentiments is not so much that preaching may be a trial, though it often is, but that the goal of preaching is so inestimably large that, apart from faith in God's redemptive work, we will sweat with despair.

Most, however, do not despair. We should be grateful to have even a single evening of Luther's despair—we would be the better for it! More likely, most of us, fearing despair and lacking the darkness of faith, choose a smaller, more manageable gospel. The gospel becomes chirpy rather than courageous, positive but not prophetic, progressive but not evangelical. According to Luther, if we resign our preaching to human works, we are sweating for the wrong thing. We need to sweat for the new thing, the impossible thing, and the wildly incongruous thing of the prophet. Lest the vocation of preaching be reduced to works, those who labor with the word are summoned to reenter, to remember, to experience an anamnesis of the womb of God's commissioning, where we are drawn near to the largeness of our calling.

Perhaps our calling is not as efficient as our world of Ethernet connections and preoccupation with speed might lead us to believe. The church's witness does not come with the easy mechanical clarity of a "snap and a click" but, instead, with something like the sharp, sometimes quite sudden, pangs of labor. There is with this announcement an edge that cries into the streets, like a woman in labor would cry, indifferent to her surroundings, unapologetic in her agony, the sweat of labor produced by the pushing of the mother, the wooing of midwife community, all yearning for the first bawling expression of mystery. It is this kind of wild, sometimes polemical, agony that leads the prophet to reverse the usual order of the world, giving birth through the prophetic imagination to a new community lathered with the blood and water/sweat of promise, making the despised into the honored and the abhorrent into the worthy.

Psalmody
Psalm 40:1-11 (RCL)
Psalm 40:2, 4, 7-8, 8-9, 10 (LFM)

If one's interpretive path led to reflection on verse 4 of Isaiah, Psalm 40 might be especially instructive, particularly as we attempt to understand the peculiar nature of Christian lament, something we sometimes hear at funeral services, "We do not grieve as those without hope," recalling Paul's words to the church at Thessalonica (1 Thess. 4:13b). Likewise, Psalm 40 contains both thanksgiving and supplication expressing the community's complaint even as it expresses a very present hope. According to Walter Brueggemann, "It is this capacity for receiving newness unextrapolated from present circumstance that makes Israel's complaints acts of abrasive hope and not statements of resignation or cynicism."[8] For the psalmist, the song of complaint is a song to the One who hears and redeems in steadfast love and faithfulness: "As for me, I am poor and needy, but the Lord takes thought for me. You are my help and my deliverer; do not delay, O my God" (v. 17).

Second Reading
1 Corinthians 1:1-9 (RCL)
1 Corinthians 1:1-3 (LFM)

Opening to the first words of 1 Corinthians 1:1-9 we are introduced to the peculiar practice of Christian gathering: "Paul, called to be an apostle of Christ Jesus by the will of God, and our brother Sosthenes, to the church of God that is in Corinth, to those who are sanctified in Christ Jesus, called to be saints, together with all those who in every place call on the name of our Lord Jesus Christ, both their Lord and ours" (vv. 1-2). Compressed into this greeting we find a grammar whose root cause is God, through whose Son, Jesus Christ, the apostle was called along with "our brother Sosthenes." Paul is not alone but bound by and in a community of affection and responsibility. Paul's greetings are never complete without thanksgiving, which, in the present pericope, is abundant (e.g. vv. 4, 5a, 5b, 6, 7). Paul's greeting and thanksgiving are a welcome corrective to a tendency among preachers and congregations to take for granted the gathered community, neglecting the holy greeting of the gathered church as well as remembering with rich thanksgiving the outpouring of God's Spirit on the people. These expressions of thanksgiving are at the heart of the "contrast community" of the church that, though often troubled from within as well as without, nevertheless gathers in triumphant thanksgiving.

Gospel
John 1:29-42 (RCL)
John 1:29-34 (LFM)

John's gospel introduces a different voice to the lections assigned for this season, particularly as John tells a story that is, as Raymond Brown argues, both historically situated *and* theologically rich. Brown worries that too many interpreters miss the historically grounded nature of John's gospel, mistaking it for an almost Gnostic meditation on the *logos* of God. Brown makes a compelling case that the Gospel of John is, in some ways, even more historically rooted than the Synoptics. Even if we tend to prefer the historicity of the Synoptics, John's almost pedantic inclusion of historical details speak against reading John as an ahistorical meditation on the *logos* of God in Jesus Christ. John's gospel, though different in language and emphasis from the Synoptics, nevertheless expresses a strong preference for historically grounded narrative over and above mystical experience.[9]

Be that as it may, John's gospel does, in fact, present interpreters with a shift in emphasis and mode of communication. Regarding emphasis, while Matthew concentrates on how the servant community becomes faithful by obeying the high moral-ethical code described in the Sermon on the Mount, John moves us directly to Jesus as the Christ. Where the Synoptics *narrate* the unfolding narrative of Jesus' identity as the Christ, John *proclaims* that identity. John says, through John the Baptist, "Behold the Lamb of God who removes the sin of the world!" We get nothing like this in the first chapter of Matthew, Mark, or Luke. Matthew, in fact, waits until 16:16, where we hear Peter's confession, "You are the Messiah, the Son of the living God!" John's directness may actually be an important christological signpost as the listening community makes the sometimes difficult journey through Matthew's Sermon on the Mount.

Closely bound up with John's peculiar emphasis is his mode of communication. John uses language in ways that depart sharply from what we grew accustomed to in Matthew or in any of the other Synoptics. Whereas Matthew begins with material grounded in a historical narrative, John's gospel begins with the almost mystical lyricism of John 1:1-5, a *logos*-based meditation on Genesis 1:1-5. While Brown's reminder that John does, indeed, employ historical narrative for his account of Jesus, John introduces us to a quite distinct literary style that, in turn, presents the listening community with specific interpretive challenges. My own experience is that while most of us move into the parables of the Synoptics with something resembling familiarity, we may, for example, be less confident when entering the complex rhetorical arguments of Galatians. We may experience something analogous with John's gospel, particularly when he employs theologically potent expressions like "Lamb of God" and the play on the divine name, "I am." To coin a phrase from Matthew, every jot and tittle of John's gospel taps into a deep theological narrative. Consequently, John presents interpreters with the problem of theological richness at virtually every word. Maybe we could liken the language of John's gospel to a wind instrument, an organ perhaps, where each word is an individual pipe, some deeper and taller than others, some narrower and more high pitched. The instrument itself excites and intimidates. Yet, as interpreters, our excitement finally tilts against intimidation—we begin rapping our interpretive knuckles against the words of John. Richard Hays says that we should learn to "inhabit" John's world, becoming intimately familiar with the language world that was native to John's telling of the gospel.[10] Maybe it is somewhat like my toddler daughters, who "play" the piano, a scattering of notes but not much music. With skill and practice, however, they may one day "inhabit" the instrument in ways that express its particular richness with skill. If we allow ourselves, we may well find John's gospel sounding us out in deeper ways than we imagined possible.

Unlike the previous lection from Matthew in which there was an account of Jesus' baptism, in John's account the baptism is recorded rather more emphatically in the act of proclamation: "The next day [John the Baptist] saw Jesus coming toward him and declared, 'Here is the Lamb of God who takes away the sin of the world!'" (1:29). One could say this is the proclamation into which John "baptized" Jesus—almost as difficult to say as it would be for John actually to baptize Jesus into the waters themselves! Difficult or not, the proclamation that begins this pericope acts like wildfire, as it leaps from the lips of John the Baptist and into the hearts of those who had, up to that time, counted themselves as the Baptizer's disciples. With that proclamation, repeated again at verse 35, a massive realignment begins, with the disciples joining Jesus, never looking back.

At verse 30, John begins to supply the historical background that culminated in the proclamation of verse 29. John's writing seems almost like an echo, as the language of before and after, knowing and not knowing reverberating throughout. One could hear this as John's way of narration through proclamation: narrative is incomplete without proclamation. Proclamation, for John the Baptist, concerns testimony to the One upon whom the Spirit descends (vv. 32-34). What John the Baptist "sees" is also bound up closely with his testimony: the one leads to the other. And yet, it would be a mistake to replace the act of "hearing the Word," which introduces John's gospel: "In the beginning was the Word …" Before we "see" the Word proclaimed, we hear the Word proclaimed. This expression of liturgical order may be suggested by John's stress on hearing as preceding the insight or knowledge of the disciple: "The two disciples heard [John the Baptist] say this, and they followed Jesus" (v. 37). John the Baptist saw and spoke, whereas the disciples heard and followed. Even with that note, strewn throughout this pericope we find events of sight or insight (e.g. vv. 29, 32, 34, 36, 39, 42, et al.), making John's part in the season of Epiphany a crucial one.

Listening to John in the context of the liturgical season suggests a "transfiguration" of sorts, where, to use the language of the transfiguration, the disciples "see" Jesus' face as it "shone like the sun" (Matt. 17:2). John gives us the precious gift of illumination, an illumination that lights up the rest of the gospel if not the entire season of Epiphany. Something else happens as well: John excites the disciples' curiosity (v. 38); the presence of Jesus himself forms their flickering curiosity into an abiding community of faith (v. 39). When Jesus "looks" at "Simon son of John" and gives him a new name, "Peter," we witness not only the illumination of Christ as the Lamb but the transformation of shifting uncertainty into the rock of God's salvific work. That community of faith crackles with testimony, as news of Jesus rumbles through the Gospel of John.

Reflection

Part of the challenge of reading and preaching from John's gospel is the sense that it speaks its own language—we have to learn the deep symbols that pervade this text if we are to begin to preach it faithfully. I am reminded of how it was for me during my wife's pregnancy. While she felt movements, flutterings, and, later on, rude limbs pressing against her belly, crowding her internal organs, I was one step removed. Her "deep symbols" (or "deep discomfort"!) were more difficult if not impossible for me to appreciate fully. Sometimes, at night, she would drag me out of a peaceful slumber saying, "She's moving, feel it!" placing my hand on her belly. Although I could not "inhabit" pregnancy, Rebecca did her best to keep me connected with what was happening on the inside. In a way, that was how it was, from the day that she became pregnant: *we*, in a manner of speaking, were pregnant. I don't say that to take away anything from women who bear children but only offer that as a reflection on women's generosity in sharing their experience of pregnancy with the likes of me. Whether I am like most men or not, my "pregnancy" or sense of deep connection did not start until I "saw" the baby. Then what I "heard" sank in deep.

While I realize this sounds a bit Advent-esque, the sense I get is that John, a witness of the light, invites us to see Christ fully, to abide with him in deep ways. As preachers, we are often in community with people who may or may not feel deeply connected to the symbols of the faith. We may feel that way from time to time ourselves. Perhaps this was John the Baptist's relationship to the disciples, when he cried out, "Behold the Lamb!" as if he felt within the womb of the creation the sudden movement of God's coming. Perhaps in an analogous way, while respecting different seasons of life, we can guide our congregations to a sense of anticipation, gently guiding their hands to movements in the womb of God's new creation.

Notes

1. Martin Luther, *Lectures on Isaiah, Chapters 40-66*, vol. 17 of *Luther's Works*, ed. Hilton Oswald, trans. Herbert J. A. Bouman (St. Louis: Concordia, 1972), 178, 179 (my italics).
2. Paul D. Hanson, *Isaiah 40–66*, Interpretation: A Bible Commentary for Teaching and Preaching (Lousiville: John Knox, 1995), 126.
3. Luther, *Lectures on Isaiah*, 169.
4. Ibid.
5. Hanson, *Isaiah 40–66*, 130.
6. Ibid., 127.
7. Luther, *Lectures on Isaiah*, 173-74.
8. Walter Brueggemann, *The Psalms and The Life of Faith*, ed. Patrick D. Miller (Minneapolis: Fortress Press, 1995), 177-78.
9. Raymond E. Brown, *The Gospel According to John I-XII*, The Anchor Bible (Garden City, N.Y.: Doubleday, 1966), xli.
10. Richard B. Hays, "The Materiality of John's Symbolic World," in *Preaching John's Gospel: The World It Imagines*, ed. David Fleer and Dave Bland (St. Louis: Chalice, 2008), 6.

January 23, 2011
Third Sunday after Epiphany
Third Sunday in Ordinary Time

Revised Common Lectionary (RCL)	**Lectionary for Mass (LFM)**
Isaiah 9:1-4	Isaiah 8:23b—9:3
Psalm 27:1, 2-9	Psalm 27:1, 4, 13-14
1 Corinthians 1:10-18	1 Corinthians 1:10-13, 17
Matthew 4:12-23	Matthew 4:12-23 or 4:12-17

For most of us, Matthew's account of the call of the disciples will be the dominant text for the Third Sunday after the Epiphany/in Ordinary Time. After all, it concerns homiletically as well as vocationally familiar themes of discipleship. However, we should not be deceived by the familiarity of the topic: these texts force us to reflect on the costly relationship born out of the collision of the kingdom of heaven and the kingdoms of this earth. We witness a transformative birth: messianic light shatters political and spiritual gloom; the call of discipleship leads erstwhile fishermen to drop the symbols of a needs-driven present to follow One who speaks in the language of future promise.

First Reading
Isaiah 9:1-4 (RCL)
Isaiah 8:23b—9:3 (LFM)

Isaiah addresses a community shaken to the heart by war and rumors of war, political intrigue, and whispers of betrayal: "When the house of David heard that Aram had allied itself with Ephraim, the heart of Ahaz and the heart of his people shook as the trees of the forest shake before the wind" (7:2). With that social-political experience as backdrop, part of the function of chapters 7 and 8 is to offer comfort to the community: "The young woman is with child and shall bear a son, and shall name him Immanuel" (7:14). At the same time, the prophet aims at more than comfort. Against the tendency to fear unworthy powers, the prophet declares, "But the LORD of hosts, him you shall regard as holy; let him be your fear, and let him be your dread" (8:13).

The experience of God's entrance into the contest of powers is unambiguous: "But there will be no gloom for those who were in anguish" (9:1 [8:23 Heb.]). This sentence marks an abrupt transition between the darkness of confusion and the announcement of God's light made visible. It is not a partial claim of victory, but a complete one, marking a dramatic break from what was to what shall be and in a sense what has, by virtue of God's promise, already become: "In the *former* time he brought into contempt ... but in the *latter* time he will make glorious the way of the sea, the land beyond the Jordan, Galilee of the nations" (9:1b [8:23b Heb.]).

While the text is best translated as a contrast in time, Brevard Childs believes the prophet means "more than a chronological sequence" of events. Instead, according to Childs, the prophet is contrasting two qualities of time, *judgment* and *redemption*, themes that have been in development since chapter 7.[1] However we choose to read that contrast, it explodes like fireworks against a night sky, the horizon of gloom streaked with the sounds and smells of celebration, abundance, feast, harvest, and exultation "as people exult when dividing the plunder" (9:3b [2b Heb.]).

By now, the suspense should be unbearable: What, we might ask, is the cause of all this celebration?

Something like this happened to me, although in the opposite direction, since what I witnessed was more the residue of fear than joy. I was walking through the central part of Paris late at night, not far from the Louvre, returning home after having drinks with a friend, when through the streets, running toward me and past me, I saw people scattering, fleeing in what appeared to be a panic. I managed to ask one of them what was happening, and he paused long enough for me to hear the words "tear gas," and then I got a whiff of the gas itself. I witnessed the symptoms of fear but did not see their cause.

Likewise, we may be curious as to the source of the rejoicing announced by Isaiah. Childs provides a homiletically tempting structure for preachers who like sermons with three points, noting that verses 4, 5, and 6 are each introduced with the Hebrew word *kî*, translated as "because" or "for": God breaks the yoke of burden, your enemies will be destroyed, and a child, Emmanuel, is given to you.[2] This last "for" is the theological hinge point of the text, since the messianic son carries forward a new form of government, one whose characteristics are embedded in the titles assigned to him: Wonderful Counsel, Mighty God, Everlasting Father, Prince of Peace. What he brings is peace, justice, and righteousness, and the assurance that the "zeal of the LORD" will accomplish his rule from "this time onward and forevermore" (v. 7 [6 Heb.]).

Interpreters may encounter the question, "About whom does the prophet write? Who is the child-king of whom Isaiah speaks?" One could conclude that Isaiah has in mind the good king, Hezekiah. Against this view, Childs cites the excessiveness of Isaiah's poetry, concluding, Isaiah's "language is not just of a wishful thinking for a better time" but a confession in the faithfulness of God to provide a divine ruler for the people of Israel.[3]

Reflection

"We *believe* life, glory, righteousness, and peace but on the contrary *feel* death, shame, sin, and trouble."[4]

Martin Luther said these words, and I suspect he knew of what he spoke: we feel more deeply the gloom of our times than we do the credo of our churches. There is often a disconnect between what we believe and what we feel, particularly in a church that experiences itself ever more uncertain in a world of power politics, intrigue, environmental collapse, global warfare, and sociocultural decay. Still, from time to time, we glimpse communities that nurture a vital connection to their holy referent, engaging in the dance of faith where one would least expect to find it, even a public pool in the former U.S.S.R. For most of the people who used the pool, it was a place of recreation, but re/*creation* separated from any deliberate connection to the Creator. But some came to those same waters with another memory, the memory of a church which had once stood in that place before it had been razed to the ground by political ideology. And yet, though the edifice was gone, the sacred memory persisted and the people gathered according to its prompting: they gathered in public and yet in secret, with their babies, their priests, their community, and they gathered together in those waters, like they gathered years before, to baptize while others merely bathed.

Psalmody
Psalm 27:1, 2-9 (RCL)
Psalm 27:1, 4, 13-14 (LFM)

Entitled by one NRSV edition as a "Triumphant Song of Confidence," Psalm 27 expresses Israel's inspiring confidence in God's assurance of triumph and salvation. Again, like the reading from Isaiah, the psalmist delights in the unlikely contrast: the invisible God is the "stronghold" of life, making the psalmist unafraid of those who are visible in the power of their threat, assault, and false witness (vv. 2, 3, 6, 12). "The psalm," according to James Mays, "is a refusal to let falsehood become the language world of existence. In its praise and prayer it evokes the reality in whose life faith chooses to live—the salvation of the Lord."[5] With the language of faith there comes a future, a future so wondrous that all present sufferings are nothing in comparison: "One thing I asked of the Lord, that I will seek after: to live in the house of the Lord all the days of my life, to behold the beauty of the Lord, and to inquire in his temple" (v. 4). God's *shalom*, like light breaking after a long night, moves the psalmist to sing to his soul, "'Come,' my heart says, 'seek his face!'" and the response, "Your face, Lord, do I seek" (v. 8). If the summons came from within, an inward illumination, then the response was an act, as the heart, the seat of the will, rose up out of the waves of despair into the radiant light of God's benedicting face.

Second Reading
1 Corinthians 1:10-18 (RCL)
1 Corinthians 1:10-13, 17 (LFM)

The dominant problem or challenge facing Paul and the Corinthian church was the question of unity. The Greek word translated by the NRSV as "united" may, according to Richard Hays, "carry the connotation of restoration to a prior condition, the putting in order of something that has fallen into disarray."[6] What, in this instance, has caused the disarray of the Corinthian church? Paul's rhetorical questions, "I belong to Paul" and the like (vv. 12-13), point to partisanship in the community. With regard to partisanship, perhaps one of the factors at play within this pericope is the question of the role of persuasion, which, by definition, creates a community that is looking to be "won" by one argument or another. Paul says, in essence, our proclamation is not persuasive but, rather, grounded in the reconciling work witnessed by the cross. In verse 18, Paul says something like, "Look at the cross: When we came together, we came as people who saw promise where others saw only despair, as people who rejoiced in a landscape that seemed only to offer sorrow." Hays amplifies the christological content of Paul's argument: "… [Paul] points to Jesus Christ as the one ground of unity."[7]

Gospel
Matthew 4:12-23 (RCL)
Matthew 4:12-17 (LFM)

This lection begins with John the Baptist's arrest, which might come as a sharp blow to the community, sending shivers of fear into the followers of Jesus. Matthew, however, in keeping with his gospel's sense of dramatic reversal, chooses this moment to introduce Jesus' preaching ministry as well as his assembling of the kingdom community. In fact, the text dramatizes the contrast between the world's apparent victory against the kingdom of heaven (v. 12) and the peculiar force of the kingdom to turn fear or resignation into decisive action in service of God's reign (vv. 18-22). What is more, the writer of Matthew, knowing his prophetic literature, situates Jesus' withdrawal to Galilee in Isaiah's prophetic witness to the one who "will make glorious the way of the sea, the land beyond the Jordan, Galilee of the nations" (Isa. 9:1b [8:23b Heb.]).

There is an interesting textual detail here, noted by Douglas Hare: "It is not clear," he writes, "why Matthew selects the verb 'heard.'" Hare speculates that, as in John's gospel (cf. 4:1-3), Jesus and John the Baptist "have parallel but independent ministries."[8] Walter Ong provides a more phenomenological interpretation when he notes that unlike witnessing some event with our eyes (the event is in front of us, within a frame of reference), sound is dynamic rather than static: "Sound cannot be sounding without the use of power. A hunter can see a buffalo, smell, taste, and touch a buffalo when the buffalo is completely inert, even dead, but if he hears a buffalo, he had better watch out: something is going on."[9] Warnings and whispers of threat waft through the air and John's arrest "rings in our ears." But at that precise moment, with John's arrest "ringing in our ears," Matthew cries out with the words of Isaiah: "… the people who sat in darkness have seen a great light, and for those who sat in the region and shadow of death light has dawned" (v. 16). At verse 17, Matthew reports that "from that time," Jesus began preaching. Hare points out that this formula occurs again at 16:21, demarcating the beginning of the Passion narrative.[10] One senses, then, that whatever else the preaching ministry may be, the kingdom Jesus announces is the kingdom that he himself inaugurates. Yet he does not do so alone: the inauguration contains a calling.

One interpretive tradition of Jesus' call of the disciples stresses the "common man" myth, that what is amazing about this story is that Jesus didn't go to the scribes but to common, uneducated fisherman. While this may be a "contrast" (i.e., educated versus uneducated) it is not the most startling contrast within this call narrative. This text contrasts the future of the kingdom drawing near in Christ in opposition to the kingdoms of this earth—those that are bound by tribe, class, ethnicity, education, wealth, status—all these are like the "nets" that are left to sink into a sea, abandoned, even as the disciple community follows Christ into the future. In a similar way, we might even recall the story of the resurrection, where the power of the kingdom of the tomb is completely shattered. Indeed, an empty tomb is, in an eschatological sense, no tomb at all.

Reflection

Matthew's community lived in the shadow of empire: a shiver in the world of empire often meant terror in the streets of Jerusalem. Given the historical and political climate that prevails in Matthew's narrative, our conventional interpretations of the call of the disciples seem politically naïve. Conventional interpretations might view the disciples as apolitical, engaged in wholesome work with their father, laboring at a trade they inherited from their father and his father's father. According to this image, the disciples were "common men," innocent of the political climate in which they lived. And yet, this prosaic image obscures the very presence of Jesus who hardly commends the economic system they serve; rather, Jesus' mere presence blows apart the edifice of peace with the very presence of the peaceable kingdom, its reality and imperative "heard" through the Sermon on the Mount.

Notes

1. Brevard S. Childs, *Isaiah*, Interpretation: A Bible Commentary for Teaching and Preaching (Louisville: Westminster John Knox, 2001), 80.
2. Ibid., 79.
3. Ibid., 81.

4. Martin Luther, *Lectures on Isaiah, Chapters 1–39*, vol. 16 of Luther's Works, ed. Jaroslav Pelikan, trans. Herbert J. A. Bouman (St. Louis: Concordia, 1969), 101.

5. James L. Mays, *Psalms*, Interpretation: A Bible Commentary for Teaching and Preaching (Louisville: John Knox, 1989), 133.

6. Richard B. Hays, *First Corinthians*, Interpretation: A Bible Commentary for Teaching and Preaching (Louisville: John Knox, 1997), 21.

7. Ibid., 25.

8. Douglas R. A. Hare, *Matthew*, Interpretation: A Bible Commentary for Teaching and Preaching (Louisville: John Knox, 1993), 27-28.

9. Walter J. Ong, *Orality and Literacy: The Technologizing of the Word* (London: Methuen, 1982), 32.

10. Hare, Matthew, 29.

January 30, 2011
Fourth Sunday after Epiphany
Fourth Sunday in Ordinary Time

Revised Common Lectionary (RCL)	Lectionary for Mass (LFM)
Micah 6:1-8	Zephaniah 2:3, 3:12-13
Psalm 15	Psalm 146:6-7, 8-9a, 9b-10
1 Corinthians 1:18-31	1 Corinthians 1:26-31
Matthew 5:1-12	Matthew 5:1-12

These days, the church speaks of change all the time. If we don't change, goes the conversation, inevitable consequences will follow: dwindling and aging membership, cultural irrelevance, sociopolitical marginalization, and so forth. What is ironic about this talk of change is not that change is necessary—most of us, even those who resist it, admit as much. Rather, the curious thing about these conversations is how little they actually reflect on the *change of redemption*, the story of God's saving acts, which are at the heart of the life of the church. It is almost as if we have been seduced by the marketing of change rather than the substance of change.

The novelist Jeanette Winterson describes our contemporary fascination with the transformations of the unreal: "The life plans, guru weekends, self-help manuals, get rich/thin/happy programs are no different than upgrading the car/house/job/wife/ boyfriend ethos that confuses surface activity with change. Art isn't a surface activity. It comes from a deep place and it meets the wound we each carry."[1] If change is the order of the day, and it is, we would benefit from reflecting on the root of Jesse, a root that introduces change from the depths of God's Spirit. Change worthy of the name will be grounded in a *response* to the activity and presence of the Spirit rather than merely a *reaction* to real or perceived changes in society and culture.

First Reading
Micah 6:1-8 (RCL)
Zephaniah 2:3, 3:12-13 (LFM)

According to W. Eugene March, the historical setting assumed by chapters 6 and 7 of Micah "is best understood from the perspective of the sixth or early fifth century B.C."[2] One can conceive of this text as a theological interpretation of the suffering experienced by Judah and Israel after the destruction of Jerusalem by the Babylonians in 587 B.C.E.

Micah's lawsuit calls on the mountains and the hills, and the foundations of the earth to "hear … controversy of the LORD" (v. 2). Something like an intrusion takes place here, an intrusion into what might otherwise have been a dispute between God and Israel: it is not a controversy *between* the Lord and his people but, rather, it is a "controversy *of* the LORD" and a controversy the Lord "has … with his people … *he* will contend with Israel" (v. 2). And in verses 3-5, the Lord assumes the voice of the defendant: "O my people, what have I done to you? In what have I wearied you? Answer me!" (v. 3). The Lord, according to March, speaks as both plaintiff and defendant.[3] To what end this controversy of the Lord? The creator of controversy stirs up the memory of the people, bringing to mind the history of the saving acts of God (v. 5).

One might say, left to our own resources, the human community would never look for, much less demand, the justice the prophet demands—only the Lord manifests this longing and it is a "controversy" created by God. And yet, if it is created by God, we are not thereby excused from responding to the questions that the prophet levels at the people. Of course, if it is in fact a controversy of the Lord, it will be a dispute that swirls out of our creaturely control, outstripping our moral imagination with the Lord's own unquenchable zeal.

This, it seems, is about the sum of it, when we hear the poetic expressions that come in verses 6-7, as the people struggle to answer the controversy of God. From the seemingly possible (burnt offerings, what the law required), to the absurd (thousands of rams and ten thousand rivers of oil), to the unbearable (the fruit of my body for the sin of my soul), Micah moves us steadily to the calling with which we have been called: do justice, love kindness, and walk humbly with our God (6:8). Again, Micah says, "[The LORD] has told you," which is to say, "You know already, it is the covenant between the Lord and Israel, remember the change that I wrought in you and in your people in the history of my saving acts. Make these practices a vital expression of your life together."

While Micah speaks in the period after the Babylonian destruction of Jerusalem, Zephaniah speaks in a time of relative political peace for Judah, in the period around 640 B.C.E. Like Micah's setting, however, the people were in danger of losing their identity through the historical influence of Assyria's domination of the kingdom: "Canaanite Baal worship flourished, with its abominable practices of sacred prostitution and child sacrifice, and those prophets who objected were persecuted or killed…. . The first two chapters of Zephaniah reflect the corruption in Judah before [King Josiah's] reform."[4] Repentance is thus the primary goal of the second chapter of Zephaniah. Repent, says the prophet, and "perhaps you may be hidden on the day of the LORD's wrath" (v. 3).

Reflection

At first a theological explanation of the catastrophes experienced by Israel seems a straightforward act: we should expect this from a prophet. However, the reality on the ground would likely speak against the prophet's interpretation, which, in a political climate defined by conquest and exile, would have been a form of revisionist history. Actually, it would probably be better to describe Micah's speech as something akin to religious graffiti, indecipherable to all but those it was intended to address. Seen this way, Micah's oracle uses unlicensed speech to provide a theological rather than merely sociopolitical account of catastrophic times.

One of the interesting characteristics of graffiti is its paradoxical character: scrawled onto concrete walls supporting an overpass built with taxpayer dollars; spray-painted onto the side of a passing train, the symbol of legal commerce; or cut into the sides of a bathroom stall, it claims public space for its illicit acts of communication. Maybe there is something of that going on here, with Micah choosing the image of a public lawsuit as the medium to scrawl out the dispute of the Lord. That dispute has to do with the submergence of the theological account of Israel's story beneath other nationalistic claims. It may be the case that the theological narrative lacks official authorization, it lacks citizenship papers, it exists as an "illegal" in the world but speaks with the confidence of a citizen of the kingdom.

Playing on the wording of Zephaniah, the prophetic voice urges the community of faith, *gather twice* ("Gather together, gather, O shameless nation"). What I mean here is that in the act of gathering, the church gathers *to* God's presence as well as gathers *against* the prevailing patterns of society. On the one hand, the church gathers as an affirmation of God but, on the other hand, it gathers, to use baptismal language, as a renunciation of the principalities and powers of the world. The art of repentance gathers us twice, the church authenticating and rehearsing its language as a peculiar community, so that, in the liturgical act of worship, it learns a tongue that may well be forbidden but, by God's grace, shall never be forgotten.

Psalmody
Psalm 15 (RCL)
Psalm 146: 6-7, 8-9a, 9b-10 (LFM)

The fifteenth psalm would exclude everyone I know, including the one I know best, from "abiding" in God's tent. I don't know anyone who "walks blamelessly" or does what is right and speaks truth from their heart, or at least not on a consistent basis. Carroll Stuhlmueller helps us with this text, grouping Psalm 15 with a liturgy used for entering one of the Temple gates: "Psalm 15 … enabled a person once guilty or at least under suspicion to be declared worthy of acceptance."[5] With this in mind, we hear a psalm written not for the healthy but the sick.

Psalm 146 begins what Stuhlmueller calls the "doxological" section of the book of Psalms, including 146-150.[6] Although the lection offers only verses 6-10, it makes more sense to include verses 1-2: "Praise the LORD! Praise the LORD, O my soul! I will praise the LORD as long as I live; I will sing praises to my God all my life long." These verses seem to infuse the rest with the richness of someone who is not only singing the song but one in whom the song continues to sing. Augustine says this to an ancient congregation in whose ears the memory of the psalm surely still rang:

> The word "praise" is spoken, and it has died away … we have praised him, and now we are quiet again; we have sung [the psalm] and now fallen silent. We are off to see other business we have in hand, and other activities demand our concentration. Does this mean that divine praise has ceased in us? No, certainly not, for, though your tongue praises him for only an hour or so, your life should praise him all the time.[7]

This text stresses just practices that go along with worship. Augustine puts it this way: "A man or woman can find praise delightful when listening to someone offering it in elegant, finely honed phrases and with a well modulated voice, but praise must be delightful to our God, whose ears are sensitive not to the mouth but to the heart, not to the tongue but to the life of the one who praises him."[8]

Second Reading
1 Corinthians 1:18-31 (RCL)
1 Corinthians 1:26-31 (LFM)

Ironically, in a setting of divisiveness, Paul actually underscores the witness of the cross as a more basic division than the divisions created by different loyalties. These loyalties, he seems to say, are actually superficial compared to the divisive power of the cross, which is "foolishness to those who are perishing, but to us who are being saved it is the power of God" (1:18). The community is gathered, as it were, in the witness of the cross that, while it judges us, also announces our salvation. Apart from the reconciling act of God in Jesus Christ, the judgment of the cross scatters rather than gathers: its meaning can only be apprehended by the faith community. It is merely a controversy but never an occasion for communion. One could read Paul as saying to the church, if you're going to be divided, divide around the basic scandal of the cross, for it shows not a creaturely division (which is what the world sees) but, in Paul's view, the divine-human controversy (God's judgment), which is reconciled in Christ's work on the cross.

Gospel
Matthew 5:1-12 (RCL, LFM)

Saying this text is "significant" in the narrative world of Matthew vastly understates its role in the Matthean imagination. Not only is it a text that resonates in our collective imagination, it is deliberately set apart by Matthew as Jesus' inaugural sermon. The beginning of this pericope, 5:1-2, sets Jesus' words apart as those of an authoritative teacher who draws people to himself, where he speaks from "the mountain" a detail, according to Douglas Hare, that is meant to recall the story of Moses without obscuring the new thing of Christ.[9] In effect, Matthew tells the readers that he intends this to be a christological statement: "[Jesus] is not simply 'one of the prophets' … but is the Messiah."[10]

Like Psalm 15, interpreters may be frustrated by this text since it, too, seems to set up an impossible situation: how can we say these words with integrity? We know Matthew's understanding of the coming of the kingdom: it is now and not yet. Jesus' sermon not only *commands* but, in the way of promissory speech, *effects* what he says. In promissory speech the act, for example, of declaring a couple "husband and wife" makes that obligation actual as they become husband and wife to each other. In a similar way, when Jesus says, "Blessed are the poor in spirit, for theirs is the kingdom of heaven," he is both speaking of how the disciple should be as well as naming an actuality that, by God's eschatological grace, the discipling community now inhabits.

Reflection

Modern skeptics might join with J. Paul Getty who famously remarked, "The meek shall inherit the Earth, but not the mineral rights."[11] Jorge Luis Borges writes, "Wretched are the poor in spirit, for under the earth they will be as they are on the earth" and "Wretched is he who weeps, for he has the miserable habit of weeping."[12] Poet and capitalist (strangely) concur: the claims of Jesus' Beatitudes do not agree with ordinary experience. This may lead us to talk of the "spiritual" meaning of these texts. If we go this direction, we will have to deal with the question of why Matthew puts the predictable misery of the world alongside the unanticipated promise of the kingdom. William Least Heat Moon helps us with this question as he ponders on the experience of seeing: "New ways of seeing can disclose new things: the radio telescope revealed quasars and pulsars, and the scanning electron microscope showed the whiskers of the dust mite." There is, however, another possibility: "… turn the question around: Do new *things* make for new ways of seeing?"[13]

Notes

1. Jeanette Winterson, "In Praise of the Crack-Up: A Novelist Peers through Darkness to Find Glittering Gems in Writing and Art," in *The Wall Street Journal*, October 17, 2009, W3, accessed from http://online.wsj.com/article/SB10001424052748704322004574475654003711242.html on 17 October 2009.

2. W. Eugene March, "Micah," in *Harper's Bible Commentary*, ed. James L. Mays, et al. (San Francisco: Harper & Row, 1988), 731.

3. Ibid., 734.

4. Elizabeth Achtemeier, "Zephaniah," in *Harper's Bible Commentary*, 742.

5. Carroll Stuhlmueller, "Psalms," in *Harper's Bible Commentary*, 441.

6. Ibid., 493.

7. Augustine, *Expositions of the Psalms: 121–150*, ed. Boniface Ramsey, trans. Maria Boulding, in *The Works of Saint Augustine: A Translation for the Twenty-First Century*, part 3, vol. 20 (Hyde Park, N.Y.: New City Press, 2004), 421.

8. Ibid., 423.

9. Douglas R. A. Hare, *Matthew*, Interpretation: A Bible Commentary for Teaching and Preaching (Louisville: John Knox, 1993), 34.

10. Ibid., 34-35.

11. J. Paul Getty, quoted in Peter Maass, *Crude World: The Violent Twilight of Oil* (New York: Knopf, 2009), 53.

12. Jorge Luis Borges, *Selected Poems*, ed. Alexander Coleman, trans. Willis Barnstone, et al. (New York: Viking Penguin, 1999), 293.

13. William Least Heat Moon, *Blue Highways: A Journey into America* (Boston: Little, Brown, 1982), 17.

February 6, 2011
Fifth Sunday after Epiphany
Fifth Sunday in Ordinary Time

Revised Common Lectionary (RCL)	**Lectionary for Mass (LFM)**
Isaiah 58:1-9a (9b-12)	Isaiah 58:7-10
Psalm 112:1-9 (10)	Psalm 112:4-5, 6-7, 8-9
1 Corinthians 2:1-12 (13-16)	1 Corinthians 2:1-5
Matthew 5:13-20	Matthew 5:13-16

The lections from the Fourth Sunday after the Epiphany suggested that change has come into the world by way of the new thing of God: new things, as William Least Heat Moon reminds us, can lead to new ways of seeing. If we are to talk about substantive change, then it will be the new thing we see in the inauguration of the kingdom of heaven. The lections for the Fifth Sunday after the Epiphany/in Ordinary Time continue to develop that change, not only in terms of *seeing* the new thing (and therefore seeing in new ways) but *becoming new* through practices that intensify the love, justice, and *shalom* of God. Practices of faith thread their way through the texts for this Sunday: Isaiah shouts "Loose the bonds!"; Matthew says, "You are like salt on the tongue, an unmistakable difference to the status quo." These texts continue to unfold the implications of the new thing revealed to the church in Jesus Christ by admonishing us to a new way of being in the world.

First Reading
Isaiah 58:1-9a (9b-12) (RCL)
Isaiah 58:7-10 (LFM)

This text from Isaiah starts out with a bang: "Shout out, do not hold back! Lift up your voice like a trumpet!" (v. 1a). The New Jerusalem Bible translation offers a colloquial interpretation: "Shout for all you are worth." And what is the message that summons the total exhaustion of the prophetic voice? "Announce to my people," says the Lord, "their rebellion, the house of Jacob their sins" (v. 1b). Why such a vigorous beginning to the text? Paul Hanson proposes an interpretation that may well unlock the significance of Isaiah's beginning address to the covenant community: "Its members engage in theological study, seek out divine oracles, engage in cultic rites, and fast. But … it is all a sham… . Their faith is faith in the subjunctive mood."[1] So, in sum, the point of Isaiah's outburst is not only the announcement of sin (which is obvious enough) but to *expose* baldly and loudly the quiet self-deception of a community that lives out its faith "as if they were a nation that practiced righteousness …" (v. 2b).

At this point, it would be tempting to dwell on verses 3-5b, since this is where the "exposure" takes place. Despite their protests, according to the prophet, their practices of righteousness are only superficial and, indeed, worse than superficial since these practices actually oppose the formation of the covenant community (vv. 3b, 4, 5). For most readers of this commentary, a similar catalogue of "disobedience" (maybe we would say, "nuisances") could be created for the congregations they serve: warring factions, the infamous "parking lot committee," budgets that seem more like the ghettoes of special interests rather than expressions of a whole community life, among others.

But that might not be wholly faithful to Isaiah's oracle. Something occurred to me as I played with this text, and I asked the question, "What would it look like were we to hear 58:1a as the introduction, the title, as it were, for the entire chapter?" Playing the text through my mind once more, I discovered that we could hear the "give it all you have got" in verse 1 not only as God's judgment for disobedience but also heard as incitement to the kinds of actions catalogued in verses 6-7 and 10. Surely these, too, should be "shouted out" in ways that are startlingly clear and unambiguously enacted. The oracle leans on us to imagine what it would be like to live our faith vigorously.

Reflection

Martin Luther, preaching from Matthew's introduction of Jesus' Sermon on the Mount ("And he *opened his mouth*, and taught them …"; Matt. 5:2 KJV), asserted to his listeners that preachers, after the manner of Jesus, should open their mouths "vigorously."[2] While it is impossible for us to imagine how Luther's congregation reacted to that characterization of sermonic speaking, to our ear being "vigorous" in speech may smack of something unseemly. We think, perhaps, of the overanxious sales pitch, complete with smiles too bright and greetings too warm, where effusive enthusiasm is more a symptom of greed than of an abundance of affection. If that is what is meant by being vigorous, then we would probably prefer the tepid greeting over the enthusiastic one. Yet this is not at the heart of Luther's admonishment. Rather, for Luther, it is not *our* affection or ambition for God but, instead, *God's* affection and promise to be in vigorous communion with the church. Moreover, it is worth recalling that God has nothing to gain; God has "only" everything to give. And what God gives, even everything, God gives vigorously.

Perhaps we could look again at the lection from Isaiah, look again for God's saving acts, and even God's own presence, a presence that animates the admonishment with a lively word.

Psalmody
Psalm 112:1-9 (10) (RCL)
Psalm 112:4-5, 6-7, 8-9 (LFM)

What do you do with a psalm like this one? It seems smugly sure of its claims: those who love God have lovely families, no ill health or at least plenty of health insurance, their homes are full to the brim with equity (never "underwater"), and their status in the neighborhood is that of the highly esteemed. They are the kind of people who are asked to sit on boards of trustees for universities. Their dead have high monuments in the cemetery; trusts are established in their names. They are glow-in-the-dark good people. More than their goodness, they are as generous as they are courageous. When bad times come, and we know that they will, these people never waver: they are sturdy both in times of weal and woe. And they have good reason to be confident: the psalmist assures us that they will "look in triumph on their foes" (v. 8). Why? Because their good works produce positive outcomes.

Yet here is the rub: what this psalm boasts is precisely what many in this world do not have—coherence, a moral universe that makes sense.

Psalm 112 belongs to a class of texts that, in Walter Brueggemann's phraseology, stress that "the system works."[3] The psalmist does not entertain any critical assessment, and, in fact, seems to ignore social critique of any kind. If such psalms are meaningful, it would be, according to Brueggemann, in a highly protected setting.[4] Brueggemann writes that texts like Psalm 112 assume a social web of meaning "that assures there will be no direct or visible contact with those who embody counterevidence."[5] Still, while the psalm assumes a moral universe, it is not as naïve as we might imagine, at least not in its canonical setting. Psalm 112 exists alongside other songs of lament, of grief and inner incoherence. With these considerations, interpreters may conclude that Psalm 112 is not as monochromatic as initially imagined: within the canonical setting, it operates in ways similar to Psalm 1, stressing not so much an uncritical perspective but, rather, the way readers ought to interpret the broad sweep of the psalms.[6]

Second Reading
1 Corinthians 2:1-12 (13-16) (RCL)
1 Corinthians 2:1-5 (LFM)

In effect, Paul says that as the cross is our root, our tree (in other words, the church) flourishes with improbable community. Where the world pronounced a curse, God manifests a blessing; where some snarled with the curses of final solutions, the crucified God shouts out even now with the song of victory. At the heart of Christian community is the testimony of the cross, which gathers the church (made up of people, to paraphrase Paul, who were not highly born, nor those who were wise by the world's standards) with the kingdom's *counter-coherence*. Paul might say that, unlike other communities that rely on the persuasive power of rhetoric, the church is gathered by the Spirit and power (*dunamos*) of what we proclaim (v. 4). What is intriguing to my eye is the way Paul contrasts his coming in "weakness and trembling" (v. 3), and not only in body but also in words and speech: our words, like our bodies, tremble before the "mystery of God" (v. 1b) that the church has received by way of Spirit and power. If it is a mystery of God, however, it is a mystery made, as it were, vigorous in the testimony of the cross.

Gospel
Matthew 5:13-20 (RCL)
Matthew 5:13-16 (LFM)

We have heard and no doubt reminded our congregations, not to mention our very selves, that we are, as Jesus puts it in the Sermon on the Mount, "the salt of the earth" (5:13a). When we try to describe a person we find especially good, we say that she or he is the "salt of the earth." We mean not only that they are "good," but that they are *richly* good. We mean that without these people, life would lose its flavor. While you might survive without these kinds of people, you would not flourish for very long. A community without salt is like a rose bush without the roses: it may be alive but it is not flourishing and, vastly more tragic, it is no better and actually much worse than a weed. Like salt that has lost its saltiness, it is trampled under foot (v. 13b). By contrast, a rose that flourishes kisses the sky with the once hidden, now richly visible, blood of the earth. The skin of the salty community is flush, red, rich, and ripe.

What the metaphor of salt seems to be after is the *intensification* of our being in fellowship with Christ in the world. Interpreters of Matthew may find Douglas Hare's thinking on this topic evocative for their own reflections: "We can perhaps catch its force better by substituting another seasoning: 'You are red hot pepper for the whole earth!' In this way we are reminded that the statement refers not to *status*, as if it said 'You are the world's ethical elite,' but to *function*: 'You must add zest to the life of the whole world.'"[7] Analogously, interpreters may choose to reflect on how this text, as well as the surrounding materials (e.g. 5:43-44; 6:25-33; 7:13-14), intensifies the church's way of being in the world. While, for example, praying for one's neighbors and friends may be a good thing, praying for one's enemies (5:43-44) is likely to raise a few eyebrows during the prayers of the people. If we were to enter the narrow way of Jesus, who says, "Take up your cross and follow me," it is more than likely that our hearts will skip a time or two.

In verses 14-16, Matthew says, in so many words, "You don't light a candle and then put it under a bowl. You put the candle in a place where it shines freely." At least that is the way I have heard it interpreted in the past. Augustine reads this text differently, speculating that the reference to the "bushel basket" is an allusion to economic preoccupations, or, as he puts it, "temporal concerns."[8] While we may laugh at the absurdity of burying a candle beneath a bowl, we will probably recognize the temptation of burying our vocation as disciples under "the bushel basket" of either economic scarcity or opportunity. The light of this community will not be swallowed up in the black whole of greedy ambition or fearful apprehensions of scarcity. Rather, the business of the community will be illuminated (and sometimes exposed) by "the light of the world" (v. 14).

The final part of this text, verses 17-20, reiterates the intensity of Jesus' proclamation: this is not a lessening of our obligation but an infinite amplification of the distinctive character of the covenant community. According to Hare, this is "the most difficult passage to be found anywhere in the Gospel."[9] Why? Among other things, the requirement that the righteousness of the disciples "exceed that of the scribes and Pharisees" poses an impossible condition for those who would attempt to be faithful to Christ's call to discipleship. When interpreting this text, according to Hare, we do well to stress not the *quantitative* but the *qualitative* substance implied by the comparison.[10] It is the quality of salt (or hot pepper) that is crucial, not the quantity. Other texts develop this theme further, especially the parables (13:31-32, 33, 44-50).

Reflection

Diana Butler Bass shares the story of Trinity Church on Wall Street, New York City, a church adjacent to the site of the World Trade Center. Since 2001, Trinity has opened its doors to more than two million visitors each year. Butler Bass remarks that these people seem like "spiritual tourists," people just passing through. But then her metaphor takes a darker turn, as she goes on to describe those "spiritual tourists" using words that would be more apt for refugees and exiles: "They are unmoored, nomads in a fractured world trying to make spiritual and theological sense of the changes, violence, suffering and war that have engulfed us."[11] The senior pastor of Trinity, the Rev. Dr. Jim Cooper, says, "I've got tourists galore.... . They come. They come in droves. But I don't want to let them leave as tourists. I want them to become pilgrims. I want them to connect, to know that there is something more."[12]

Back in 1999, I set off on my own pilgrimage, the Camino de Santiago, a 380-mile walk beginning in France and ending in Santiago de Compestela, Spain. The Camino is considered one of the three great pilgrimages of the world, certainly the longest, and the only one that stipulates walking as the primary mode of travel. There was a certain pride in announcing to any who asked what I was doing: "No, I'm not a tourist," I would say, "I'm a *pelegrino*." Nevertheless, I carried a camera and a backpack, as well as a "fanny pack," one of the telltale signs of the American tourist. And what is more, I began my walk alone, the way a tourist passes through the living room of other people's homes, solitary and unconnected, paying for each precious expression of hospitality.

My solitary journey was not to last for long, however. Soon, I found myself walking with an international community: Brazilians, Mexicans, French, and Spanish, as well as North Americans. But we were more varied than even our nations of origin would suggest: we were an AIDS sufferer and his partner; a Spanish grandmother and her young daughter; a businessman having an affair while his wife died of cancer; a Princeton University student, bright and full of promise; a middle-aged single mother, whose eyes seemed to always be searching for what could not be seen; and I was there, too. Whether we were walking or limping, sometimes it was hard to tell. Nevertheless, we became a community: sharing food, mending each other's blisters in the late afternoon; sometimes sharing burdens, at other times sharing silences; laughing in our companionship. No matter how sore we felt, either on the inside or outside, what was defining was how the small gestures of companionship shaped us into a people who were once no people at all.

> *She cradles my sore, blistered foot on her knees.*
> *Only a few days ago, she was a stranger to me. But now,*
> *we are strangely close.*
> *Needle in her hand, she tends to my blistered feet;*
> *she cleanses each one,*
> *each wound bandaged with compassion,*
> *each ache intensified by communion.*
> *I am not the same.*
> *And we are not alone.*[13]

Notes

1. Paul D. Hanson, *Isaiah 40–66*, Interpretation: A Bible Commentary for Teaching and Preaching(Louisville: John Knox, 1995), 204.
2. Martin Luther, *The Sermon on the Mount (Sermons) and The Magnificat*, vol. 21 of *Luther's Works*, ed. and trans. Jaroslav Pelikan (St. Louis: Concordia, 1956), 9.
3. Walter Brueggemann, *The Psalms and the Life of Faith*, ed. Patrick Miller (Minneapolis: Fortress Press, 1995), 239, 240 n.19.
4. Ibid., 240.
5. Ibid., 240 n.19.
6. Ibid., 190.
7. Douglas R. A. Hare, *Matthew*, Interpretation: A Bible Commentary for Teaching and Preaching (Louisville: John Knox, 1993), 44.
8. Saint Augustine, *The Lord's Sermon on the Mount*, ed. Johannes Quasten and Joseph C. Plumpe, trans. John J. Jepson, in *Ancient Christian Writers: The Works of the Fathers in Translation* (Westminster, UK: Newman Press, 1948), 25-26.
9. Hare, *Matthew*, 46.
10. Ibid., 49.
11. Diana Butler Bass, "Preface," in *From Nomads to Pilgrims: Stories from Practicing Congregations*, ed. Diana Butler Bass and Joseph Stewart-Sicking (Herndon, Va.: Alban Institute, 2006), xi.
12. Quoted in ibid., xi.
13. Poem by author.

February 13, 2011
Sixth Sunday after Epiphany
Sixth Sunday in Ordinary Time

Revised Common Lectionary (RCL)	**Lectionary for Mass (LFM)**
Deuteronomy 30:15-20 or	Sirach 15:16-21
Sirach 15:15-20	
Psalm 119:1-8	Psalm 119:1-2, 4-5, 17-18, 33-34
1 Corinthians 3:1-9	1 Corinthians 2:6-10
Matthew 5:21-37	Matthew 5:17-37 or 5:20-22a, 27-28,
	33-34a, 37

As I reviewed these texts I was reminded of a map, in particular the way maps guide us through unfamiliar landscapes. Perhaps this is not a bad way of thinking about the Mosaic laws or even of the Matthean expression of the law, not so much because they help us make our way in this life as because they instruct the church on how the present life can become relevant to the reign of God. Viewing it this way (that the presence of God not only illuminates the places where we live but, in fact, changes those places through the Spirit's activity) shifts our experience of the law from a static body to an active expression of the kingdom. Indeed, if the Spirit works through those who follow Christ's path, then the path itself will change because we are changed. Perhaps the most significant change held up by the texts for the Sixth Sunday after the Epiphany/in Ordinary Time is the change of reconciliation. Where we imagined a straight path of obedience we are given instead the detours, interruptions, reversals, and paradox of God's reconciling Spirit.

First Reading
Deuteronomy 30:15-20 (RCL)
Sirach 15:15-20 (RCL ALT.)
Sirach 15:16-21 (LFM)

To read the verses from Deuteronomy and Sirach, one could almost come away thinking that the world and its inhabitants were acting reasonably and decently. And even if everything was not all sorted out, at least the law of God did not leave a lot of ambiguity: "See, I have set before you today life and prosperity, death and adversity" (Deut. 30:15). Sirach does not suggest a great deal of grey either: "There are set before you fire and water; to whichever you choose, stretch forth your hand. Before man are life and death, whichever he chooses shall be given to him." (vv. 16-17 NAB).

God seems to be holding before the people of Israel two choices: one obviously wrong and the other obviously right. They seem to assume a static universe in which moral clarity is obvious. Sometimes, however, texts that seem calm on the surface are, at heart, a response to exceptionally turbulent life situations, as Richard Nelson points out in his commentary on Deuteronomy: "These verses … speak to an audience that has already experienced national destruction and exile. The path of return is set out step-by-step. Take these blessings and curses to heart in the land of exile and return to God through renewed obedience."[1] While on the surface the bold contrasts between blessings and curses seem to assume an environment where the "right way" is self-evident, closer inspection reveals a context of shifting realities.

One can look at this text and note the prominent presence of the law, the commandments, and the decrees as either static or dominant. Most of the time, when we think of the law, we think of it as we imagine it in Moses' hands: written in stone. However, the text itself expresses something of the dynamism of the law: "If you obey the commandments of the LORD your God that I am commanding you today, by loving the LORD your God, walking in his ways, and observing his commandments, decrees, and ordinances, then you shall live and become numerous …" (v. 16). One *chooses* life, *walks* in the way of God, and actively *observes* the commandments. The laws of God, one could say, sparkle with life in a world all too acquainted with the dead zones of fear and death.

As one soaks in the language of these texts, particularly Deuteronomy, what becomes increasingly evident is that obedience is not a symptom of fear but, rather, a symptom of covenantal love. Loving God, like knowing God, is not achieved through an accumulation of dutifully fulfilled requirements. If it were thus, we might expect the text to say, "Obey the decrees" or even "Obey his laws," but instead, the writer calls the people to "love the LORD your God, obey him, and hold fast to him" (v. 20). One could say that the first clause, "love the LORD your God," and the last clause, "hold fast to him," show both the origin and the character of our obedience.

Many texts—and this one can be counted among this class—seem high on admonishment and low on proclamation. With each verse, the interpreter and, eventually, the listening community is addressed by a demand. There is no getting around that fact: we belong to a covenantal God, a covenant that is not so much defined by privilege as it is responsibility. However, the longing for free proclamation of God's good work is a legitimate one and should not be simply set aside. My own theological orientation to the biblical witness inclines me to view each text as potentially breathing with the mercy and grace and love of God. There is a pneumatic pulse or pattern in each text, maybe in each word, disclosing God's active work of redemption and reconciliation. With that in mind, I attempted to lift up the "implied theological narrative" in verse 20a: "The LORD your God loves you with an everlasting love, calling out to you even when you are hidden and even when you turn, God is faithful still; God clings to you like a mother to her child, or like a child to its mother, such is the love of God for you!" When one identifies the "implied theological narrative" in texts such as this one, it becomes evident that human acts of obedience are mere echoes of God's more primary act of loving kindness, something like the blossom dancing in the abundance of the sun.

Reflection

"Our country and its congregations," writes Craig Dykstra, "are populated by a people who feel quite at sea." Our living rooms and classrooms have become forums where we wrestle with issues, or even each other, exhausting ourselves in bruising debates around difficult topics, such as human sexuality, growing distrust of governmental and religious institutions, increasing anxiety about environmental collapse, among others. We are a people at sea and the waters are turbulent and our ship, our social-moral-ethical traditions, seems ill equipped to take us through the storm. As Dykstra points out, "We would like to be sure that what we are doing—as people, as citizens, as families, as a nation—is right and good, but deep down we are not at all sure that it is. Furthermore, most people do not know where to go to find resources adequate for dealing with our personal and cultural moral ambiguity."[2] Perhaps one of the most quoted poems in this regard is W. B. Yeats's "The Second Coming," especially these two lines: "The falcon cannot hear the falconer; / Things fall apart; the center cannot hold …"[3]

When people feel as if they are at sea, they may be tempted to view the Bible, as well as the laws contained in it, as an instruction book for life. While there is clearly value in the "instructions" of Scripture, "instructions" as such cannot contain all to which Scripture witnesses. George Buttrick's criticism of the excessive claims of science could be applied to the religious community that "reduces" its yearning for communion with God to a mass of instructions:

> God cannot be spelled in blocks of logic, for God is not a theorem to be proved; and if He were, He would hardly be worth proving. God cannot be spelled with blocks of science, for God is not mainly a subject to be studied; and if He were, the studying could bring no genuine life. . . . Anyone content merely to examine a violin scientifically would never find Bach's "Air for the G String."[4]

We may apply a similar principle to the laws or "instructions" about how to live: scrupulous obedience to instructions does not necessarily lead to either God or community.

But the reverse is also true: while we may not be able to discover Bach's "Air for the G String" through scientific study of the violin, neither will we ever play or imagine something so beautiful as Bach's music if we do not become intimately and lovingly familiar with the "rules" or "science" of the instrument. Which is to say, as we look forward to the text from Matthew, Jesus insists that he is not removing one "jot or tittle" of the law: somehow the instrument becomes a witness to God's covenantal love.

What we are searching for is how the love of God and the love of learning fuse together as the music of devotion. When this fusion happens, it is like watching a gifted pianist play: his fingers move over the keys as if keys were waves of water, lifting sound-notes of music into the air, saturating everything with a sound that is more than the sum total of the separate notes, skills, hours, and years of practice which preceded that moment—it is like watching someone in love with a mystery, but a mystery that responds to our searching hand with the sound of music, just as a lover responds to the touch of the beloved. Perhaps this is one way we could come to value the law, as an instrument: it can be played badly or, as we hope, movingly, such that we do not think it is an instrument at all. Indeed, we know it is no instrument but, rather, something more like the multiplication of syllables, an expression of richness that pervades and surrounds our senses. The music of the faithful life expresses a gentle simplicity; it is a life worn by repetition, by renewal, and by repentance.

Psalmody
Psalm 119:1-8 (RCL)
Psalm 119:1-2, 4-5, 17-18, 33-34 (LFM)

Psalm 119 is an "octonary" psalm, with each of eight verses beginning with a letter from the Hebrew alphabet and then, with the next set of eight verses, beginning with the subsequent letter. Each verse of Psalm 119:1-8 begins with the Hebrew letter *aleph*. The design of the psalm encouraged those who knew Hebrew to commit it to memory. John Calvin, noting this feature of the text, says that although we may not have the linguistic "ears" to hear the aural pattern of this psalm, we should not miss the point of the Hebrew: the text of "this psalm should be carefully studied by all the children of God, and treasured up in [our] hearts, to render [us] the more conversant with it."[5] The material of the psalm was designed for "constant meditation."[6]

As interpreters pass over the words of the psalmist, they may be reminded of traditions of sung prayer, such as those present in the Taizé community of France. The words of the songs are often quite simple but never simplistic. They deepen us by their repetition, so that they become like a rosary, a rosary of words for our ears and tongues. The songs of Taizé, which are drawn from the tradition of singing the psalms, "can continue in the silence of our hearts when we are at work, speaking with others or resting. In this way prayer and daily life are united. They allow us to keep on praying even when we are unaware of it, in the silence of our hearts."[7] Sometimes, in the oddest places, the memory of the song returns to us, often when away from worship, when people feel as if the "song" has all but ceased. A simple singing of a psalm can deepen our day by adding the communion of memory to the distractions of living in our world.

Second Reading
1 Corinthians 3:1-9 (RCL)
1 Corinthians 2:6-10 (LFM)

All along, Paul has been arguing against the ordinary standards for how loyalty in a community is to be formed. Something new has transpired that upends the entire order of the cosmos. According to Paul, the community is not defined by its wisdom, its rhetoric, its particular leaders, or its particular gifts. In fact, it is solely constituted by the Christ who gathers them together in the paradox of the cross, a scandalous act. According to Beverly Roberts Gaventa, Paul's decision to image himself as a nursing mother may have scandalized his masculinity.[8] While she makes a compelling argument, the confusion he created in that rhetorical act was nothing compared to the Christ assuming the form of the crucified: "… for anyone hung on a tree is under God's curse" (Deut. 21:23). To Paul's trained eye, surely the cross was a curse. After all, he was a Jew, and he was under the law as well as the threat of its curse; but the testimony of the cross, to Paul's ear, became the mysterious music of the spheres, and he, in turn, became the servant of the Spirit's reconciling song, emptying himself after the manner of Christ's own self-emptying.

Gospel
Matthew 5:21-37 (RCL)
Matthew 5:17-37 OR 5:20-22a, 27-28, 33-34a, 37 (LFM)

If the previous lection from Matthew used salt as a metaphor for how the kingdom community brings out the richness and vitality of a redeemed creation, the salt of this text stings us with its sharp, seemingly unforgiving angularity: anger, Jesus proclaims, is no different than murder; one who "looks at a woman with lust" is the same as the one who actually commits adultery. The stridency of Jesus' "but I say to you" continues to build in verses 22-26, 29-30: "come to terms quickly with your accuser," "tear out [your eye]," and "cut off you hand," lest the whole perish for the part. Verses 31-37 only raise the stakes higher, warning those who hear these words to act quickly and hew closely not just to the letter of the law but to the spirit of the law.

At least one scholar, commenting on this text, suggests that Jesus uses this "figurative" and extreme language as "an expression for drastic action to avoid situations where temptation is likely."[9] Martin Luther, speaking in this spirit, counsels his congregation with a wise saying from one of the church fathers who likened the "stray" temptation to commit a sin to a bird flying overhead: "'I cannot … keep a bird from flying over my head. But I can certainly keep it from nesting in my hair or from biting my nose off.'"[10] As a text, this part of Jesus' Sermon on the Mount is a vigorous attack on any sin that may be trying to make a nest in the disciple's heart.

Luther, always colorful, expresses something of our modern preoccupation for "holistic" practices when he chooses to emphasize "*You* shall not murder." It is not only our hand, says Luther, but our whole person that murders:

"You shall not kill," therefore, is equivalent to saying: "You may find as many ways to kill as you have organs. You may use your hand, your tongue, your heart; you may use signs and gestures; you may use your eyes to look at someone sourly or to begrudge him his life; you may even use your ears if you do not like to hear him mentioned.— All this is included in 'killing.'"[11]

We might call this a "holistic" expression of human sin. In any event, between Calvin's plain statement of the function of the law and Luther's perceptive insight into the ways we "kill," the text speaks either a word of inescapable judgment or a word that announces the law as an instrument of grace.

Ultimately, the language of the text betrays not the clarity of our path but the passion of our repentance. It is a passionate repentance, disruptive and full of detours and unexpected turns in the road. Part of this we sense in the escalation of alarm in verse 22, where the punishment escalates with each decision to delay the act of reconciliation. Especially worthy of comment is what comes in verse 23: "So when you are offering your gift at the altar, if you remember that your brother or sister has something against you, leave your gift there before the altar and go; first be reconciled to your brother or sister, and then come and offer your gift." Even doing the *right* thing, making an offering to God, becomes the *wrong* thing without the ongoing act of reconciliation. The disciple of Jesus has to take another path, one she neither imagined nor even perhaps foresaw.

Again, where the paths of "curses" and "blessings" seem to part, in the work of repentance and reconciliation, they are joined together in the paradox of God's passionate communion.

Reflection

There is something of the impatience of Mapquest in contemporary Christian communities. Congregations want a super-highway spirituality, moving at the speed of an Ethernet connection. Some probably grew up with quips like, "What's the Question? Jesus is the Answer!" or the question (which is not really a question at all), "What would Jesus do?" Both seem to imply that ambiguities that require reflection can be reduced to a quick "directions" check, giving precise instructions for how to get from one's present ambiguity to fully realized clarity. Such "directional" questions falsify not only the complexity of the world but also the richness of following Christ in the world.

Of course, within the biblical tradition, we are obviously given "directions" or, much more significantly, the law. The problem is not the laws themselves. After all, it was through the lens of the law that New Testament writers, particularly Matthew, saw Jesus and the kingdom he inaugurated. The problem is that we reduce the laws to a mechanistic system, tempting churches into a "convenient" or "sanitized" communion with God, as if we could blot out ambiguity and blank spaces for the most convenient, fastest path to our chosen destination—and often that path is the one least cluttered with the daily work of reconciliation. By contrast, the way of Christ introduces lasting change as he reigns victorious from an unlikely throne, the cross.

Notes

1. Richard Nelson, "Deuteronomy," in *Harper's Bible Commentary*, ed. James L. Mays, et al. (San Francisco: Harper & Row, 1988), 232.
2. Craig Dykstra, *Growing in the Life of Faith: Education and Christian Practices*, 2d ed. (Lousiville: Westminster John Knox, 2005), 3.
3. William Butler Yeats, "The Second Coming," in *The Norton Anthology of English Literature*, 5th ed., vol. 2, ed. M. H. Abrams, et al. (New York: Norton, 1986), 1945.
4. George A. Buttrick, *So We Believe, So We Pray* (New York: Abingdon, 1951), 30.
5. John Calvin, *Commentary on the Psalms*, vol. 2 (Albany: Books for the Ages, 1998), 502.
6. Ibid., 501.
7. Taizé Community Web site, http://www.taize.fr/en_article338.html, accessed November 29. 2009.
8. Beverly Roberts Gaventa, *Our Mother Saint Paul* (Louisville: Westminster John Knox, 2007), 41-42.
9. Mark Allen Powell, "Matthew," in *Harper's Bible Commentary*, 957.
10. Martin Luther, *The Sermon on the Mount (Sermons) and The Magnificat*, vol. 21 of *Luther's Works*, ed. and trans. Jaroslav Pelikan (St. Louis: Concordia, 1956), 88.
11. Ibid., 77.

February 20, 2011
Seventh Sunday after Epiphany
Seventh Sunday in Ordinary Time

Revised Common Lectionary (RCL)	Lectionary for Mass (LFM)
Leviticus 19:1-2, 9-18	Leviticus 19:1-2, 17-18
Psalm 119:33-40	Psalm 103.1-2, 3-4, 8+10, 12-13
1 Corinthians 3:10-11, 16-23	1 Corinthians 3:16-23
Matthew 5:38-48	Matthew 5:38-48

The lections assigned for the Seventh Sunday after the Epiphany/in Ordinary Time extend the topic of the law, its requirements, and its radicalization in Jesus Christ. Related to that broad topic of the law, one of the pastoral issues facing interpreters who grapple with these texts is the question of how to articulate faithful obedience so that congregations can be saved from either a quiet surrender to despair (this is impossible and therefore irrelevant) or a freedom-killing legalism. To underscore the point, the interpreter himself or herself is likely be "bent double" by the stridency of these texts, particularly the admonishment to perfect holiness. If we are to keep walking with these texts, we will need to keep in our mind that the stridency of the words is ultimately a reflection of the brightness of God's appearing. If we are blinded by the piercing work of the law it is not so much the laws themselves as it is the brightness of the One who renews and faithfully inaugurates the fullness of the law. Viewed this way, the purpose of the law is not so much to drive us toward legalism or despair as it is to drive us, step by precious step, into the waiting arms of Christ.

First Reading
Leviticus 19:1-2, 9-18 (RCL)
Leviticus 19:1-2, 17-18 (LFM)

Leviticus showcases the character of God through God's holiness—a topic with which we have by now become familiar as we have worked our way through Matthew's Sermon on the Mount—which is at the heart of Leviticus. The Hebrew word for God's holiness appears 150 times in Leviticus, as a verb, noun, or adjective.[1] While all of

Leviticus deals with this topic, Walter C. Kaiser Jr. describes the phrase of verse 2, "Be holy because I, the LORD your God, am holy" as "the masthead" of chapter 19.[2] This phrase collects the spirit of Leviticus: the book of Leviticus is given not only that the people might live a holy life but that through these laws the nation of Israel could be a blessing to the nations: "Seen in this light, the Levitical laws are intended to train, teach, and prepare the people to be God's instruments of grace to others. Consequently, one of the key purposes for the law of Leviticus is to prepare Israel for its world mission."[3] Kaiser's reading reminds us of two important features of the law: first, the law is an "instrument of grace," and second, as an instrument of grace, it expresses the mission of the church to the world, which is to be as salt and light and yeast to the nations.

As to the literary character of Leviticus 19, interpreters may initially hear these laws as scattered and unconnnected. One commentary titles this chapter "Miscellaneous Instructions," reflecting the wide array of issues and relationships addressed. If the instructions seem to be all over the place, however, the repetition of the refrain, "I am the LORD your God" and the shorter from "I am the LORD," binds the miscellaneous character of the law as an expression of covenantal theology. Beyond this feature, the text, according to Kaiser, draws from the principles of the Ten Commandments.[4]

Structurally, the text is divided into three major parts, the second of which is the primary concern of this lectionary. This second attends to laws having to do with relationships to neighbors, maintaining principles of the truth, regard for the poor and for employees.[5] The climax of this text, and really the interpretive key to the text as a whole, comes in verse 18b: "… but you shall love your neighbor." This individual is called "neighbor," "brother," "fellow citizen," "people."[6]

Reflection

The prominence of the refrain "I am the LORD your God" and "I am the LORD" catches my eye as curious in its proximity to the giving of the law. Ordinarily, when I receive instructions, I am not related to the lawgiver, and sometimes I do not know the origin or rationale of the law. I am simply told to "obey" and mostly I cooperate. In either case, I am not related in any way to the lawgiver that would imply or require mutual affection. By contrast, the expression "I am the LORD *your* God" suggests something other than an absentee authority. Rather, it is almost as if the law were being given in God's own hand, something like the way Paul would sometimes close his letters, saying, "Look what large letters I use, this is my own hand, extended in brotherly love to you!" The chapter stresses not God's distance, as the lawgiver from on high who demands that we rise up to God's standards, but, rather, the lawgiver who came down from on high to be with us in covenantal love. Like Paul's letters to the churches, the law comes to the people of Israel as an expression of God's affection rather than merely God's authority. God's affection reaches not only to what we do with our hands and fields but helps us begin to amend the conditions of our hearts, particularly with respect to our neighbor.

Psalmody
Psalm 119:33-40 (RCL)
Psalm 103:1-2, 3-4, 8+10, 12-13 (LFM)

"Teach me, O LORD, the way of your statutes, and I will observe it to the end" (119:33). These words, which include "way of your statutes," also include this interesting clause, "and I will observe it to the end." Why "observe it to the end"? Would it not be enough to simply become the student of the law of God? Learn it and apply it? To my ear, the psalmist expresses not only the benefit of the law but the love of the lawgiver, indeed, that the lawgiver is more than the laws. Perhaps this is why the psalmist pleads to God and not to a mere body of knowledge. Something more than an academic interest in the Torah pervades this text. We hear evidence of this in appeals of the psalmist: "teach me" (v. 33); "give me" (v. 34); "lead me" (v. 35); "turn my heart" (v. 36); "turn my eyes" (v. 37); "I have longed for your precepts" (v. 40). Augustine moves us to the heart of this psalm:

> Let us love [God] in himself, love him in our ourselves, and love him in the neighbors whom we love as ourselves, either because they possess him or in order that they may possess him. The possibility of doing so is conferred on us by his gift, which is why the psalm says to him, *Bend my heart to your testimonies, and not to covetousness.*[7]

Psalm 103 suggests an image of a conductor, standing just above a sea of skilled musicians, instruments at the ready, but each separate and distinct from each other, gifted in themselves but not yet joined as a symphony of one. Then the psalmist begins, and like sound awakened from sleeping souls, the music begins, stringed instruments, wind, and percussion bending and building, speaking and responding, "Bless the LORD, O my soul, and all that is within me, bless his holy name" (v. 1). As in music, so also in this psalm, there is a story to be told, the story of God's benefits remembered (v. 2), God's gift of wholeness and mercy (v. 3), God's redemption through the gift of God's crown of "steadfast love and mercy" (v. 4). As if all the music of all the instruments, of all things, everything that can sing, every voice gathers together in the sweeping gift of forgiveness, "as far as the east is from the west" (v. 12a).

Second Reading
I Corinthians 3:10-11, 16-23 (RCL)
I Corinthians 3:16-23 (LFM)

Hearing the apostle speak of "foundations" and master craftsmen, each one skilled in a specific area, cooperating together, suggests something like the experience of stepping onto the scene of a massive construction project. You can almost hear the high whine of skill saws buzzing, the pneumatic bursts of nail guns driving nails into wood soft with sap and damp, the sweet smell of pine wafting through the air, worker's voices, short and abrupt, like the tools they use. Paul writes of a church under construction, a site where you might see the sign "Excuse Our Progress," as the exciting vision for the future comes into view with the dust and detritus of construction. In that spirit, Paul says more than a word or two about our work. The masthead of this text is not our work but, rather, God's gift: *"According to the grace of God given to me*, like a skilled master builder I laid a foundation, and someone else is building on it" (v. 10). Somewhere (I do not recall where) Augustine describes the Old and New Testament as the breasts of Christ. The child, the church, sucks eagerly because the milk of God's word activates and comforts, develops and deepens. The word builds by what it gives; we grow by what we eagerly and with thanksgiving receive.

Gospel
Matthew 5:38-48 (RCL, LFM)

The present text continues Jesus' elaboration of what he declares verses 17-20: "Do not think that I have come to abolish the law or the prophets; I have come not to abolish but fulfill" (v. 17). At least one commentator describes this as one of the most difficult texts in the New Testament, particularly referring to verse 20. Jesus assures us that he is not removing the law but intensifying it, as salt might intensify taste. Of course, if this text is difficult to hear, the gift of grace that introduces the text is truly amazing: "You are salt and light" in the world. In other words, the church receives its name even before it can be counted as faithful.

Ordinarily, names or titles are given upon the completion of a particular task. When I successfully defended my dissertation, I was given the credential "Ph.D." But something happened the first day of my matriculation into Princeton's Ph.D. program that I had not expected and surely had not earned: Katharine Sakenfeld, then the director of Ph.D. studies, used the words, "Welcome to the community of scholars!"—the same expression used to congratulate doctoral graduates at the time of their graduation. It would be six years before I heard those words again, but there were many times when, frustrated and exhausted, I clung to their memory, hoping to hear them again, knowing in a sense that I would hear them again. While I never told anyone, the memory of those words often sustained me as I labored toward the future.

In a much more radical sense, Matthew's Jesus does something analogous: before we merited this title as salt and light, it was given to us through Christ. Before we were a nation or were worthy of the name of the kingdom, Christ gave us that identity and now we, in fear and in trembling, live into the reality that gift creates. Again, as in Paul, grace is our teacher, opening our eyes to the new reality reigning supreme in our hearts and minds. For Matthew, that gift of a new name, inaugurated in the name of Christ, creates an utterly new world, where even the law of Moses seems, if you could say it, outdated: "You have heard that it was said, 'An eye for an eye and a tooth for a tooth.' But I say to you, Do not resist an evildoer. But if anyone strikes you on the right cheek, turn the other also …" (vv. 38-39). Perhaps one could say that while the law of Moses was progress in a relative world, Jesus' proclamation inaugurates stunning transformation.

Perhaps one of the most memorable expressions of that transformation appears in the antithesis of verses 43-44: "You have heard that it was said, 'You shall love your neighbor and hate your enemy.' But I say to you, Love your enemies and pray for those who persecute you, so that you may be children of your Father in heaven."

But what, for Matthew, does love look like? How is it manifested? How is it demonstrated?

Douglas Hare reminds us that this pericope from Matthew is not concerned with how we *feel* toward those who hurt or injure us but, rather, how we *act* toward them. The text, he points out, is silent on our feelings and highly descriptive in terms of what "love" actually does: it walks the extra mile, turns the other cheek, gives away one's extra cloak, does not refuse those who beg. Hare concludes, saying, "What is absolutely clear from the examples [Jesus] gives is that the Christian response must be *abnormal*; to *negative* attitudes and acts we must take *positive* responses."[8] The final verse of the text, "Be perfect, therefore, as your heavenly Father is perfect," may well remind us of the beginning of the Leviticus reading: it is not so much that these texts should be relevant to us but that our lives, particularly our actions relative to our enemies, should become relevant to God's reconciling work in the world.

Reflection

"We were ready for anything, except for candles and prayer."

These words were spoken by an East German police officer when confronted by the "candles and prayers" of nonviolent resistance to police brutality and government repression in the formerly Soviet-controlled G.D.R. (German Democratic Republic).

Where did these candles and prayers come from? Beginning in the early 1980s, the congregation of St. Nickolai Evangelical Lutheran Church in Leipzig gathered each Monday for prayer, reciting the Beatitudes from the Sermon on the Mount. The pastor, Christian Führer, reported that the numbers were small to begin with but they quickly grew. In the former G.D.R., where atheism was normative, the church became a sanctuary for an alternative vision for human life: "Everything that could not be discussed in public could be discussed in church, and in this way the church represented a unique spiritual and physical space in which people were free." A "critical mass grew under the roof of the church—young people, Christians and non-Christians, and later, those who wanted to leave [East Germany] joined us and sought refuge here." These vigils of prayer eventually spilled out of the church and into the streets as nonviolent protests against government oppression.

But in October, 1989, the government cracked down, beating and arresting protesters. Even so, the fear and intimidation were nothing compared to candles and prayers: "Two days later [after the start of the crackdown] St. Nikolai Church was full to overflowing for the weekly vigil. When it was over, 70,000 people marched through the city as armed soldiers looked on, but did nothing." Speaking of his experience of that night, Sylke Schumann, a college student at the time, remembers, "… it was a cold evening, but you didn't feel cold … because you saw all these people, and it was, you know, it was really amazing to be a part of that, and you felt so full of energy and hope."

According to Führer, the people "had learned to turn fear into courage.… . They came to church and then started walking …"[9]

Notes

1. Walter C. Kaiser Jr., "The Book of Leviticus," in *The New Interpreter's Bible: A Commentary in Twelve Volumes*, ed. Leander E. Keck, et al. (Nashville: Abingdon, 1994), 1:985.
2. Ibid., 1:1131.
3. Ibid., 1:988.
4. Ibid., 1:1131.
5. Ibid.
6. Ibid., 1:1134.
7. Augustine, *Expositions of the Psalms: 121–150*, ed. Boniface Ramsey, trans. Maria Boulding, part 3, vol. 20 of *The Works of Saint Augustine: A Translation for the 21st Century* (Hyde Park, N.Y.: New City Press, 2004), 392.
8. Douglas R. A. Hare, *Matthew*, Interpretation: A Bible Commentary for Teaching and Preaching (Louisville: John Knox, 1993), 59.
9. Deborah Potter, "The Church That Helped Bring Down the Berlin Wall," in *USA Today*, http://www.usatoday.come/news/religion/2009-11-05-church-berlin-wall_N.htm, accessed December 3, 2009.

February 27, 2011
Eighth Sunday after Epiphany
Eighth Sunday in Ordinary Time

The Eighth Sunday after the Epiphany/in Ordinary Time assures the faithful of God's ability to bring to completion all that God has promised and, indeed, calls the church to both look for and become instruments of this promise. Perhaps Christopher Seitz sums it up best when he compares Isaiah's servant with Moses: "Moses cut a covenant; the servant is a covenant."[1] Throughout these texts, interpreters will witness the character of the servant who brings to fulfillment all God's promises, whether that fulfillment is shown through the servant's act of deliverance, or through Matthew's reminder to reconnect with the abundance of God's creation.

First Reading
Isaiah 49:8-16a (RCL)
Isaiah 49:14-15 (LFM)

Second Isaiah imagines a "new exodus" in which the act of God's deliverance and the magnificence of the servant community will be global in a way never before foreseen. Yet, at the same time, this text remembers the voice of grieving Zion, those who experience separation and exile from their sons and daughters in the midst of the Babylonian deportation: "But Zion said, 'The LORD has forsaken me, my Lord has forgotten me'" (v. 14). That is, even though the new exodus is global in scope, the grief of those who are separated from those they love is always particular and local. The Lord answers Zion's pain, asking, "Can woman forget her nursing child or show no compassion for the child of her womb? Even these may forget, yet I will not forget you.

See, I have inscribed you on the palms of my hands; your walls are continually before me" (vv. 15-16).

Although the new exodus imagined by Isaiah multiplies the old exodus, it is still rooted in that ancient covenant between Israel and Yahweh. And yet, something has clearly changed, part of which is manifest by the absence of any further references to Israel or the house of Jacob after 48:14. Israel and Jacob are replaced by a "personified Zion."[2] Likewise, the servant seems to be changing, from being a corporate Israel to an individual person or, on some occasions, the prophet himself.

Yahweh speaks to the servant, in verse 8b, saying, "I have kept you and given you as a covenant to the people, to establish the land, to apportion the desolate heritages …" The language here, covenant, is well known, but we know it as the Decalogue cut into stone, held aloft by Moses, an understanding that we hear (or see) reiterated often enough. Only this afternoon, while reading from an illustrated children's Bible, my youngest daughter, pointing to the tablets held in Moses' hands, asked, "What is that?," the law separate and distinct from his person. With Moses the law or the covenant was a *thing,* but in Isaiah's vision the covenant is a *person* or community.

It strikes me that amid the confusion of Babylonian deportation, there were many who kept their heads low, suffering the exploitative behaviors of governments and employers as a modest price to pay in comparison to losing everything. And, according to Paul Hanson, some of those who survived the Babylonian deportation may well have enjoyed some personal profit, as they were given "considerable freedom to enter into business relationships."[3] While some may have profited from "cutting deals" with their new bosses, there might have been a larger cost, namely the loss of social reform as a serious option.

The servant of Isaiah, however, expresses both God's righteousness and God's compassion, showing pity as well as leadership for a people who are, by virtue of their political and economic circumstances, no people at all. They are people who dwell in darkness, probably out of fear. They are people who are in prison, without right of appeal. The wilderness journey imagined by Isaiah will not be the forty-year wandering of Israel but, instead, they shall be well looked after (vv. 9b-10). It will be a deliverance of many nations, peoples will come from all around the earth, only this time they will not be driven by economic necessity or political fear, but in the triumphant song of the free, which comes to include the entire creation (v. 13a). Isaiah sees an exodus of staggering proportions, one that not only releases the captive but the slaveholder; not only the propertyless but the capitalist; not only the city dwellers but the creation itself.

Amid the songs of holistic rejoicing, the following verse is unexpected: "But Zion said, 'The LORD has forsaken me, my Lord has forgotten me.'" Seitz ties this text back to themes present in the book of Lamentations. These words, he says, recall the felt losses of a people who have experienced traumatic deprivation and separation.[4] It reminds me of the criticism of the story of Job, particularly the last part of Job where Job's family is restored, only now it is multiplied many times over. Those who have lost family, sons or daughters, look at such texts in disbelief, since they seem to paper over the loss with no real compassion. Isaiah's servant does not forget those who grieve, particularly those who grieve for lost generations.

Reflection

"Comfort," writes Christopher Seitz, "is more than emotional understanding; it entails restitution and explanation—from God."[5]

She was a mother and yet the sign of her motherhood was dead. Her child was killed when he ran into the road near their home and was struck by a police vehicle. The police officer was held not responsible for the boy's death; it was ruled an accident. The mother, however, cried for an explanation. She told me once that even then, three years later, when she saw the police officer who hit and killed her son, it was like being kicked in the stomach. As she said this, she placed both her hands on her stomach, the place of her womb.

She seems to embody the spirit of the bereaved mother, whose children are taken away, either by violence or accident of history. She demands someone speak to her, concretely. It does not matter to her that the world has moved on, that it has been three years, that it was not the officer's fault. That which came from her, a child to whom she was once joined, is now gone, making her an exile in life even as her son is an exile in death. Her memory comes to mind as I think about Native peoples, their descendants, many of us more familiar with the city that absorbed us than with the land that bore us; I think of the people who stay on at the reservation or in the village, seeing the young people leave, knowing that they often never come back. Indigenous peoples, displaced peoples, slaves of the sex trade, they are people who have been dragged by violence or necessity out of their mother's wombs, leaving an ache that pleads for an answer.

Psalmody
Psalm 131 (RCL)
Psalm 62:2-3, 6-7, 8-9 (LFM)

Augustine offers the following insight into the text, and particularly what it means for the weaned child: "It cannot see the Word; it cannot yet see the equality between the Word and the Father or how the Holy Spirit is equal to the Father and the Son. Let it simply believe this and go on sucking."[6] When we are weaned, as children, our exile from our mother is almost complete. Yet, as weaned children, we suck on faith, nourished by being kept near its presence, through the act of remembering our kinship with God through Jesus Christ.

Tracy Letts's play *August: Osage County* tells the story of an American family's implosion, as members of that family violate, viciously twist, and destroy the connections that bind them together. At the quiet center of this lurid account of a family's self-destruction there is Johnna, a Cheyenne woman hired to look after the house and prepare meals. Jean, a high-school-age girl and granddaughter to the drug-addled Violet, notices that Johnna wears a necklace with a beaded pouch:

Jean: I like your necklace.
Johnna: Thank you.
Jean: Did you make that?
Johnna: My grandma.
Jean: It's a turtle, right?
Johnna: Mm-hm.
Jean: It feels like there's something in it.
Johnna: My umbilical cord.
(Jean recoils, wipes her hand on her pants leg. Johnna laughs.)

Johnna goes on to explain why she wears the memory of her birth: "Because if we lose it, our souls belong nowhere and after we die our souls will walk the Earth looking for where we belong."[7]

We are a nation of wanderers, tourists, the cords that tied us to the creation and Creator forgotten or indistinct. Augustine views the calm of the psalmist christologically, as binding us to God's love: "Our Lord Jesus Christ made the bread that was himself into milk for us by becoming incarnate and appearing as mortal man, so that in him death might be abolished and we, by believing in the flesh which the Word took to himself, might not wander away from the Word."[8]

Psalm 62 expresses unambiguous confidence in God: God is the rock of my salvation. Though God is silent, I will wait for him. To God alone I belong. The psalmist boasts of a confidence in God's power to save and God's compassion to hear. Rather like Psalm 131, though expressed in the vigorous language of confession, the psalmist proclaims his unwavering trust in God and calls others to do the same: "Trust in him at all times, O people; pour out your heart before him; God is a refuge for us" (62:8). Everything else, according to the psalmist, is passing away. It may seem like it is powerful, it may seem like it will last forever, but even together—add them up, skyscrapers, corporations, civilizations, and histories—"they are together lighter than a breath" (v. 9). One wonders whether the psalmist spoke to those who knew what it was like to see once hallowed institutions swallowed up in disillusionment; the psalmist speaks to the longings of many when he proclaims that God's salvation is a sheltering rock amid shifting sands.

Second Reading
I Corinthians 4:1-5 (RCL, LFM)

"Think of us in this way …" Paul seems to search for an image or analogy for how apostles should be seen by the community of faith. And well he might search, especially given the way he characterizes his coming to the Corinthians: Paul comes with neither eloquence nor plausibility; he comes to the Corinthians in weakness and trembling. Paul comes as an infant or, as he describes himself in another letter, an orphan. Not exactly the "strong leader" or the "wise teacher" or "great orator" the Corinthians had hoped for.

Who, then, is Paul? And who, in turn, are we? And perhaps what is most important, who is God that he should send one like Paul?

Paul answers this question, saying, "Think of us in this way, as servants of Christ and stewards of God's mysteries" (v. 1). Stewards, Paul writes, should be found trustworthy (v. 2). While Paul does not disregard those who judge him, he nevertheless puts their judgment in perspective: "But with me it is a very small thing that I should be judged by you or by any human court. I do not even judge myself" (v. 3). We should not hear this as Paul disparaging the appropriate discipline of the community (this would go against the spirit of his letters to the Corinthians as well as others) but only his attempt to place that discipline under the sign of God's redemptive judgment. God sees the "purposes of the heart" and will, in God's own time, "bring to light the things now hidden in darkness and will disclose the purposes of the heart" (v. 5). Paul, we might say, lives under the sign of God's reconciling work, under the judge who was judged in our place. The servant does not "judge" the heart of the One he serves but, rather, finds his or her vocation by being stewards of the testimony, engaging in the language of the liturgy, "For what I received from the Lord, I also pass onto you …"

The church and its leaders often make edicts with such stridency that the edicts themselves obscure the more important witness to God's reconciling work. Paul speaks sense, chastening our proclivity to sever relationships by issuing harsh judgments and calling the church to be patient with others as well as ourselves, confident of God's reconciling work in the world.

Gospel
Matthew 6:24-34 (RCL, LFM)

If there were a title for this pericope, it might be found in the first verse of this lection: "No one can serve two masters; for a slave will either hate the one and love the other, or be devoted to the one and despise the other. You cannot serve God and wealth" (v. 24). Wealth, or the love of money or our need to constantly acquire it, can blind us not only to the richness of life but also to the God who gives us abundant life. Interestingly, it seems that the people who seem most "detached" from that knowledge are those who are absorbed by the search for more. They walk hurriedly, cell phone or Blackberry held close to their ear, talking to no one who is near, caught up in the adrenalin rush of the acquisitive spirit. And this is not the lone problem of businesspersons; they are only the most obvious victims. Rather, we all struggle with this ailment: our hearts are bent in the way of selfish gain. To put it another way, our hearts feel more deeply and respond more readily to scarcity than abundance. Jesus says, reflect on the place where you are, see it deeply.

One commentator, reading this text, believes that Jesus counsels "detachment" from worldly concerns. My own feeling is that the notion of detachment itself does not square very neatly with Matthew's interest in creating a kingdom community that is, in a radical sense, *attached* to the teachings and person of Christ. If Jesus' homily is about detachment, it is even more an expression of profound attachment.

"Look," says Jesus, "at the birds of the air" and "Consider the lilies of the field"— all connect (or reconnect) the listener with the abundant provisions of the kingdom of God. These two words, *look* and *consider*, come in a veritable storm of anxious distraction. The word *worry* appears frequently in this short text, in verses 25, 27, 31, and 34. It can be translated as anxiety, concern, or distraction. Jesus seems to say, you are being drawn away from my abundance, attaching yourself to a world of scarcity. Turn your eyes to my richness and you will know my abundance … and abundance poured out upon you, the church.

Reflection

My sense is that most of have not seen the world in a very long time—at best, we are passing through the world at the speed of a blur, our wake of wind creating untold turbulence and roadkill, passing enormous swathes of land and ways of being with barely more than a nod. We think our cars, rigged with GPS, power windows, and heated seats are symbols of our worldly import, justifying the urgency of our tasks; maybe they are important, but what about the hour itself, what about the land we live in, what about the community to which we belong? Matthew's Jesus says twice, "look" and "consider"—it almost echoes Isaiah 48:20-21, where Zion sees children she did not imagine existed and yet, in some profound way, children she knows as her own. She who experienced barrenness and grief becomes one who is inexplicably rich in the promises of God. At another level of interpretation, our "worry" and "anxious" labor are symptoms of a people detached from what is true and what is lasting and what is deep. We may also see in Matthew the deliverance of the creation: the creation is not merely something to be exploited, genetically modified, or turned into a profitable monoculture, but it witnesses to the sublime diversity, generosity, and inner coherence of God's creation.

Notes

1. Christopher R. Seitz, "The Book of Isaiah 40–66," in *The New Interpreter's Bible: A Commentary in Twelve Volumes*, ed. Leander E. Keck, et al. (Nashville: Abingdon, 2001), 1:430.
2. Ibid., 1:431.
3. Paul D. Hanson, *Isaiah 40–66*, Interpretation: A Bible Commentary for Teaching and Preaching (Louisville: John Knox, 1995), 1.
4. Seitz, "The Book of Isaiah," in *New Interpreter's Bible*, 431.
5. Ibid.
6. Augustine, *Expositions of the Psalms: 121–150*, ed. Boniface Ramsey, trans. Maria Boulding, part 3, vol. 20 of *The Works of Saint Augustine: A Translation for the 21st Century* (Hyde Park, N.Y.: New City Press, 2004), 152.
7. Tracy Letts, *August: Osage County* (New York: Theatre Communications Group, Inc., 2008), 44-45.
8. Augustine, *Expositions of the Psalms*, 149.

March 6, 2011
Transfiguration of Our Lord
Last Sunday after Epiphany (RCL)
Ninth Sunday in Ordinary Time (LFM)

Revised Common Lectionary (RCL)	Lectionary for Mass (LFM)
Exodus 24:12-18	Deuteronomy 11:18, 26-28, 32
Psalm 2 or Psalm 99	Psalm 31:2-3a, 3b-4, 17+25
2 Peter 1:16-21	Romans 3:21-25, 28
Matthew 17:1-9	Matthew 7:21-27

While mountains are beautiful, they are not often tender: they do not kneel down to us but, rather, summon us to their lofty heights, and even then something of their spirit remains elusive, never to be touched by the hands of mortals. Mountain peaks are lonely places, their solitude and solemnity almost regal in nature. Most of the time, we are content to admire them from a distance, the way we might admire a saint: their features, like the names of the saints, are familiar, but familiar only as landscape, never as habitation. Only rarely do we attempt to scramble up their steep shoulders and onto their crowns, and then always as guests but never as tenants. Mountains may be the habitation of the Spirit, but for mortals, for those of us easily confused in sweeping clouds, vulnerable to making small mistakes with tragic consequences—for us, mountains are easier honor than they are to inhabit.

It is not an exaggeration to say that through the season of Epiphany, interpreters have been confronted with texts that look for the high mountain of God's habitation: the mountain of God's law climbed higher, becoming more inaccessible with each word, jot, and tittle summoning us on an upward way. Lections assigned for Transfiguration Sunday take us up the last bit of this mountain but, even more remarkably, God makes the steepest, most treacherous journey imaginable: God condescends to us. After this journey, a journey characterized largely by command, we find ourselves wrapped in holy presence. Atop this mountain, in the words of Ernest Nicholson, we may fix "gloating eyes upon the Divine Presence."[1]

First Reading
Exodus 24:12-18 (RCL)

While the lection assigned for the RCL begins with verse 12, it would make sense to include verses 9-11, as they seem to operate as a fulcrum between verses 1-8 (which recall God's commandments (e.g., "All the words that the LORD has spoken we will do"; v. 3b) and Moses' entrance into the cloud (v. 18). As in Matthew's account of the transfiguration, God appears to the elders of Israel: "… they beheld God, and they ate and drank" (v. 11). Summarizing the chapter, Walter Brueggemann writes, "This chapter … holds together *awesome presence* and *covenantal demand*."[2] Given past lections assigned for this season (which were high on covenantal demand), it makes pastoral sense to include verses 9-11.

Juxtaposed with the unexpected apprehension of the Divine Presence, a presence that ordinarily corresponded with the death of mortals, is the ordinary act of taking food. Curiously, I am reminded of the way, in the baptism account of Matthew, the ordinary and the sacred interpenetrate each other and, remarkably, those involved live to tell the tale. Likewise, in this text: in a place ordinarily beyond reach there is, unbelievably, communion. Within this nearness is a paradoxical remoteness: "… the narrator invites us to an irreducible moment that allows no useful probing."[3] God's holy mountain has become, by God's gracious decision, a peculiar habitation for mortals. Like the invitation to the Lord's table, being in the presence of God mingles awe with the sacramental act of communion, real presence with ordinary bread.

The next scene suggests that this is not an expression of divine egalitarianism since the Lord says to Moses, "Come up to me on the mountain, and wait there …" (v. 12). Moses, following the command, climbs further. In verse 13, Joshua makes an unexpected appearance that goes unexplained by the immediately surrounding material. In any case, Moses is again alone by verse 15 and, ominously or mysteriously, "the cloud covered the mountain" (v. 15). Of course, this is no ordinary cloud, but "the glory of the LORD" settles on Mount Sinai, and the "cloud covered it for six days; on the seventh day he called to Moses out of the cloud" (v. 16). It is hard to resist the connection between this text and Genesis, where "darkness covered the face of the deep, while a wind from God swept over the face of the waters" (1:2b). Just as in Genesis, the dark and quiet of God's hovering Spirit presages God's speech: "[the LORD] called to Moses out of the cloud," *ex nihilo*.

The final scene shifts from Moses and the Lord to the people down below, looking upward to the mountain: "Now the appearance of the glory of the LORD was like a devouring fire on the top of the mountain in the sight of the people of Israel." For Moses, however, it was different: he *enters* the cloud. The text intimates something other than climbing a mountain, even a very steep mountain. As Brueggemann notes, "[Moses] goes where no one has ever gone. He leaves the zone of humanness and enters the very sphere of God. And there he stays, forty days and forty nights—i.e. a very long time. No one … knows whether he will ever come out again."[4]

Deuteronomy 11:18, 26-28, 32 (LFM)

A little before the pericope assigned by the LFM in verse 8, Yahweh commands the people to "keep ... this entire commandment that I am commanding you ..." These words follow the scene of chapter 10 where Moses receives from God the Ten Commandments (for the second time). After rehearsing the law and exhorting the people to fulfill all its commands, chapter 11 opens by narrating the history of God's deliverance of Israel out of bondage (11:1-7). Israel saw this happen, "every great deed that the LORD did," with their "own eyes" (v. 7). But what they witness with their eyes must now be internalized as the memory of their hearts: "You shall put these words of mine in your heart and soul, and you shall bind them as a sign on your hand, and fix them as an emblem on your forehead" (v. 18). The proper habitat of the Lord's story of deliverance and faithfulness is neither on the pages of a book nor even on the lips of the scribe but, rather, in the hearts and on the hands of the people.

However deeply lodged in the heart, this memory should not be confused with a sentimental admonition: "See, I am setting before you today a blessing and a curse" (v. 26). To continue the metaphor introducing the lection, God says, "Look here, you see, this is the path, sure, it is narrow, but look to one side, and there you get the alternative: a sheer drop." The recipients of this command know "what time it is," the hour is late. One walks the path of redemption and salvation history with care. A couple years ago, while I was visiting the United Kingdom, the evening news carried reports of a walker who had fallen to his death from one of the high ridges leading to Northern England's rugged mountain peaks. Having been on some of those paths, I can testify that they are narrow and sometimes quite unforgiving. But my father-in-law, himself an avid walker, offered a response that was pretty straightforward: "You simply think about each step you take."

Walking, as it happens, exists as a prominent theme in the immediately preceding chapter: Moses goes up the mountain (10:3); he comes down the mountain (10:5); the Lord commands Moses, "Get up, go on your journey" (10:11a); the people's journey in the wilderness is recounted (11:5a), as is the anticipation of coming into the promised land (11:8b) and future thresholds, "when you cross the Jordan" (11:31). They say that a thousand-mile journey begins with one step; it also ends with one step. But before it becomes a journey, beginning or ending, we must imagine "the thousand miles" as such, otherwise it is merely wandering. One could say that the law recounted in this text and the admonishment to bind them to one's heart is both an expression of each step as well as a vision for the journey itself.

Reflection

If the law of Moses is a tangible expression of Israel's closeness to God, the mystery of God's presence with Israel could never be reduced to those stone tablets, however much wisdom they may have contained. Finding our particular expression of faithfulness to God's covenant love today may be like the labor of walking, always done carefully, placing each footstep with care. Whether we walk with care or not, God comes with compassion, surrounding us, creating a "theophanic tent" that shelters us and even encourages us to keep pointing in the direction of our high calling, ever mindful that, as Paul once wrote, we have not achieved it, but we press on to the high calling of God in Christ.

Psalmody
Psalm 2 (RCL)
Psalm 99 (RCL ALT.)

Both these psalms speak of the awesomeness of God. Psalm 2 does so, in part, by mocking the arrogance of nations "who conspire" and peoples who "plot in vain" (v. 1) against the Lord and his anointed. While those who conspire against God may do so with utmost seriousness, their conspiracy is more comedic than ominous: "He who sits in the heavens laughs; the LORD has them in derision" (v. 4). God's anointed king is far above the nations, on the Lord's "holy hill" (v. 6). Then, in verse 7, the tone of the psalm changes, addressing the anointed one, "You are my son; today I have begotten you." If the Lord is infinitely removed from those who are against the Divine, God is intimately close, even as a mother is to a child, to the one God calls his anointed. The final verses close by admonishing that the kings of the earth to "be wise" and "be warned" (v. 10). The last words of the psalm assure happiness to those who seek refuge with God.

Psalm 31:2-3a, 3b-4, 17+25 (LFM)

Belonging to the genre of lament, Psalm 31 follows a familiar pattern: the lament describes the experience or situation that occasioned the "crying out" to God and, in turn, expresses the psalmist's particular petition.[5] Psalm 31 describes the experience of abandonment or betrayal. The words of the psalmist convey utter exhaustion: "My eye wastes away with grief, my soul and body also" (v. 9). Not only does the psalmist feel "wasted" on the inside, the light of his eye grows dim with affliction. The psalmist literally seems to collapse: he is a "horror to my neighbors" and a "dread" to others; at the sight of him strangers "flee" (v. 11). The public abandonment experienced by the psalmist is so complete that even ordinary niceties, never mind hospitality, are denied. The petition of verse 2 comes out of this wounded state, an open wound through which the psalmist cries for refuge and dignity (vv. 1, 17), a safe place ("rock of refuge" and "strong fortress") and a reliable guide (v. 3), escape from entrapment (v. 4), and hospitality (vv. 11-13). Between cries for God's saving presence, the psalmist expresses confidence in God's deliverance (vv. 3-5, 7, 14-16, 19-24). Our wounds, as they cry out to God, may also become our witness, remembering and trusting in God's steadfast love.

Second Reading
2 Peter 1:16-21 (RCL)

The lection from 2 Peter follows the assurance of the writer that "I intend to keep reminding you of these things" (1:12), namely the character of those who have received the gospel (e.g., vv. 5-7). However, this part of the letter has to do with reiterating the testimony of Jesus Christ's transfiguration as confirmation of the church's continued hope in his return, the latter topic being the preoccupation of chapter 3.[6] The writer implies the nature of the doubts about Jesus' return when he writes, "we did not follow cleverly devised myths" (v. 16). Rather, the basis of their faith is that they "had been eyewitnesses of his majesty" (v. 16b), a foundation that is reiterated in verse 18: "We ourselves heard this voice from heaven, while we were with him on the holy mountain."

Romans 3:21-25, 28 (LFM)

"But now"—by using this expression in the lection assigned for the LFM from Romans, Paul introduces what Ernst Käsemann calls the thesis that answers the antithesis, that is, the wholesale failure of humankind, both Jew and Gentile, to fulfill all righteousness.[7] "For 'no human being will be justified in his sight' by deeds prescribed by the law, for through the law comes the knowledge of sin" (v. 20). The "but now" suggests that something genuinely new has happened, and the happening consists in the disclosure of "the righteousness of God through faith in Jesus Christ, for all who believe ..." (v. 22b). The inclusion of the testimony of the law and prophets (v. 21b) is not a case of proof texting, according to N. T. Wright, but "signals the continuity and reliability of God's purpose, which is part of the meaning of God's covenant faithfulness itself."[8] Isaiah longed for the servant who would not fall short of the glory of God but, rather, would bring God's glory by "showing" (v. 25) his righteousness. This is accomplished through Christ's crucifixion seen now in the light of his resurrection.

Gospel
Matthew 17:1-9 (RCL)

The writer of Matthew signals a significant change of scene at 16:21, where he writes, "From that time on ... ," the same formula employed to demarcate the beginning of Jesus' preaching ministry (4:17).[9] Immediately prior, Matthew records Peter's confession, "You are the Messiah, the Son of the living God" (16:16). Then, following Jesus' description of his suffering, death, and resurrection, he calls them to a life of discipleship (16:24-25). Peter's confession and the growing darkness of the crucifixion narrative seem to build toward the event recorded in the transfiguration account of Matthew 17:1-9.

As in the past, Matthew deliberately calls to mind the memory of Moses and Aaron, Nadab, and Abihu who went up the mountain of God in Exodus 24:9-18.

Unlike before, however, this event, according to Douglas Hare, is not so much a *theophany* as it is a *christophany*.[10] In other words, Matthew sets our eyes on Jesus as the Anointed One: "And he was transfigured before them"; "his face shone like the sun"; "his clothes became dazzling white" (v. 2). As in the Exodus account, where those who witnessed the event of God's appearing used similes to describe what they were seeing (e.g. Exod. 24:10), so also in this text, the appearance of Jesus as the Anointed surpasses our capacity for description. Likenesses appear for a moment before they collapse through intrinsic deficiency; other likenesses surface, which in turn vanish in the ever-growing light of revelation. In the transfiguration Jesus appears as genuinely new, and not merely novel, as the "sudden" appearance of Moses and Elijah seems to suggest (v. 3). Their presence provides narrative rootage in the covenant between Yahweh and Israel. However, when Peter proposes building "three dwellings here, one for you, one for Moses, and one for Elijah," he is interrupted in verse 5: "While he was still speaking, suddenly a bright cloud overshadowed them, and from the cloud a voice said, 'This is my Son, the Beloved; with him I am well pleased; listen to him!'"

This text has a superabundance of imagery, implied by the "high mountain" but also by the insufficiency of human speech, the presence of Moses and Elijah, and a "bright" cloud that covers them in its mystery. As in the Exodus account, just as Yahweh called to Moses out of the cloud, God commands the disciples out of the mystery of the cloud, "Listen to him!" The majesty of this text can be overwhelming and, for interpreters, intimidating. Wordsmiths by nature, preachers will find their tools too short, too rude to approximate this text. We may throw our voice into the mystery but our soundings will likely be swallowed up into something deeper than we know. And we, indeed, are afraid, even unto death …

But Jesus …

In an action that foreshadows Jesus' resurrection as well as ours, Jesus comes to the disciples in their silence with the word of his touch: "But Jesus came and touched them, saying, 'Get up and do not be afraid.' And when they looked up, they saw no one except Jesus himself alone" (v. 7). This, I would say, is the climax of this text, the conjoining of the vision with the touch of the One who is the Christ. Combining sacramental touch with Divine Word, the church answers no other voice but Christ's own voice.

However, this pericope includes verse 9, in which the disciples are instructed to not tell anyone about this "vision" until after the resurrection. Which is to say, Matthew steers the church away from a merely mystical experience of Jesus Christ but, rather, would have the church view Jesus by way of the cross and tomb, where the concrete realities of suffering and death are met and conquered in his resurrection. Just before this important chapter closes, Jesus speaks of how "Elijah has already come, and they did not recognize him," and then, saying that his fate will resemble John the Baptist's, he adds, "So also the Son of Man is about to suffer at their hands"

(v. 12b). Ironically, Jesus speaks of those who set their hands on him, touching him yet not knowing him. Yet, as he touches us, so also we come to know him.

Matthew 7:21-27 (LFM)

The Sermon on the Mount ends at 7:12, with the Golden Rule: "Do unto others …" The subsequent material accentuates *doing*, the Greek verb for "to do" or "to make" appearing nine times between 7:12-29.[11] One who is faithful will "enter through the narrow gate" since that is the gate that leads to life and the wide path leads to destruction. The faithful community will bear the fruit of their doings. But all this comes with a warning: "Not everyone who says to me, 'Lord, Lord,' will enter the kingdom of heaven, but only the one who does the will of my Father in heaven." Then, after warning of the consequences for evildoers, Jesus contrasts those who merely hear with those who hear and respond with the story of the wise person who built his house on a rock (and prospered) and the foolish person who built his house on sand and the house collapsed mightily. One almost gets the impression that the house built on the sand had every appearance of success: after all, its fall was "great"—everyone noted its collapse.

This text has obvious connections to the failure of the real-estate market, which produced not only both supersized McMansions and supersized profits, but a mind-boggling economic collapse for the global economy as well: and great was its fall. By contrast, one could almost read the wise person as one who nurtured a moral-ethical root for the formation of a local economy. Profit was not a matter of capturing a market of scale but, rather, in doing one's work with care and reflection. Don't simply throw something up because there is an opportunity but think rather about the community: How will your work contribute to a habitat in which loving one's neighbor is as important as loving oneself?

Jesus' words "astounded" the crowds, according to Matthew. He spoke, they said, "as one having authority," not like the scribes (v. 29). Jesus' words were bound up in his work in the resurrection when he declared: "All authority in heaven and on earth has been given to me. Go therefore and make disciples of all nations" (28:18b-19a).

Reflection

Mount Eccles … more than the name of that mountain in my memory is its outline, the way the clouds that announced the coming of rain would pour like a thick river over its peak and down its rim, down into the small fishing town of Cordova, Alaska. It was the mountain that filled my vision when we went trout fishing at the reservoir, where we could see it more closely because the reservoir was nestled at the top of a lower ridge of coastal hills. It was also the mountain that cast its shadow over my grandmother's grave—Mount Eccles presence was regal, never to be forgotten, removed, and distant, while my grandmother's grave and the tragic memory of her life were intimate, having a smell like my own, even if it was a smell buried beneath dirt and years.

Death, oddly enough, seems to have been at back of these texts all along. Exodus 24 recounts that the men on the mountain with Moses "saw God" and did not die. Even more importantly, they ate in the presence of God, a confirmation of life. Yet, as Moses "enters the cloud" there is, in a sense, something resembling death. He dies to creaturely light just as his eyes are opened to God's uncreated light. Perhaps this "entering of the cloud" is somewhere at work in Paul when we hear him say, "It is no longer I who live, but it is Christ who lives in me" (Gal. 2:20) and "I die every day!" (1 Cor. 15:31). Paul's expressions and the ordinary act of eating in the otherwise terrifying presence of God suggest that something has changed in our experience of death, an event that otherwise, as the poet Louise Glück writes, "terrifies us all into silence."[12] But now, to borrow from Paul's language in 1 Corinthians, far from being silent, the church gathers around the Lord's table to celebrate the Eucharist, as the church "*proclaims* the Lord's *death* until he comes" (11:26b). Where, at the tomb, we were once silent in wounded loss, our mouths open boldly to witness not only to the resurrection of Christ but our resurrection in Christ. As Matthew reports in the transfiguration, the disciples, overshadowed by a bright cloud, heard the divine voice, and "fell to the ground and were overcome by fear" (17:6b).

In a manner of speaking, they died: "But Jesus," says Matthew, "came and touched them, saying, 'Get up and do not be afraid'" (v. 7).

Notes

1. Ernest Nicholson, "The Interpretation of Exodus XXIV 9-11," *Vetus Testamentum* 24 (1974): 89-90, quoted in Walter Brueggemann, "The Book of Exodus: Introduction, Commentary, and Reflections," in *The New Interpreter's Bible: A Commentary in Twelve Volumes*, ed. Leander E. Keck, et al. (Nashville: Abingdon, 1994), 1:881.
2. Brueggemann, "The Book of Exodus," *New Interpreter's Bible*, 1:882.
3. Ibid., 1:881.
4. Ibid., 1:882.
5. Walter Brueggemann, *The Psalms and the Life of Faith*, ed. Patrick D. Miller (Minneapolis: Fortress Press, 1995), 70.
6. Bo Reiche, *The Epistles of James, Peter, and Jude: Introduction, Translation and Notes*, The Anchor Bible (Garden City, N.Y.: Doubleday, 1964), 156-57.
7. Ernst Käsemann, *Commentary on Romans*, ed. and trans. Geoffrey W. Bromiley (Grand Rapids: Eerdmans, 1980), 91.
8. N. T. Wright, "The Letter to the Romans: Introduction, Commentary, and Reflections," in *The New Interpreter's Bible* (2002), 10:469.
9. Douglas R. A. Hare, *Matthew*, Interpretation: A Bible Commentary for Teaching and Preaching (Louisville: John Knox, 1993), 29.
10. Ibid., 199.
11. Ibid., 81.
12. Louise Glück, *A Village Life* (New York: Farrar, Straus, & Giroux, 2009), 63.

Lent

Susan Marie Smith

The words were simple, but profound. I didn't expect to be so moved—by a children's lesson. Speaking of the three great feasts, Christmas, Easter, and Pentecost, Jerome Berryman said, "Some people walk right through these feasts and don't even know what's there! It takes time to get ready to come close to a great mystery. . . . The time to get ready to come close to the mystery of Easter is called Lent …"

It was a Christian education workshop, and the author of *Godly Play*[1] was demonstrating one of his children's lessons. His eyes were focused on the props, "the story," which drew in the hearers' attention as well. It worked. I was filled with a sense of awe and holy desire to "come close to the mystery of Easter." And I am astonished to find that I have held that anticipation ever since.

Easter and the Great Feasts are not the only holy moments for which we must prepare. We are both privileged and obligated to place ourselves in the way of openness, so that when the moment, the day, the sacrament comes and the Spirit is more active than ever, we will have the possibility of receiving the gift—the Gift—our souls have hoped for. In Lent, our early Christian forebears prepared intently, not only for Easter, but for *baptism*.

Preparation is a way of taking seriously what is to come. It creates suspense and anticipation, like a child watching the Christmas tree go up, blinking as the lights go on, helping with ornaments, placing nativity figures. There is time to wonder and to ask questions. There is time to ponder the meaning, talk to friends, and spend oneself in reading or praying or making or giving—until the eagerness builds up to all-night preparation and celebration, and sleepy feasting the next day.

It is good to prepare for baptism, because this sacrament utterly changes one's identity. Once, one's life had no meaning. One belonged only to the people one knew. One's life had no purpose beyond what one could see. One's own finitude, and others' limitations, defined the limits of one's life. But in preparing, whether for forty days or four years, an awareness begins to dawn of the joy and gravity of this freedom, this life offered *en Christos*. It's not just study, but life change—conversion—formation. *Catechesis* was the Greek word for this process of mind-stretch and soul-tend and heart-open. What helps? The love of sponsors, the prayer of the congregation, the study of God's creation and redemption, the growing intimacy with Jesus. Especially, the practices: *fasting, praying, sharing with others; serving, tithing, worshiping; holy reading, living simply, cultivating Christian friendships.* Especially, renewing our commitment annually, in Lent.

Lent is a time to prepare. It is a gift of time to "get ready to come close to the mystery of Easter." Many churches are returning to the ancient practice of baptizing at Easter, or *Pascha,* since the meaning of baptismal immersion into the life, death, and resurrection of Jesus Christ is made so vividly real at the hinge of history that is Christ's Passover (*Pascha*) to *new life.*

But whether or not a church will baptize or renew baptismal vows at Easter, the mystery of Easter is still the mystery of Christ, the Son of God, whom death—even painful crucifixion—could not hold, but who is resurrected from the dead, to reign in glory at God's right hand! Lent is a time to enter the mystery of who Jesus is. And as followers of Jesus, the first question of identity leads to the second: *Who are we? What does it mean to be human?*

The readings in both lectionaries for Lent, Year A, are geared to the exploration of both Jesus' and our identity: *Who is Jesus?* and *Who are we? What is our relationship with him? How can we be most fully human?* The authors of the lectionaries, with wisdom from the liturgical reform of the 1960s to 1990s, have drawn the readings of paschal identity—that of Jesus and of those baptized in his name—from the early church's use, and have placed them here, in Year A.

In particular, Antoine Chavasse, a French liturgical historian, has reconstructed the early lectionaries to identify the particular readings selected for the third, fourth, and fifth Sundays in Lent, from at least the fifth century (and beyond). These stories are given to the church again on these same three weeks: the Woman at the Well (John 4:5-32), the Man Born Blind (John 9:1-38), and the Raising of Lazarus (John 11:1-54).[2]

In the course of liturgical renewal and reform in the latter twentieth century, there was a renewed emphasis on the ministry of the laity and the importance of baptism as a sacrament of Christian identity and ministry. These readings, then, arouse those preparing to come close to the mystery of their baptism to learn who Jesus is; to prepare to be washed in living baptismal water (John 4); to be healed in recognizing that Christ is the light of the world (John 9); and to connect the baptismal life with life in communion with the risen Christ, who is the resurrection and the life (John 11). Ideas for making these connections are offered in this commentary.

There is reason to think that the twenty-first-century Western world is hungry for *meaning:* for a Mystery greater than ourselves for which we can offer our best and deepest. Something that is not "whatever," relative, or under our control; but something—or Someone—we can utterly trust, give ourselves to, stand for, honor, and live into. Someone we would be willing to proclaim publicly. Someone Lent would prepare us to meet. Here are two cultural examples.

In the first decades of the twenty-first century, it is hard to miss the appeal of J. K. Rowling's *Harry Potter* series, in which the hero, a wizard living among those who do not recognize his identity ("muggles"), has a sign imprinted on his forehead indicating that he is alive because of the self-giving love of his mother, who gave her life to save him.[3] It is hard to avoid the connection with the cross of Christ, imprinted upon the baptized,[4] and renewed every Ash Wednesday, when ashes are inscribed on the foreheads of Christians, called to bear the cross of Christ. Harry's sign, visible where Christians' signs are invisible, sets him apart for a particular life and mission. The scar hurts when evil comes near; yet even in the pain, it serves to guide him to help himself and others through evil to the right and good. Do Christians realize that they are set apart, effectively "wizard" living in a muggle world? The wild popularity of Harry Potter might suggest that people, including Christians, are hungry for higher stakes—worth dying for—and a life that counts for something: for the One whose self-giving love, even unto death, gave his life to save us.

The crosses on Christian's foreheads at their initiation into Christ are invisible—which means that few know when this sign of identity is violated. Yet in addition to Harry Potter, it is another interesting sign of the times that tattoos are on the increase. Young and old have signs of significant life moments engraved in color on leg, shoulder, arm, and back—where they can be seen. A colleague told of the irony of a frustrated youth, complaining because the tattoo artist did not have the particularly shaped cross used by his denomination, and he had to have a generic cross indelibly marked on his arm. What does this indicate? Is it possible that not only do persons want their identity in Christ to matter and to mean something, but also that they are ready to come out publicly, indelibly, so that there is no way to hide their commitment?

Identity and commitment in Christ must occur every day. But periodically folks need a reminder, a renewal, an encouragement. They need self-examination, course correction, spiritual practices that enable the Word of God to penetrate busy lives. This is the purpose of Lent. And renewal in light of who Jesus is, and in relationship to baptismal identity and who we are, is the orientation of the lections for Year A.

Even nonchurchgoers know that Lent is a time for habit changes. They may not understand, however, that Christians practice Lenten discipline not only to get healthy, but to fulfill their baptism into a life of holiness, deepening their relationship with the Holy One and intentionally growing toward the likeness of God (Gen. 1:26-26), the mind of Christ (Phil. 2:5). They may not grasp that, like the pilot of a small plane or jetliner, Lent is a time for feedback in order to make course corrections in our lives: to pay particular attention to our inner instrumentation so that we can land safely at this year's destination on the joyous Easter *terra firma* of Christ's resurrection.

The tried-and-true course corrections are the three classic spiritual disciplines to which God's people are called by both Scripture and tradition: fasting, prayer, and almsgiving (see the Ash Wednesday commentary, below). Yet congregations vary, and Lent keeps coming around every year. What matters most is that good pastors seek fresh ways to invite their people to renewal of faith and spiritual practice. In the early church, these weeks of holy work to cleanse them for the intense paschal presence of the Holy Spirit were called "the forty days." The name *Lent* comes from Middle English *lente*, meaning "springtime," since (from the third century) baptisms happened on the day of resurrection (always occurring near Passover, which in the northern hemisphere is always spring). With the memory of the crucifixion still fresh, baptizing at Easter is a powerful symbol to *make real* what and Who it is they are being baptized into. Lent began, then, as forty days of intense spiritual preparation for baptism, the rite that makes a person part of the Easter people.

Intentional reempowerment of baptismal living in Lent, especially in Year A, could change the post-Christendom church's role in the world. These commentaries are offered to you to support your intentions for the people in your care, whom God saves in Christ, empowers by the Spirit, calls and continues to set apart, temper, love, and send forth. May this be a holy Lent for you and for your people.

Note

1. Jerome W. Berryman, *The Complete Guide to Godly Play: An imaginative method for presenting scripture stories to children*, Vol. 2 (Harrisburg, PA: Morehouse Continuum, 2002).
2. "La structure du Carême et les lectures des messes quadragesimales dans la liturgie romaine," *La Maison-Dieu* 31 (1952) 76-120; «La préparation de la Pâque, à Rome, avant le Ve siècle. Jeûne et organisation liturgique,» *Memorial J. Chaine* (Lyon: Facultés catholiques, 1950) 61-80; and «Temps de préparation à la Pâque, d'après quelques libres liturgiques romains, » *Rech. de Sc. Relig.* 37 (1950) 125-45. Cited in Maxwell E. Johnson, *The Rites of Christian Initiation: Their Evolution and Interpretation* (Collegeville, MN: Liturgical Press, 1999) 164, and 164 n. 14, 15.
3. There is no indication that Rowling intended this association; but for those who reflect theologically on contemporary culture, it is astonishing the number of signs of people's hunger and God's word of grace.
4. Signation of the cross is typically placed on the forehead, where in the Roman Empire a brand was burned with the symbol of the master whom one served. In the Roman Catholic Church since the 1960's, signation of infants at Baptism is on the top of the head; signation on the forehead occurs at Confirmation which is initiatory.

March 9, 2011
Ash Wednesday

Revised Common Lectionary (RCL)

Joel 2:1-2, 12-17 or Isaiah 58:1-12
Psalm 51:1-17
2 Corinthians 5:20b—6:10
Matthew 6:1-6, 16-21

Lectionary for Mass (LFM)

Joel 2:12-18
Psalm 51:3-4, 5-6ab, 12-13, 14, 17
2 Corinthians 5:20—6:2
Matthew 6:1-6, 16-18

First Reading
Joel 2:1-17, 12-17 (RCL)
Joel 2:12-18 (LFM)

The Text.[1] The prophet Joel summons God's people to repentance: "Blow the trumpet in Zion; sound the alarm on my holy mountain! Let all the inhabitants of the land tremble, for the day of the LORD is coming; it is near …" (2:1). Missing from the lectionary are verses 2-11, Joel's fearful description of the day of the Lord, the *eschaton*, the end time, with fire, earthquakes, darkness—"terrible…. Who can endure it?" (v. 11c).

These verses for Ash Wednesday dramatically contrast the terror of doomsday with God's true desire for God's people. Like Jonah to the Ninevites, Joel speaks on behalf of God to call the people of Judah (and current readers) to *Return! Repent! Return to me, the* LORD, *with all your heart.* God desires salvation for the people. God's priests are called to mediate for the people ("between the vestibule and the altar"), and to weep and cry out, begging God to "spare your people" (v. 17).

What will be the outward sign of the people's repentance? Sackcloth (1:8, 13) is the ritual sign, but the Lord is calling for a change in behavior. If the sign is not connected to the behavior, then God prefers hearts be mortified over clothing (2:13a), and whole-heartedness at that: honest (even if painful) awareness of shortfall, deep desire to be one with God, change of practices ("all your heart," v. 12). And the sign and means of turned hearts are "fasting," "weeping," and "mourning" (v. 12c). The whole assembly is called, including the elderly and children (v. 16b), and those who might seem exempt (bridegroom and bride, v. 16c; see Deut. 24:5).

The Preaching. This call for repentance and return through Joel continues to be a compelling call today. It is fitting to remind Christians that the solemn, holy fast begun on Ash Wednesday and lasting a traditional forty days is the same repentance and return to which priests and prophets of God have called the covenanted people whenever needed (like Joel), and always annually during the ten High Holy Days of fasting and repentance between Rosh Hashanah (New Year) and Yom Kippur (the Day of Atonement): "Blow the trumpet … sanctify a fast; call a solemn assembly; gather the people. Sanctify the congregation; assemble the aged; gather the children, even infants at the breast …" (vv. 15-16b).

Verse 18, added in the Roman lectionary, proclaims trust in the outcome: "the LORD… had pity on his people."

Isaiah 58:1-12 (RCL ALT.)

The Text. The alternative RCL reading from Third Isaiah, dated after the restoration from Babylonian exile, is, like Joel, a call to repentance and return. It, too, begins with a trumpet announcing the fast, or, at least, voices shouting like a trumpet. Isaiah, too, proclaims God's call to fast as a means to return to their practice of "righteousness" (v. 2). However, Third Isaiah sounds a strong call to the righteousness of *social justice.* Reminiscent of Micah 6:6-8, God here calls the covenanted people not to self-satisfaction having lain "in sackcloth and ashes" (v. 5), but

> …to loose the bonds of injustice, …
> to share your bread with the hungry,
> and bring the homeless poor into your house; …
> and satisfy the needs of the afflicted. (vv. 6-7, 10b)

The Preaching. Right relationship with God requires inner integrity, a life of prayer, spiritual peace, mental discipline, and a heart full of love and light. It *also* requires the outward manifestation of this inner life, in relationships with God's people and other creatures whom God called good (cf. Genesis 1) and beloved. The two are part and parcel of each other. This reading will support a preacher who intends to lead the congregation to a Lenten focus not only on inward self-examination and turning from sins of body and soul, but also on outward care of neighbor and the vulnerable. Increasing numbers of churches are finding ecumenical inspiration in working together on Lenten projects, and then conducting an ecumenical Easter Vigil together.[2] This passage is a reminder that the fruits of return to the Lord are mercy, hospitality, sharing, and social justice.

Psalmody
Psalm 51:1-17 (RCL)
Psalm 51:3-4, 5-6ab, 12-13, 14, 17 (LFM)

The Text. Psalm study still benefits from the important work of Hermann Gunkel, whose use of form criticism identified genres in the psalter.[3] In his typology, Psalm 51 is identified as an individual lament. Later, others have subcategorized it as one of seven penitential psalms (Psalms 6, 32, 38, 51, 102, 130, 143).

Verses 1-13 are a lament for sin, and indeed are a general confession. Yet, while acknowledging one's sinful state and expressing authentic desolation and sorrow, these verses are full of hope and utter trust in the God to whom they are addressed. God's nature is "steadfast love," "abundant mercy" (v. 1), and "wisdom" (v. 6); and God can be trusted to "cleanse" from sin (v. 2), "purge" so that we shall be "clean" (v. 7), our sins washed away. God's desire is "truth in the inward being" (v. 6) and the blotting out of all iniquity (v. 9).

Given the awareness of this beauty in God's nature that the psalmist proclaims, it is apparent that the speaker has an intimate relationship with this God. There is knowing, and trusting, and appreciating, and proleptic celebrating (i.e., "Let me hear joy and gladness" [v. 8], "Create in me a clean heart, O God" [v. 10], "Restore to me the joy of your salvation" [v. 12]).

The psalmist, who takes seriously this relationship, however, freely and painfully acknowledges sin and the failure to keep the human side of the covenant. In the face of the adored Holy One, the psalmist confesses (vv. 3-4a). The intimacy of the relationship is expressed not only by the aching honesty, but also by what the psalmist prays for: "blot out all my iniquities" (v. 9b); "put a new and right spirit within me" (v. 10b);[4] "sustain in me a willing spirit" (v. 12b); "deliver me from bloodshed, O God" (v. 14a). Some think that the psalmist is ill ("bones ... crushed," v. 8; translated elsewhere as "body ... broken"), but even so, the psalmist is much more concerned about the stained or soiled conscience than the healing of the body.[5]

Finally, verses 16-17 echo the call of Joel 2:12-17 and Isaiah 58:1-12 that what finally matters to God is not a mindless action (in this case, buying animals to be sacrificed for one's sins without actually noticing one's sins, without remorse, without amendment of life). The psalmist repeats before the Holy One (also confirming in the psalmist's heart, and ours) the truth that God indeed seeks our change in behavior, but not only that: the inner spirit matters ultimately. As if the deep longing in verse 6 were not enough ("You desire truth in the *inward* being; therefore teach me wisdom in *my secret heart*," emphasis added), the penitent's cry in verses 16 and 17 in the repetition of parallelism proclaims yet again: "if I were to give a burnt offering, you would not be pleased.... [Rather, it is] a broken and contrite heart, O God" that you desire.

The Preaching. The throb of the spiritual life is reflected in this psalm: like so many of the lament psalms to this loving and merciful God, this psalm ends in praise. Such is not only Christian theology ("even at the grave, we sing our Alleluia!"), but the practice of honest lament and contrition before our God releases and frees us to return to right relationship: ethics toward one another, and praise toward God.

A preacher might invite the use of this psalm daily during Lent. In fact, verse 15 has been commonly used at the beginning of Morning Prayer (*Lauds*) services since the *Rule of Benedict* (chapters 12-13) in the sixth century: "O Lord, [if you will but] open my lips, … my mouth will declare your praise" (v. 15).

In worship, parts of Psalm 51 serve well as confession of sin, using the psalmist's words to express our own penitence, and engendering solidarity of the present congregation with generations of Jewish and Christian penitents through the ages. Further, because it is a *psalm* (song), it is fitting to sing or chant this psalm, or to invite a cantor to offer the verses while the congregation responds with a refrain, such as verse 10.

As a response to the reading from Joel (or Isaiah), the psalmist enables the congregation to enter into confession and restoration: this honest, penitent, and confidently hopeful relationship to which those covenanted to God are called—including Christians covenanted to God through baptism.

Second Reading
2 Corinthians 5:20b—6:10 (RCL)
2 Corinthians 5:20—6:2 (LFM)

The Text. This lection follows Paul's statement that "if anyone is *en Christos*, there is a new creation" (v. 17). Immediately before verse 20, Paul claims that God "reconciled us to himself through Christ, and has given us the ministry of reconciliation; that is, in Christ God was reconciling the world to himself … and entrusting the message of reconciliation to us" (vv. 18-19). Without constant attention and renewal, however, reconciliation with God and one another can be lost. Paul "entreats"—"beseeches" (RSV), "implores" (NEB)—the Corinthians to come again to reconciliation. This is a call to repent and return to right relationship with God, replacing sin with "righteousness" (5:21), and accepting grace and forgiveness in Christ Jesus (6:1). Grace-filled living shows forth in righteous life patterns; therefore, he exhorts them "not to accept the grace of God in vain" (6:1), but to be renewed.

At 6:2a, Paul quotes Isaiah 49:8a in which the Lord says, "In a time of favor I have answered you …" In a prolepsis of the eschaton, a realized eschatology, Paul proclaims that the time of favor is *now;* the acceptable time is *now;* the day of salvation is *now.*

In the continuing section, used in the RCL, Paul refers to his own ministry, showing his own willingness to endure afflictions from others and from bodily wants (e.g., hunger, sleepless nights), for the sake of the gospel. He endures through the power of God (6:7a). In this testing, his love and faithfulness are proven.

The Preaching. This reading on Ash Wednesday contributes not only an urgency to be about the work of repentance, renewal and righteousness during these short forty days, but suggests that God has given an opening, a window of opportunity. *Reconciliation* is the ministry of the Christian family, and this grace has been given to the body of Christ to be shared in and with the world. There is no other, no better time to fast from excesses and distractions, to let go of cheap grace, and to return to the primary purpose for which Christ's body is covenanted to God. Paul's list of difficulties can be a strong encouragement not to give up, nor shirk, nor weaken; for in purity and patience, holiness and truth, one's reconciliation—and one's baptism— is renewed. And in the face of death, we are alive! For even when we are sorrowful, in Christ we are always rejoicing.

Gospel
Matthew 6:1-6, 16-21 (RCL)
Matthew 6:1-6, 16-18 (LFM)

The Text. In this section of the Sermon on the Mount (Matthew 5–7), Jesus names the three classic Jewish spiritual practices (all of which became standard in both Christianity and Islam): almsgiving, prayer, and fasting. These practices are *signs* of righteousness, and also help *effect* right relationship with God. Almsgiving is a way of loving God through loving neighbor; prayer is done several times a day to stay in contact with God, such that the divine relationship becomes the context for the rest of life (1 Thess. 5:17); and regular abstinence from food can strengthen discipline, turn one's attention to God, and liberate the mind-heart to deepen the inner holy connection. It was assumed that those devoted to the Lord would practice these disciplines.

Jesus, however, adds a new meaning by insisting on a particular *spirit* of the disciplines. The temptation to practice devotion for an audience, showing off one's piety, is an easy one to fall into. The word *hypocrite* (6:2) originally meant "actor," one who plays to an audience, who intends to be seen.[6] Piety for the public does *not* lead to righteousness. Jesus makes a sharp contrast between the show of piety and the gift of self-emptying, between meeting others' expectations and a quiet, personal outpouring for the Divine Lover. In this sermon, the longing of God's heart is clear: when *you* give alms, pray, and fast, do it *for the sake of relationship,* Jesus exhorts his disciples. And protect yourselves from temptation: act quietly, in your closet, with unburdened eyes, so that you *cannot* succumb to proving your religiosity to others.

The Preaching. Since this reading, like all the other lections for Ash Wednesday, does not follow a three-year cycle but is read on this day every year, faithful churchgoers will hear again and again the admonition to give alms (money, but also the things money can buy, to those who need it), to pray, and to fast. This is not about proving one's religiosity. This is about one's heart returning to the Lord in purity and holiness.

But year after year, it can be a challenge to be inspired, much less to inspire one's congregation, to a productive and inspiring Tithe of the Year (as Lent was called)[7] that will really renew their hearts and their relationship to the God revealed in Christ Jesus by the Spirit.

Some preachers suggest taking on something—a practice—instead of giving up something. The gospel suggests *both,* since prayer is a spiritual practice that takes many forms, and the invitation here is to take on renewal of openness to and relationship with God, which is the spirit and purpose of prayer. Further, the section not read today (vv. 7-15) is the Lord's Prayer with seven petitions, a good subject for a Lenten series. The "giving up" practice is the fasting.

Feminist readings may challenge the heavy penitential tone year after year, especially when many women's lives are heavy all year long. The goal of Lenten self-examination is life-giving contrast in order to renew the joy of living in constant connection with God. The leader of a women's religious order once invited the (very disciplined) women not to burden themselves with abstinence, but to "take on something which will give you joy." In this case, the spirit of righteousness and right relationship with God would indeed be fulfilled by a ritual contrast to the traditional fast.

In a glut culture that eschews abstinence, however, preachers may have difficulty imagining themselves "sanctifying a fast" or even taking one seriously, much less calling their people to give up anything. In comparatively wealthy North America, a creative preacher may have less difficulty preaching the first two: "almsgiving" (earnest submission of time, talent and treasure to God's needy people for one-tenth of the year's weeks) and "prayer" (additional or renewed spiritual practice for the purpose of deepening relationship with God, the author of all goodness, grace, and gift). But *fasting* is harder to preach, especially in churches that do not know how to engage in lavish celebration at Easter. The benefit of Lent, as Catherine Bell has noted, is its strategic contrast with the rest of the year.[8]

In an auditory presentation called *Midlife and the Great Unknown,* poet David Whyte reminds his hearers that "life [is] a nourishing repast."[9] But living in circumstances where one always has what one needs and usually what one wants, in a glut of abundance and "affluenza," one loses one's sense of appreciation. We forget. The fact that everything has been provided by God, and that all we have is not deserved but is *gift,* becomes lost on us. And words alone are inadequate. However forcefully we tell ourselves that this food, this bed, this apartment, this family, this job, this unemployment payment, is a gift, it is difficult to believe ourselves if we do not experience it as gift.

The point of fasting is to enable the actual experience of gift. When we fast from meat, or treats, or food, we cause ourselves to actually experience a bit of longing or desire, a bit less expectation and demand. We keep an edge, says Whyte, that enables us to have a taste for real life, to see the gift, and to enjoy both the freedom of *not* having, as well as the freedom of having. Even more is the freedom of seeing, of noticing, of enjoying, of appreciating the juiciness of the peach, the softness of a daisy's petals, the kindness in a stranger's voice. This practice of awareness, this paying attention, must be cultivated in Lenten times if God's people would come to the full Easter relationship with the Creator-Redeemer-Sanctifier to which they are called. Ironically, the ability to recognize—to taste, feel, and hear—God's gifts, absolutely requires a fast; for fasting creates a contrast with drudgery, lulled complacence, dull routine, or glutted numbness.

Brother Roger Louis Schütz-Marsaucher (1915–2005), founder of the Taizé community in France, understood the critical importance of such simplified living, "edge living," and the need to avoid the self-indulgence of too much, too easy, or too familiar. He demonstrates such wisdom at twenty-five years old at his first stop in France from Switzerland seeking to form a community:

> In August 1940, I set out from Geneva by bicycle to look for a house. Not far from the border, I went through a village called Frangy. Less than a mile after the village, I saw on the left a large house and a farm. The owner, an elderly lady, showed me the house where she lived, a fine Savoy house with a chapel. She told me: "Saint François de Sales once celebrated mass in this chapel." She wanted to leave the house and settle down near the centre of the village. . . . "If you want to buy the house, all I'll ask is an annuity, a little rent." The annuity was tiny, so she was almost giving me the house. I was very touched by such a welcome and by the woman's trust. But I thought that the place was too well-off, and that if things were too easy that would not lead me to be creative. And again, the house was too close to Geneva. I was afraid of being too close to the people I knew to be able to find my own way. So I went on further.[10]

God's people are called to this edge, this lean emptying, this willing engagement. *Gift* is not easy indulgence or facile acquisition. The edge of self-denial is also the edge of appreciation.

And the time to begin again to practice this living is *now*, here, in Lent, on this day, for this is the way to return to the Lord of our salvation. And *now* is the acceptable time.

Notes

1. For exegesis on Joel, I'm following Geoffrey E. Wood, "Joel," in *The Jerome Biblical Commentary* (Englewood Cliffs, N.J.: Prentice-Hall, 1968), 439-43.
2. My thanks to the Rev. Bill Doggett for sharing one example of a weekly ecumenical clergy lectionary group that led to friendship, common congregational projects, and shared annual celebration of the Easter Vigil.
3. Hermann Gunkel's (1862-1932) commentary on the Psalms was first published in 1926. See Hermann Gunkel, *The Psalms: A Form-Critical Introduction*, trans. Thomas Horner (Philadelphia: Fortress Press, 1967). Gunkel's psalm genres include hymns, songs of Yahweh's enthronement, community or individual laments, thanksgiving psalms, royal psalms, cultic psalms (used in liturgy), and blessings.

4. Note the parallel request for a new covenant, new heart, and new spirit in Jer. 24:7; 31:33; and Ezek. 36:25-33, esp. 25-29a.

5. See Roland E. Murphy, "Psalms," in *The Jerome Biblical Commentary*, 585, §67. On how sin is sickening, keeping the psalmist from rest and peace, he refers the reader to E. Dalglish, *Psalm Fifty-One in the Light of Ancient Near Eastern Patternism* (Leiden: Brill, 1962).

6. John L. McKenzie, "The Gospel According to Matthew," *The Jerome Biblical Commentary*, 73, §43.

7. This was John Cassian's designation (c. 360-435), as Lent is approximately 10 percent of the year. In Thomas J. Talley, *The Origins of the Liturgical Year,* 2d ed. (Collegeville, Minn.: Liturgical/Pueblo, 1986, 1991), 221.

8. "Strategic contrast" is one of the four attributes of ritual identified by Catherine Bell in *Ritual Theory, Ritual Practice* (New York: Oxford University Press, 1992), 81-82, 90-91.

9. David Whyte, *Midlife and the Great Unknown: Finding Courage and Clarity Through Poetry,* CD (Boulder: Sounds True, 2003), disc one, tracks 19-22. Whyte may be contacted through Many Rivers Company, P.O. Box 868, Langley, Washington 98260. Tel: 360-221-1324.

10. *Choose to Love: Brother Roger of Taizé, 1915-2005* (Taizé: Ateliers et Presses de Taizé, 2006), 27-28.

March 13, 2011
First Sunday in Lent

First Reading
Genesis 2:15-17, 3:1-7 (RCL)
Genesis 2:7-9, 3:1-7 (LFM)

The Text. All the lections today point to the human problem of living the moral life we are called to live, especially resisting temptation toward self-indulgent desires. This challenging text is foundational to the biblical understanding of creation, and of the gift and problem of human morality.

The LFM text (2:7-9) emphasizes creation. God created an "earth creature"[1] (Heb. *adam*) out of the substance of the earth (*adamah*). The earth creature was placed in a beautiful garden with other creatures, a place of life—unending life. The RCL text (2:15-17) emphasizes the earth creature's moral responsibility to be obedient to the Creator, who admonishes this creature not to eat of the tree of mortality, which is "the tree of the knowledge of good and evil." When God sees that the (perhaps androgynous) earth creature is lacking in relationship with its own kind, God splits the creature in two, male (Heb. *ish*) and female (*ishshah*) (vv. 18-23).

The story then jumps (3:1-7) to the core issue of human relationship with God, each other, other creatures, responsibility for the garden, as well as relationship with their own freedom, desires, intellect, and curiosity. How can they work all these out in an integrated whole? What does it mean to be human? The answer arises out of response to a terrible challenge: a tempter, in the form of a serpent, preys upon their freedom, their relationships with God and each other, and especially their desires—even desires they may not have known they had: for instance, for power, or limitless options, or knowledge, or infinite freedom without responsibility.

First, the tempter breaks the boundary of Eve's sense of moral limitation, by challenging God's word on the basis of reason (v. 4b, "You will not die …"). Then the tempter helps her visualize what it would be to be like God (v. 5)—the ultimate misplaced desire: for the creature to become the Creator. Having now imagined being more than a finite human can ever be, Eve turns away from the covenant with God and toward her own desires (v. 6), and eats of the tree, sharing with her husband, who accepts and eats as well. The result is a fall from innocence; what once seemed free and natural is now a source of shame.

Reading beyond today's pericope reveals all the consequences of disobeying God. But even here, the sin is clear: seeking to transcend our finitude, bearing with dissatisfaction the human place in creation, and preferring to act like the Creator (vv. 8-24). However, the word *sin* is not used in this text. The first time "sin" is used in Scripture is in chapter 4 when Cain murders Abel.

The Preaching. 1. *Adam and Eve.* Contrary to some thinking, Adam and Eve are not enemies to humanity but truth bearers of the human condition. Indeed, they are the prototypes of humanity. Christ has been called the Second Adam. In parts of Europe, and in the East, Adam and Eve are considered saints. In Dublin there is a church named after them (the Church of Adam and Eve), and their feast day is December 24 (which is the reason many Christmas trees are decorated with apples or red balls).[2] Adam and Eve "are us," and a preacher might remind hearers that neither they, nor we, are the enemies. Rather, the enemy is blindness (ignorance and hubris), and the loss of faith and hope to keep leaning into the relationship with God that has been prepared for us, which requires moral living and resisting temptation. In Christ through the power of the Holy Spirit, resisting temptation will continue to be difficult, but is possible. Lent is the time to practice.

2. *The Garden of the Soul.* A garden is often a symbol for the soul, the place that provides for us, where we meet God who speaks with us. But it is possible to disrespect, even to abuse, the garden of one's soul. Antonio Machado's short poem, "The Wind, One Brilliant Day," would be a heart-stopping sermon beginning: The wind (Spirit) calls to the soul, but the person confesses "all the flowers in my garden are dead."[3] Faced with failed stewardship, the person cries the self-honest question, "What have you done with the garden that was entrusted to you?" Similarly, some hearers will remember the story *The Shack* in which the protagonist encounters his blooming but weed-infested soul and, with the help of the Spirit, begins to do important soul weeding (a good Lenten practice).

3. *Temptation.* It is not sinful to be tempted — but it matters utterly how we respond to temptation. Persons who face temptation are not bad people: they are *us*. Adam and Eve remind us that the moral problem is an endemically human problem. The prurient self-dare to claim the power of God and to live beyond our finitude is a universal and ongoing challenge (cf. the film *Bruce Almighty*).

Resisting temptation is extremely difficult. A preacher might call people to be attentive to tempters in unexpected forms, to self-indulgent desires to "be more, have more," and to the temptation to transcend normal human finitude. The forces against breaking bad habits and addictions are tremendously strong. And we all fall short from time to time.

But the inner and outer effort to resist and overcome is necessary and important. The community of faith must assist. Strategic actions include:

- praying;
- helping one another to resist;
- boldly naming addictions to Internet, computer games, gambling, pornography, gossip, and fast "soul food," and facing them in solidarity;
- encouraging one another to eat more healthy foods, exercise, watch less television, spend more time with family and friends, stop drinking or smoking, and embrace other positive habit changes;
- noticing temptation (even unwitting or unconscious) to join with others to disparage, defame or dismiss, deflate, discourage, or otherwise "diss" another human being;
- seeking help for one's own feelings of temptation; and
- using humor! Laughter is anathema to all tempters.

Psalmody
Psalm 32 (RCL)

Having invited recitation of the primary penitential psalm on Ash Wednesday, the RCL suggests another penitential psalm as response to the first reading. Psalm 32 expresses a dramatic plot of the human condition, which can be read in three voices:

Narrator's introduction (vv. 1-2)
Individual's prayer to God (vv. 3-7)
God's assurance and counsel (vv. 8-9)
Narrator's conclusion and praise (vv. 10-11)

In a sermon calling for penitence and confession, the psalmist is a role model to "not hide my iniquity" but boldly to "confess my transgressions to the LORD," trusting that God will forgive "the guilt of my sin" (v. 5). The call to repentance would be enhanced if the psalm is proclaimed with the people reciting verses 3-7.

Alternatively, placing the Lord's words in the people's mouths can make real to them God's presence, guidance, and desire for their responsive obedient participation. This would support a sermonic call to courageous confession, trusting in the presence of the Spirit who ministered to Jesus in the desert.

Psalm 51:3-4, 5-6, 12-13, 14, 17 (LFM)

For commentary on this text, see the Ash Wednesday entry, p. 141.

Second Reading
Romans 5:12-19 (RCL, LFM)
Romans 5:12, 17-19 (LFM ALT.)

The Text. The first part of Romans 5, to be read on the Third Sunday of Lent, is about the righteousness of Christ, by which Jesus' followers are justified (made righteous or upright) through faith in Christ.

Here, Paul builds on that good news, showing again and again the abundant grace available in Christ (vv. 15-17), and how sin (*hamartia*), death (*thanatos*), and the law (*nomos*) are all overcome by Christ. Paul proceeds by drawing a parallel between Adam, "the first parent," and Christ, the "head of a new humanity."[4] Through the disobedience of "one man" (an expression used twelve times in this passage), sin and its result, death, entered humanity. (A lovely parallel to this story of new creation infected by sin can be found in C. S. Lewis's *The Magician's Nephew*.)

While *hamartia* (sin) is an archery metaphor, referring to "missing the mark" (that is, the target's bull's-eye), Paul expands the concept of sin to alienation of humans from the God who created and is redeeming them. Through sin came death (v. 12b), referring not only to physical death but to the spiritual separation of humanity from God, the Source of Life. At the time of our first parents, there was no law. In fact, rabbis "often divided their 6000 years of [human] history into three periods: from Adam to Moses, 2000 years of chaos [v.14]; from Moses to the Messiah, 2000 years of Law; from the Messiah on, 2000 years of blessings."[5] *Nomos*, law, was intended to bring life—but though showing the way to life, Paul says it was unable itself to bring life, and served only as informant and condemner.[6]

Ernst Käsemann explains the stark contrast by which Paul is trying to express the utter freedom and life—eternal life—given even now *en Christos*:

> The spheres of Adam and Christ, of death and life, are separated as alternative, exclusive, and ultimate… . An old world and a new world are at issue. In relation to them no one can be neutral. There is no third option… . Hence Paul is definitely not speaking of personal guilt or naturally necessary death but of *the forces of sin and death which have invaded the world*… . [Death spreads] across the generations like an infectious disease. It is a curse in the texture of earthly life which ineluctably affects every individual.[7]

But thanks be to God, however great sin is, Christ's power, Christ's free gift of grace and righteousness, is much greater, and will "exercise dominion in life through the one man, Jesus Christ" (v. 17).

The Preaching. Paul creates a sharp contrast between the one man, Adam, and the new Adam, Christ, so that readers can discern: Who is Jesus? And who are we, followers of Jesus, baptized into Christ, seeking to be fully human? The glory and grace of Christ is emphasized by this contrast:

- Woman was born out of man (Adam) in Genesis; yet in Christ, man was born out of woman;
- Adam and Eve sought to take, for their own sake, while Christ gives, for others' sake ("free gift," vv. 15-19);
- implied in the epistle is Eve's and Adam's succumbing to temptation, and Jesus' resisting.

By this contrast Paul also emphasizes Christ as liberator from sin. Paul's sin language in this passage is strong, and led others to induce the doctrine of original sin from Paul, beginning with Augustine. Paul does not intend to formulate a doctrine of sin here, however, but if anything, a doctrine of Christ. Paul challenges readers to comprehend that Jesus is the Christ, whose free gift (*charis*, "grace") overcomes our failure, our separation from God, and our inhuman alienation from ourselves and all creation. In Christ is righteousness: Jesus is the role model for choosing obedience, and also the means by which Christians are enabled to do the same.

Gospel
Matthew 4:1-11 (RCL, LFM)

The Text. The story of Jesus' temptation in the wilderness is also recounted in Mark 1:12-13 and Luke 4:1-13, and is referred to twice in Hebrews (2:18; 4:15). In all three Gospel accounts, it is the Spirit who sends Jesus into the wilderness for forty days. In Matthew and in Mark, the temptation is placed immediately after Jesus' baptism— right after "a voice from heaven said, 'This is my Son, the Beloved, with whom I am well pleased'" (3:17). And the one who tempted him was "the devil" (4:1). Major issues of Jesus' identity, his spiritual relationship with God, and the nature of "his" ministry are revealed:

1. *Jesus' identity.* Scriptures this season raise the question of Jesus' identity, inviting the response given at Jesus' baptism (3:17), "This is my beloved Son." Now the devil tries to twist the meaning, and says twice, "If you are the Son of God …" Jesus is called to face for *himself* whether this is true, and what this means for him.

2. *Jesus undoes the devil and distinguishes God's ministry from a "Jesus agenda."* First, Jesus does not answer the tempter's question, but responds with a reason why the question is irrelevant. Second, Jesus draws upon the authority of the law to show what *is* relevant. Each of the three temptations is met by Jesus with a verse from Deuteronomy (= "second law") (Deut. 8:3b; 6:16; 6:13).

The first temptation is *physical*. When Jesus is at his hungriest, the tempter preys upon the power he must have "if you are the Son of God" to make bread out of stone. Jesus draws upon the word of God, not to answer or address the question, but to name what truly matters. Jesus does not allow the evil one to dictate the terms of the conversation.

The second relates to *power and identity*. The devil tries to use Jesus' own strategy of Scripture (Ps. 91:11-12) to tempt him: "If you are the Son of God," prove it by showing that God will protect you from harm. Again, Jesus sidesteps the question, quoting Deuteronomy to show that such questions are contrary to right relationship with God.

Shifting strategies a third time, the devil tempts Jesus not in relationship to himself—his needs, identity, or power—but *in relationship to others*. Some see this as appealing to his loving kindness: "If you'll bow down and worship me," I'll give you the world —implying, "imagine how much *good* you could do!" Others say Jesus was tempted to overlook God's priorities, in which it's not just the result that matters, but the means which is important. God's means are neither violent nor "bottom line" ("just worship the devil, get the world, and be done with it"), but loving and honoring of human free will.[8]

However, Jesus does not confuse himself as human with the Lordship of God. The world is the Lord's, and is not the devil's to give. Further, no one "may inherit the promises [of God] without obedience to the Word of God."[9]

According to Peter Doble, "each of the words of temptation refers to the sonship revealed in the Baptism." Jesus' ego is not piqued; in fact, he does not need to act like the Son of God. Rather, he keeps his focus on God, showing that he *is* the Son of God. Jesus submits to the Father. And his ministry is to listen to the word of God, and hearing it, to obey and follow.

The Preaching. This text reveals much about the human condition, the purpose of Lent, the identity of Jesus, and the identity of Jesus' followers, symbolized and represented by baptism. Whether preaching to baptismal candidates, persons already baptized, or nominal or non-Christians, a preacher has a range of rich options for a sermon. Here are several.

1. Identity:

a. *Jesus' identity.* A preacher might pose the question, Who is Jesus for you?, and invite hearers to be Christians by imitating how Jesus honored the Father: by turning back all power and status and glory to God. Perhaps a recalibration of values or practices is needed. Lent is a good time to begin.

b. *Baptism as a sign of our process toward fully human identity in the divine nature (2 Pet. 1:4).* Jesus' identity became clear at his baptism. So does ours. When persons are baptized into Christ Jesus, they are baptized into his death and resurrection (Rom.

6:3-5), into his ministry, and into the proclamation of the word and Holy Spirit into which he was baptized: "This is my Beloved: *with you I am well pleased.*" A preacher might remind hearers of the process of baptismal identity that is not only individual but communal, and that the whole family of faith are called to grow and be sent to continue Christ's ministry. Jesus' three responses to the tempter make a powerful claim on baptismal living.

2. Spiritual Practice: *Doing—Jesus is an example in dealing with sin.* As noted at the first reading, it is not sinful to be tempted. The problem leading to sin is succumbing to temptation. A still relevant book describing the strategy of temptation from the devil's perspective, worth rereading, is C. S. Lewis's *The Screwtape Letters.*[10] A preacher might encourage hearers to the steps of first *noticing* temptation (even as simple as desiring to pop into a fast-food place or wanting to make an impulse purchase), then *resisting it,* and importantly, *sharing the success or failure with another,* perhaps a Lenten prayer group.

Spiritual disciplines are essential (see below). And the first spiritual practice is the prayer Jesus taught his disciples, including a petition directly related to this dire danger: "Lead us not into temptation," or, as Hans Dieter Betz once translated it, "Rescue us from temptation."

3. Spiritual Practice: *Being—spiritual practices are essential disciplines for being sons and daughters of God.* We know that the temptation for Jesus was real, because temptation is endemic to being human. Jesus, fully divine but also fully human, was really tempted, like we are.

Yet temptation is extremely difficult to overcome. Eve was not able to do so, nor was Adam. What, then, enabled Jesus' resistance that Adam and Eve did not have when the serpent tempted them? What do the baptized have that Eve and Adam lacked? For what Jesus had, we also have. A preacher might use or expand upon these:

a. Jesus had the *covenant and the covenanted people*, which had not yet been formulated when Adam and Eve lived. He knew that he was part of a covenanted people, whose prayers sustained him, and whose practice had developed over thousands of years. This covenant was written down in Scripture, which Jesus knew (and quoted to the devil), and it was made real and concrete in the law, so that he could know how he was supposed to act. Jesus was not alone; he had the covenanted people with him, and he knew the ethics of the covenant God had made with the people, and that God is faithful. This was of tremendous support in resisting the tempter.

b. Jesus had *spiritual practices* that he inherited and learned and developed from the covenant and covenanted people, an advantage Eve and Adam did not have. He kept the Sabbath, for example, read Scripture, and regularly practiced prayer, fasting, and generous giving to the poor and widows. These habits were strong patterns in his life, and not easily overturned in vulnerable moments. Yes, he was hungry—but he was used to being hungry, because he was used to fasting. So when he was really vulnerable, even on the edge of giving in, the regular practices of his faith family and his related individual practice helped him resist.

Because Lent is set aside specifically as a time to deepen the spiritual practice of individuals, congregations, and the Christian faith family, a preacher might urge the people to follow Jesus by being faithful in the practice of spiritual disciplines.

c. Jesus had *memory*. He remembered God's lovingkindness and mighty acts. Through Scripture, story, and worship, Jesus knew salvation history. He remembered what God has done in creation and in the prophets and judges; he remembered God's faithful redemption through the exodus and journey to the promised land; he remembered God's restoration of the people following the Babylonian captivity. He remembered that the desert is a place of testing, but also of giving (manna, the law). He remembered the psalms of praise of his people, and God's lovingkindness. And he remembered his own particular experience of God in his life and prayer.

A preacher might remind hearers that the evidence of God's love and faithfulness comes through reconnecting with, *re-membering,* what God has done, over and over and over. Such storytelling and sacramental action is foundational to Christian worship. It's also the basis of Christian covenant and faith-sharing circles. What God has done, God continues to do. Living steeped in the reality of God's ongoing action then, as well as now, is a tremendous power against temptation. And the longer history goes on, and the longer we live, the more evidence there is.

4. Ministry: *Jesus' ministry is God's work.* Jesus was very clear that he was about his Father's business, not his own. He was able to resist the evil one partly because the devil tempted Jesus with ego desires. But Jesus was not oriented toward ego, self-indulgence, nor even toward his own agenda.

A preacher might contrast Jesus' experience with that of someone in the newspaper. When the tempter invites Jesus to "satisfy your hunger and your doubts by turning these stones into food,"[11] what do people do when they have real doubts and real hunger? The cultural version is often equally subtle: "If you'll just stretch these numbers, we'll come out even. If you'll just sell your name, you can pay for your child's college! We'll give you all this if you simply … If you really care about your children, then sign up for this … If you were a responsible spouse, or parent, or citizen, of course you'd want to …"

In World War II Vichy France, two pastors were imprisoned for leading the people of Le Chambon to hide Jews and rescue them from the Nazis. After a month, they were unspeakably glad to be told they were being released. But on the way out, there was a formality of signing a paper. It exacted the promise to obey unquestionably any orders "for the good of the National Revolution occupying goverment …" It brought them up short, and they replied, "We cannot sign this oath. It is contrary to our conscience." The camp director was incredulous, and began shouting. Finally, he calmed down and "became confiding. 'Look, be reasonable. I appreciate your courage, but this is—Look, you have wives and children. Sign. It's just a formality. Later, no one will notice what you did here.' [Pastor] Trocmé replied, 'If we sign, we must keep our word; we must surrender our consciences to the marshal. No, we will not bind ourselves to obey immoral orders.'"[12] Thus they remained in prison for many more months before their release.

Jesus is our role model for what it means to be fully human. What matters to Jesus is his relationship with the Father. Jesus trusts God, and relies on his promises; but the promises, like all gifts, are "obligatory generosity"[13] calling for a response. No one "may inherit the promises without obedience to the Word of God."[14] Upon this, Jesus stands. Upon this we, too, may stand.

Notes

1. Phyllis Trible, *God and the Rhetoric of Sexuality*, Overtures to Biblical Theology (Philadelphia: Fortress Press, 1978), 75-115, esp. 76-78.
2. "Christmas Eve is the feast of our first parents, Adam and Eve. They are commemorated as saints in the calendars of the Eastern churches (Greeks, Syrians, Copts). Under the influence of this Oriental practice, their veneration spread also to the West and became very popular toward the end of the first millennium of the Christian era… . In many old churches of Europe their statues may still be seen among the images of the saints… . In Germany, the custom began in the sixteenth century of putting up a 'paradise tree' in the homes to honor the first parents. This was a fir tree laden with apples, and from it developed the modern Christmas tree." Francis X. Weisner, *Handbook of Christian Feast and Customs,* quoted in *An Advent Sourcebook* (Chicago: Liturgy Training Publications, 1988), 154-55.
3. Antonio Machado, "The Wind, One Brilliant Day," in *Times Alone: Selected Poems of Antonio Machado,* trans. Robert Bly (Middletown, Conn.: Wesleyan University Press, 1983).
4. Joseph A. Fitzmyer, "The Letter to the Romans," in *The Jerome Biblical Commentary* (Englewood Cliffs, N.J.: Prentice-Hall, 1968), 306, §52.
5. Ibid., 308, §58.
6. Ibid., 308, §60.
7. Ernst Käsemann, *Commentary on Romans,* trans. and ed. Geoffrey W. Bromiley (Grand Rapids: Eerdmans, 1980), 147 (emphasis added). For eschatological life already present now, in the reign of Christ, see ibid., 146.
8. W. Powell, "The Temptation," response to Peter Doble, "The Temptations," in *The Expository Times* 72 (Oct. 1960-Sept. 1961): 248.
9. Doble, "The Temptations," 92.
10. C. S. Lewis, *The Screwtape Letters and Screwtape Proposes a Toast* (New York: Macmillan, 1961).
11. Doble, "The Temptations," 92.
12. Philip Hallie, *Lest Innocent Blood Be Shed* (New York: HarperCollins, 1979), I.5.
13. Louis-Marie Chauvet, *Symbol and Sacrament* (Collegeville, Minn.: Liturgical Press, 1995), 101.
14. Doble, "The Temptations," 92.

March 20, 2011
Second Sunday in Lent

Revised Common Lectionary (RCL)

Genesis 12:1-4a
Psalm 121
Romans 4:1-5, 13-17
John 3:1-17 or Matthew 17:1-9

Lectionary for Mass (LFM)

Genesis 12:1-4a
Psalm 33:4-5, 18-19, 20, 22
2 Timothy 1:8b-10
Matthew 17:1-9

First Reading
Genesis 12:1-4a (RCL, LFM)

The Text. This story marks the beginning of God's new approach to salvation history. Instead of continuing to try to covenant with all humanity (cf. Adam and Eve, Genesis 2; Noah, Gen. 5:28—9:17), in Genesis 12 God turns to one faithful man, Abram, for covenant relationship, and to the patriarchs descended from him. In this call and Abram's acceptance, God creates and covenants with a *people*, intervening in their lives to love them, call them to ethical living, and save them, that through them the world might be saved.

The epic of Abraham begins today with God's call and promise—and equally significantly, Abram's obedient response. Verses 1-4a are the first part of what is commonly called the "call of Abram" (vv. 1-9), though the covenant of Abram, and the change of Abram's and Sarai's names to Abraham and Sarah, won't happen until Genesis 17:1-27.

This passage is in the vibrant storytelling mode of the Jahwist writer (c. 900s B.C.E.). Several aspects are worth noting:

1. It is God who seeks Abram out and initiates the call. God acts first.

2. God bids Abram to leave all that he knows behind: his "country and … kindred and … father's house"—in other words, his world. His patterns. Everything familiar. He was called to take his nomadic family and their possessions (so that in community they could survive), and to go forth.

3. But God does not tell Abram where he and his family will be going. Abram is called to leave for a new home, but he won't know he has arrived until he gets there (v. 1b). The invitation is to walk out into the unknown, in faith, trusting in God alone.

4. God promises to make of Abram "a great nation" (v. 2a), and commits to Abram, not just through his journey from Haran, but into all history: "and I will bless you …"

5. Even here, God's call and promise to Abram is not only for his sake, but for a wider and ethical purpose. God will bless Abram "and make your name great, so that you will be a blessing" (v. 2).

6. Not only that, but the blessing to Abram involves protection, and an implied covenant, since God "will bless those who bless you, and the one who curses you I will curse" (v. 3). Yet again, this blessing and protection is not only for Abram: "In you all the families of the earth shall be blessed" (v. 3b). The particular and the universal are connected, here in God's call and promise to the first patriarch.

7. Abram goes (v. 4a). There is no questioning or arguing. There are many reasons why Father Abraham is honored in the three great religions of the Book (Judaism, Christianity, and Islam)—not least of which is Abram's trust and obedience, right here from the start.

The Preaching. Neither Abram's identity, nor his covenantal initiation, has yet been established. Yet God calls Abram, offering him a challenge (which God expects him to accept) as well as a lavish promise on which to lean. In accepting God's challenging invitation, in responding to this *call* with its imbedded promise, Abram ties his future to this God, and makes himself open to God's already-beginning salvific work to be accomplished through him.

Abram's story of going out in faith to the unknown could pose a set of challenges to the congregation. In this time of Lenten renewal, those who are baptized are challenged not to take this covenantal union with God-in-Christ-by-the-Spirit for granted, but to allow Abram and Sarai to live in them, reviving their faithfulness, increasing their trust, and as Christians, walking by Christ into the world unknown.

Those who are not baptized, including visitors, guests, seekers, and lurkers, have in Abram a wonderful role model. There is no name for this faith at the story's beginning. There is no name for this people. In the fullness of time, Abraham's sons will be called Isaac and Ishmael, and his grandson will be called Israel. In the fullness of time, the stories will be written down, and three great faith families will call Abraham their father. But here, there is only a promise of blessing, provision, protection, and a relationship with the One who calls and promises, so that those called may be a blessing. This promise is a life of meaning, a life that makes a difference, in relationship with mighty, merciful, trustworthy God, and with a whole people who will carry on after we die. Is this not true for seekers today? This covenantal relationship is a holy and worthy way to live. Given innumerable areas of broken devastation in the lives of people who may show up at church, seeing how the promise to Abram continues anamnetically[1] as a promise to each of us, here and now, is nothing but good news.

For those preparing for baptism at Easter, preachers will be able to connect their story with Abram's following of God, who leads him into an unknown land. They, like Abram, are already called, already offered the promise of new life in Christ Jesus to be made real in the sacrament of baptism, already expected to be living a life of faith and trust in God. Like Abram and Sarai, baptismal candidates do not yet have their new names, nor do they know into what ministries God may lead them. Yet Abram and Sarai leave home anticipating the adventures God will give them. What a strong model is Abram for baptismal candidates—and all followers of The Way.

Psalmody
Psalm 121 (RCL)

Psalm 121 is a psalm of comfort to one in need of help: "From where is my help to come?" The psalmist is as certain of "God's presence and assistance"[2] as Abram, and feels proleptic[3] comfort now, already, though full help is yet to come. Such trust makes the psalm a fitting response to the Genesis text. Placing these verses in the mouths of the congregation could help them "try on" and embody the faith and trust to which they are called, so that they, too, can walk out into the utter unknown, their whole trust in God.

Psalm 33:4-5, 18-19, 20, 22 (LFM)

Psalm 33 is usually accepted as a psalm of praise, probably used in worship. Its twenty-two verses match the number of letters in the Hebrew alphabet (though it is not an acrostic). The six verses selected here are a fitting response to the hearing of Abram's going forth, showing reasons for trusting in "the word of the LORD [which] is upright" (v. 4a), for the lovingkindness of the Lord fills the whole earth (v. 5b), and "the eye of the LORD is on those who fear" God (v. 18). A preacher may select a refrain related to the sermon, perhaps the closing prayer (v. 22), or verse 20, placing in their own mouths the same faith that was in Abram: that it is God who is "our help and shield."

Second Reading
Romans 4:1-5, 13-17 (RCL)

The Text. Paul, apostle to the Gentiles, uses Abraham as example in discussing the relationship of law to gospel and promise in this, his most systematically theological epistle (written 54-58 C.E.). In sum: the Jews were chosen by God, and lived their intimate, covenantal relationship with God through following the law. The gift of the law, spirit and letter, was testified to in the Scriptures, particularly the Torah ("teaching" or "law," Genesis through Deuteronomy). The people's part was to follow this law, all 613 commandments found in the Torah. But what about non-Jews? Paul's problem was, How would Gentiles be grafted into the salvation mediated by Jesus Christ when they didn't follow the law? And, conversely, would the Jews be left out because they *did* follow the law?

Today's text grants hearers a summary of his answer, with Abraham as Paul's case study. Abraham was upright[4] before the Lord, not because he followed the law (which had not yet been formulated), but because of his *faithfulness* to God's *promise*. And whoever "lives by faith, lives by grace."[5]

The words *upright*, *righteous*, and *justified* all come from the same root. Yet because of the lack of a single English verb for "to be made righteous," the verb *justify* is used to mean "to make right" (we have no English word *righteousize*[6]). The goal of holy living is to be "made right" with God, to be in "right relationship" with the Holy One. How? Paul's answer before his conversion was that one is made righteous (justified) by following the holy law. But afterward, Paul found the possibility of moral living and right relationship with God even without the law through faith in God's promises, in Christ.

Later, Abram entered into formal covenant with God through circumcision (Genesis 17). But before that, Abram followed God's call to leave his homeland of Haran and go where the Lord would show him, a response based purely on faith and trust in God's promise. And for this, Abram was "reckoned as righteous."

"Reckoned" can also be translated "accredited"; the Greek[7] is a bookkeeping term, implying keeping a record of gains and losses. Paul asserts that Abraham's faith was a gain; it "counted" as upright; for believing in God's trustworthiness and obeying God's word, even without knowing where one is going, is part of right relationship with the Holy One. The response to God must be free, unlike a laborer who is owed wages (v. 4). God owed nothing to Abraham. Rather, God's call was a gift, and Abraham's response was also freely offered. It is this that makes it upright. This is the meaning of the technical language: "Abraham was justified by faith." Paul points to Abraham as the "father of all of us" (4:16; *Abraham* means "Father of many nations"); for through his example, all are called to trust in the graciousness of God's promises, and respond in faith. As Joseph Fitzmyer's synopsis puts it: "Abraham … (1) … was declared upright because of his faith (4:1-8); (2) not because of his circumcision (4:9-12); (3) nor in dependence on the Law, but in virtue of a promise (4:13-17). As a result, (4) he is our father, and his faith is the 'type' [example, precursor] of Christian faith (4:18-25)."[8]

The Preaching. By extrapolation, the Romans as well as today's hearers can also trust in God's promise. Relationship is a two-way street—and if they respond in faithfulness, freely, they, too, will be able to do their part to be in right relationship, by God's grace through their faith.

Father Abraham is revered among Jews (and Christians and Muslims) as their father in the faith. It needs to be said that Paul does not intend his assertion of faith over law to be anti-semitic (after all he, like Jesus, was Jewish). Paul affirms the law's value as moral guide and conscience former (cf. Rom. 3:19-20). Yet Paul's word points not only to freedom in Christ, but to the universality of God's grace.

Since Lent is a time of self-examination and renewal, it is a fitting time to revisit one's trust in God, one's attentiveness to God's grace, faithfulness, and abundant blessing moment by moment, so often missed by humans distracted by lists of demands and expectations. This passage fits naturally with the Genesis passage, enabling a preacher (like Paul) to lift up Abraham as an example of trust, faithfulness, and obedience.

The focus on Abraham is also fitting for a sermon that honors the three religions of the Book, all of whom strive for holy living and right relationship with God. Not only Christians, but Islam in its five "pillars" of the faith calls persons to pray five times a day, fast, and give alms—the three traditional Lenten disciplines (see Ash Wednesday), along with pilgrimage once in a lifetime (*Hajj*) and the profession of faith.[9] Judaism, the religion of Jesus of Nazareth, calls for daily prayer from two (e.g., Exod. 29:38-39; Ps. 55:17; Dan. 6:10) to seven times daily (Ps. 119:164); fasting for closer connection with God (e.g., Judg. 20:26; Est. 4:16; 2 Chron. 20:3); and giving to the needy as part of "doing justice" (e.g., Deut. 24:21; Mic. 6:6-8; Isa. 58:3-9a). Love for God includes ethical care for neighbor, which is essential for right relationship with God (i.e., the Decalogue, Exod. 20:1-17; Deut. 5:1-21).

The idea of one acting on behalf of many, as Abraham did, invites words on the importance of every faithful person keeping covenant, for one does so not only for oneself, but also for those not able to do so. God is faithful, and God's people are called to be faithful, when it is easy and when it is hard, when the way is clear and when, like Abraham, one is called to leave the familiar without knowing where one is going, or why. Lent is a good time to call people to renew their spiritual lives, and their dual call to love God and neighbor, including self and those close to home. And like Abraham, we, too, act not just for ourselves, but on behalf of the whole people.

Abraham's covenant of faithfulness also invites a sermon related to Lenten practices of renewing baptismal promises and baptismal living. Those baptized into water and the Spirit (John 3) and into the death and resurrection of Christ (Rom. 6:3-5), as infants or adults, are covenanted into the body of Christ to live not for themselves but for those Christ loves and for whom Christ died. We dis-integrate our part of the covenant inasmuch as we do not listen for and obey God's voice like Abraham did. A preacher may want to call persons to become baptized, call the baptized to live their baptism, and call those preparing for baptism or baptismal renewal at Easter to deepen their practices and receive from the faithful who have gone before, like our father, Abraham.

2 Timothy 1:8b-10 (LFM)

The Text. Like Genesis 12:1-4a, this section of the very personal letter to Timothy is about call. Verses 7-8a suggest Timothy may be timid, but that God gives power, love, and self-discipline for the sake of the work to which he is called. Here, too, the author refers to salvation by grace: "saved us … in conformity with his own design and the grace given us in Christ Jesus" (vv. 9-10).[10] The call is part of grace. Timothy and Paul have a "holy calling," holy and gracious because of the one who issued it from the beginning of time, revealed and made apparent now in the epiphany of God in Christ Jesus (*epiphaneia,* "appearing").

The Preaching. Abraham and Timothy and those hearing the sermon, have all been called. The present assembly follows in a holy line from before Christ to the eschaton. Initiation into Christ Jesus is immersion into this same call. Therefore, all the baptized may be called to renew their covenant to join with the apostles "in suffering for the gospel, relying on the power of God, who saved us" by God's grace. This call can be preached in relationship with the Genesis reading, both to those preparing for baptism and to those preparing to renew their baptism at Easter.

Gospel
John 3:1-17 (RCL)

The Revised Common Lectionary, following the lead of the Roman lectionary, claimed the importance of the transfiguration narrative, a presage of the resurrection, as a source of revelation and hope for the Lenten journey with Jesus to the cross. The RCL prefers to proclaim transfiguration on the Sunday before Ash Wednesday, the last Sunday after the Epiphany. But its Lenten importance in recognizing Jesus' identity is such that if missed on the earlier Sunday, it is offered as an alternative here (see commentary below). The preferred reading for RCL users today is the story of Nicodemus, rabbi of Jerusalem,[11] Pharisee, member of the Jewish Sanhedrin, who comes to Jesus under cover of darkness to sort a few things out.

The Text. Nicodemus is portrayed as a foil for Jesus, a Johannine device creating almost slapstick misunderstanding in a character, in order to invite clarification by which Jesus' word may sound starkly. One can imagine Nicodemus' raised shoulders and clueless tone, "Can one enter a second time into the mother's womb … ?" (v. 4).

And what is Jesus' word here? One could identify at least four points:

1. To enter the kingdom of God, one must be reborn, of water and the Spirit (vv. 3, 5; cf. Matt. 18:3 and par.). To be a child of God so as to participate in God's reign then and now, requires the gift of the Spirit. Evidence of this Spirit-creating relationship is also found in the First Testament apocryphal book of Jubilees 1:23-25: "I will create in them a holy spirit and I will cleanse them.… . I will be their Father and they shall be my children."[12] Qumran scrolls also show that all who entered this Essene community learned the Spirit's role in purification which was needed to become God's children: "[God] will cleanse [them] of all wicked deeds by means of a

holy spirit; like purifying waters [God] will sprinkle upon [them] the spirit of truth."[13] Being able to worship God as God deserves, and to live in God's way, and be cleansed of sin so as to live in holiness, and to participate in the divine life as children of God, requires the Spirit.

2. The children of God may have eternal life, not only then, but now (vv. 15-16).

3. While the familiar passage, John 3:16, proclaims God's love and the promise of eternal life, it is followed by a strong statement of the divine intention, or purpose, or mission of God in Christ Jesus: that the whole world might be saved through him (vv. 16-17; cf. Isaiah's servant songs, 42:1-4; 49:1-6; 50:4-11; 52:13—53:12).

4. *There is a relationship between water and the Spirit* (v. 5; see Ezek. 36:25-26). The Spirit purifies and cleanses, which both figuratively and literally implies washing. This passage is followed by accounts of both John the Baptist and Jesus baptizing (3:22-23, 25-30); Jews practiced baptism of converts apparently from the first century C.E.[14] This passage, then, suggests baptism. From "the earliest days this passage was thought of in a baptismal context," as testified partly by "the early baptismal use ... in catacomb art and inscriptions ..." of verse 5.[15]

The Preaching. The story of Nicodemus affords many sermon options. A preacher might identify the church with Nicodemus, a person of status who wants to understand the truth, but cannot fathom the unusual, unexpected nature of God's word, for all (v. 17).

Further, the text offers two approaches in support of the Lenten journey in which the people follow the Lord in renewed purification and holy living. On the one hand, being born of the Spirit can happen "only as a result of Jesus' crucifixion, resurrection, and ascension." "That the Son must be "lifted up" (vv. 14-15) on the cross as the Spirit's means of eternal life makes this passage especially fitting for Lent: we are walking the way of the cross with Jesus.

On the other hand, to be able to walk this journey, and to live as children of God, requires a renewal of commitment to holy living, purification, honest self-evaluation, and openness to the Spirit to renew and guide God's people—as a whole, and as individuals.

In addition to encouraging the people in their cruciform walk, a preacher might remind them of their role as Christ's priestly people (1 Pet. 2:9-10), through whom God is working "that the world might be saved through him" (John 3:17). The baptized are "signed on" as God's agents in Christ to serve as bridge builders, reconcilers, truth tellers, lovers of creation, and mediators by the Spirit for the sake of God's reign. God's people live no longer for themselves, but for Christ in them—yet they need regular reminders and seasons of detachment from cultural temptation.

And finally, the passage points directly to baptism, which is ecumenically understood as a moment in which the Holy Spirit is given in a renewed, intensified way, and as a sign of the kingdom of God.[17]

Matthew 17:1-9 (RCL ALT., LFM)

The Text. Jesus, transfigured, appears in glorious fulfillment of the Law and the Prophets with Moses (giver of the law) and Elijah (greatest of the prophets). A voice from heaven pronounces, "This is my beloved Son." And Jesus' "face shone like the sun, and his clothes became dazzling white" (v. 2; other trans.: "white as light")—so that the disciples were given a vision of Christ in his glory. He says, "Tell no one about the vision, until after the Son of Man has been raised from the dead" (v. 9). Thus, Jesus' transfiguration prefigures the resurrection. The journey to Jerusalem and the cross is framed by these two images of Jesus as the Christ in his glory: transfiguration before, and resurrection after. And this vision makes plain his identity: *Jesus is the Christ.*

One cannot miss the connection with the other time this Voice said, "This is my beloved Son": it was at Jesus' baptism (Matt. 3:17). Unlike Mark and Luke, Matthew recounts the voice of God speaking in the third person, not to Jesus but to the disciples. At the transfiguration, God adds, "Listen to him" (17:5).[18]

The Preaching. The story of the transfiguration of Jesus occurs in all three synoptic gospels, always just before Jesus begins his journey to Jerusalem (Matthew 19-20), and the cross (21-27). While its placement on the Sunday before Ash Wednesday (RCL) enables hearers to have a prefiguring of the resurrection before beginning the Lenten journey, thus "remembering forward" that the One to be crucified is the Son of God, its placement here in early Lent creates a strong connection between Jesus beginning his descent, and the hearers beginning theirs.[19]

That is, Lent is a time of attentive self-examination and repentance for the sake of inner peace. It is hard to have an honest look at oneself, strengths and weaknesses, guilt and shame. It is hard to identify bad habits and take real, disciplined steps toward changing them. It's humbling. It's embarrassing. But the process, as Twelve Step programs reiterate, includes making a searching and fearless moral inventory,[20] admitting to God, yourself, and another person the "exact nature of your wrongs," and making amends (Steps 4-5, 8-9). It calls for honest confession, receptive absolution, and active reconciliation. This is its own kind of cross; but the resulting freedom and newness of life is its own kind of resurrection as well. Such a process is grounding, and can eliminate the self-anxiety of, say, Peter, who, far from taking in the wonder of Christ's glory in silence, babbled so much that God had to interrupt him to get him to stop talking and *listen.*

A preacher, then, might remind the assembly who it is they have been—or will be—baptized into: the very Son of God. As Jesus' identity is made real at the transfiguration, so our identity is made real at baptism, when the voice of God also claims each of us as Christ's own, forever. The descent into repentance, fasting, almsgiving, prayer, as well as service and joyful disciplines, is hard work, but *good work*—work that is necessary for us to actually live into the fullness of our identity. Not only that, Christ has promised that we will be raised up on the last day (see the Fifth Sunday in Lent). This story is a reminder that the blessed self-emptying each year is for us, as for Jesus, a foretaste of the glory to come.

Notes

1. *Anamnesis* is a kind of *remembering* (the opposite of "amnesia") in which the power and meaning of the past is unleashed into the present (such as Christ's presence at the eucharist, or here, God's ongoing promise to those with whom God covenants).
2. Susan Marie Smith, "Hermeneutics of the Psalter: Toward a Critical Pastoral Approach," *Doxology* 25 (2008): 101-132; here, 122.
3. *Prolepsis* is the anticipation of the future in such certain hope that one begins to live its reality in the present.
4. Joseph A. Fitzmyer uses this term, which I find a helpful alternative for skirting confusion and myriad associations with the word *righteous*. See "The Letter to the Romans," in *The Jerome Biblical Commentary* (Englewood Cliffs, N.J.: Prentice-Hall, 1968), 304, *passim*.
5. Ibid., 304, §47.
6. This point was made by Charles Talbert in a class lecture, "Introduction to New Testament," at Wake Forest University, Winston-Salem, N,C., 1966-1967.
7. *Elogisthē* = "was accredited."
8. Fitzmyer, 303, §43.
9. "There is no God but Allah, and Muhammad is his prophet."
10. Trans. from George A. Denzer, "The Pastoral Letters," in *The Jerome Biblical Commentary*, 357-58, §38.
11. Raymond E. Brown, *The Gospel According to John (I–XII)*, The Anchor Bible 29, 2d ed. (Garden City, N.Y.: Doubleday, 1980), 184-85.
12. Ibid., 140.
13. 1 QS 4:19-21; quoted in ibid.
14. Brown, *The Gospel According to John*, 142.
15. Ibid., 143. He cites F.-M. Braun, *Revue Thomiste* 56 (1956): 647-48.
12. Ibid., 145.
17. *Baptism, Eucharist and Ministry*, Faith and Order Paper #111 (Geneva: World Council of Churches, 1982), "Baptism" II.C ("The Gift of the Spirit"), and II.E ("The Sign of the Kingdom").
18. The only difference is that in 3:17 the voice is from "heaven," while in 17:5 it is from "the cloud."
19. The Feast of the Transfiguration remains on August 6 on many calendars, when this text will be heard again.
20. Honest self-examination must also include the good that is happening, the accidents that do not happen, examples of redemption and God's ongoing presence and continuing work on earth.

March 27, 2011
Third Sunday in Lent

Revised Common Lectionary (RCL)

Exodus 17:1-7
Psalm 95
Romans 5:1-11
John 4:5-42

Lectionary for Mass (LFM)

Exodus 17:3-7
Psalm 95:1-2, 6-7, 8-9
Romans 5:1-2, 5-8
John 4:5-42 or 4:5-15, 19b-26,
    39a, 40-42

First Reading
Exodus 17:1-7 (RCL)
Exodus 17:3-7 (LFM)

The Text. Immediately after the exodus from Egypt and slavery, the children of Israel dance and celebrate (15:1-21). But then comes their trek toward the promised land—and *water* was their first concern. Three days into the wilderness, they found no water (15:22). They got thirsty and scared. They quarreled and complained to Moses. Moses cried out to God on their behalf, and God granted their needs. Moses then called the people to trust the God who loves and freed them. This pattern is repeated three times: complaining for water (15:22-27), then for food (16:1-36), then again in today's story, for water (17:1-7).

The weight of the people's complaint and lack of trust in God is evident in the names Moses gives the place where the Lord gave water from the rock: *Massah* (= "test," for the people tested their God) and *Meribah* (= "quarrel," from the Hebrew root *rib,* which means "quarrel"[1]).

Consistent evidence of God's faithfulness is insufficient to cause the people to trust. From liberation from slavery and escape from the Egyptian charioteers, to sufficient food and water in the desert, God provides; yet the people will not be won from their doubt and fear.

The Preaching. See below, under the Psalm.

Psalmody
Psalm 95 (RCL)
Psalm 95:1-2, 6-7, 8-9 (LFM)

The Text. The first seven verses of Psalm 95, called the *Venite* (= "Come," its first word), is commonly used as a praise hymn for Morning Prayer or Praise, because it is an expression of God's people's pure worship and joy! Here in Lent, however, the whole psalm is used, including the last four verses (vv. 8-11), which change to God's voice. In these verses, referring directly to Exodus 17:7-9, God says, "Do not harden your hearts, as at Meribah … in the wilderness, when your ancestors tested me … though they had seen my work." The RCL continues with God's expression of anguish, even anger, that the people God had saved were faithless, untrusting, and disobedient—"wayward in their hearts"—an outward sign that "'they do not know my ways'" (v. 10).[2]

Preaching Exodus and the Psalm. A preacher might invite hearers to take the perspective of one of the characters in these readings: God, Moses, or the recently freed slaves.

1. *God's Perspective.* A sermon could invite hearers to identify with God. Particularly interesting in the psalm is the suggestion of how God feels when God's people do not trust (vv. 8-10), followed by anger in verse 11. What a human response! The question could be put: When have you—teacher, lawyer, parent, friend, pastor, nurse, retail salesperson—faithfully cared for someone, poured out your time and creativity, given yourself, only to have them resent or ignore you or, worse, act as if you were the enemy, untrustworthy, uncaring? Is there a greater insult, a deeper pain, a more numbing rejection, after all you've done for someone, to have them doubt your loyalty, commitment, love? How does it feel to imagine God enduring such an experience?

Such empathy may lead to two points: the call to trust and hear/obey and the call to give thanks. The first, "trust and obey," as the refrain goes in the old hymn, or "faith and follow," if one wants to draw in today's epistle, is the call of all those covenanted to God, as difficult as it can sometimes be. Yet in spite of the dire and fearful circumstances around us, the evidence of God's faithfulness is available to us through recognizing and remembering (anamnesis). The Bible is the account of God's consistent and faithful acts of creation and redemption, as are the testimonies of members of the congregation, and even news reports. There is evidence everywhere that God is at work in the world today, averting the accident, reconciling parent and child, healing, opening a second chance—in individuals, neighborhoods, and nations. Sunday worship *recounts the story* of God's faithful salvific action. But also, God's people are impelled to tell and live the continuing story day by day in words and witness. A preacher could invite hearers to remember (and share) accounts of trusting in God, and of God's faithfulness.

Such testimony leads beyond trust to thanks. Whether sharing one's own story or hearing another's, witnessing God's constant and loving creation and redemption necessarily erupts in praise and thanks! This relationship of trust and thanks works in both directions. If one gives thanks, both for the gifts one receives and for the gifts one hopes to receive, trust is built up. In this part of the exodus story, there are not accounts of the people thanking God for the water (or the quail, or the manna, or for Moses, or for freedom). They do not give thanks. And they do not trust.

To trust is to receive, resulting in thanks. To thank is to be open to the gift, resulting in trust. A preacher might remind hearers that the lack of thanks and trust *makes full receiving impossible,* whether from family, friends, Moses, or even God. The full giving-receiving of God's blessings is blocked when the intended recipients are not open to them. Trust and thanks are essential for this openness and this receptivity.

2. Moses' Perspective. What insights are revealed if we imagine ourselves to be Moses? Moses recognized the people's pattern: when they need water, they ask for it, and God gives it. Moses trusts God and sees the evidence that God is trustworthy: this now-liberated people is on the way to a land promised by God, a fulfillment already assured! So when they don't see water and assume God must have abandoned them, Moses is frustrated. Then, when they blame Moses, he is beside himself with irritation and frustration, both for himself and for God.

It must have seemed unfair. Moses heard and obeyed God, leaving his family in the desert to speak truth to pharaoh's power. After arduous weeks and a dramatic escape to freedom, does Moses get any thanks? Does he get appreciation, gratitude, support? No. He gets whining and complaints, murmuring and quarrels. The people blame him even while they cling and seek his mediation.

A preacher could ask, "When have you done something selfless and good, only to 'pay' for it? Have you ever invested in a limited project, and then found yourself committed up to your eyebrows, when you hadn't bargained on so much more work? Or poured yourself out, and no one noticed, but only demanded more?" Books and films are full of unappreciated, unnoticed redemptive leaders.[3]

Still, Moses is listening more to God than to the people, and he continues to be their God go-between. He strikes the rock (v. 6)—and there is water. But Moses' own pain is found in the name he gives that rock-place. He could have called it "God provides" or "Water at last!" But *Massah,* also translatable as "proof," and *Meribah,* also translatable as "contention," reveal his—and God's—strongest memory of that experience, a memory repeated in Deuteronomy 6:16 and in today's psalm.

The way of the servant leader is not safe, smooth, or simple. The pain of loving is real. But a good servant leader, like Moses, leans on God's faithfulness, and continues to trust and give thanks—even in the midst of complaint and quarrel. When we love, in pain and joy, we're in good company—and by God's grace, the result for us, as for Moses, may be life and freedom for God's people.

3. *The Children of Israel.* A preacher could invite hearers to identify with the people in the wilderness. The call upon the soon-to-be covenant people is to trust God, and obey. God specifically requests that the people *hear* (which implies "obey," 15:26; Decalogue, chaps. 19-20), *receive* God's gifts no matter how far beyond human comprehension they may be (e.g., water from a rock), and *trust*.

But the Exodus lection shows their inability and unwillingness to trust—the same two problems we have today. A preacher might lead the congregation to see ways in which we are complainers, missing the facts of God's power and provision right before us. Yet we, living on this side of the resurrection, have even more reason to trust than they.

Some people do not trust because they are unable. Slaves—victims—those coerced, beaten, or belittled—learn wariness and anxiety as a way of life. In fact, it is right not to trust one's oppressors. There will be members of every congregation who will be able to identify with this experience in one way or another (e.g., childhood or spousal abuse, war, conflict, homelessness).

The blindness that continues the oppression, however, is treating God like the oppressor. God is not like a finite human being with self-interest, who can use power for other purposes than love. Trusting God is unlike trusting another human being. The willingness to be dependent upon the Lord is very different from putting one's whole trust in any lesser being, for God is love in power. Trusting the Holy One is the way to true freedom.[4]

To get at this, a preacher might first invite identification with the children of Israel. "What have been the circumstances in which you have been reduced to mere survival? In war? Abused in a relationship? Have you ever been without enough to eat, even for a short time?"

While trust is not gained overnight, the sermon might then challenge hearers to make a list of times God provided, intervened, lavished grace, shifted circumstances. Noticing, then giving thanks, are the first two steps toward becoming able to trust our great and gracious God.

Other people would be able, but do not trust because they are unwilling. They may be skeptical because of lack of evidence, or they may refuse because of blindness. It is easy to trust that God will give you water when you're staying in an oasis; but when you can't see the goal, it is very human to turn instead toward fear. A preacher might point out, however, that the evidence of God's trustworthiness is always available through remembering God's salvific deeds in the past, and by witnessing to God's actions in the present. Moses' frustration was that the people who had already received water and food in the desert refused to trust that it would come again. Trust is necessary for freedom. Until this people could place their whole trust in the Holy One, they would retain slavery within themselves. Trusting God *now* based upon God's record, in spite of the apparent lack of current evidence, is called faith (see Heb. 11:1, and today's epistle). Thus, remembering is the way toward becoming willing to trust our faithful God.

Becoming willing and able to trust God is essential in order to receive God's grace fully. In this story, thirst without trust in God utterly distracted the people from the gift of freedom they had just received. Ask: "Have you ever been given a blessed gift, but been so distracted by the unfamiliar, the change, the adjustment, that you failed to notice the gift? Or perhaps seen the gift but in frustration called it 'bad' or 'unwanted'?"

Second Reading
Romans 5:1-11 (RCL)
Romans 5:1-2, 5-8 (LFM)

The Text. This first part of Romans 5, describing the gracious effects of uprightness by faith through Christ, is built upon Paul's discussion in the first four chapters of how one is "made right" with God ("justified"). Is it through the law as Paul had always thought?

No, he concludes—it is through faith. He argues that circumcision (part of the law) is not the *cause* of covenant with God, but its *sign*. Yet if the covenant is not kept, the sign is empty: outward life and inward life—the letter and the spirit of the law—must match in any kind of ethical living (Rom. 2:25-29). But in Christ, Paul goes on to show, "the righteousness of God has been manifested apart from law ... through faith in Jesus Christ for all who believe" (Rom. 3:21a, 22a, RSV). And "since all have sinned and fall short of the glory of God, they are justified by his grace as a *gift, through the redemption which is in Christ Jesus ...*" (3:23-25). In last week's reading, Paul used Abraham as an example of faithfulness (4:13). Now we see that Jesus Christ, crucified for the forgiveness of sin, through resurrection redeemed our relationship with God, making it right—a process continued through faith (4:25; see the discussion of the second reading for the Second Sunday in Lent), above.

Chapter 5, then, reiterates that "we are justified by faith." Paul gives three effects of this making right with God through God's grace in Christ Jesus, made available to us by faith:

1. *peace* (5:1-2), a gift of grace (*charis*), which includes reconciliation (5:11).
2. *hope* (5:2-5). These come from the gift of love given through the Holy Spirit (5:5). This love is not earned, but comes when we are weak and sinful (5:6-9).
3. *participation in the risen life of Christ* (5:10-11).[5]

The Preaching. This, then, lends itself to a sermon on grace, and the freedom we have through faith in Christ to be made right with God. The relationship of peace to reconciliation, both as gifts from God, is especially fitting in Lent when our self-examination calls us to attend to broken relationships, whether we have been guilty (e.g., ignoring, hurting, violating, gossiping, withholding compassion), victimized (e.g., therefore angry, resentful, self-absorbed, weak, fearful, unable to trust), shamed (e.g., thinking too little of ourselves, isolating, unable to discern or receive), or otherwise unable to fully receive God's love and reconciliation.

Receiving God's good gifts in right relationship contrasts with the Exodus story of lack of trust in God or God's loving provision, and sets the stage for today's Gospel's promise of living water. The epistle fits particularly with God's grace (*charis*) given at baptism, for the sacrament or ordinance of holy baptism is the sign of our participation in the death (Rom. 6:3-5) and in the risen life of Jesus Christ (Rom. 5:6-9). While we are all tempted to fear and complain, and to rely on rules and legalisms, our baptismal identity in Christ is both God's call to live a redeemed life in faith, and our promise made at baptism to do so. Baptismal identity is also an already gift of the Holy Spirit, constantly working within us in peace and hope to lean into trust of the God who has already initiated the reign of God through Christ in our very midst. It is a commitment for the covenant people baptized into Christ and anointed by the Spirit together to live this life.

Gospel
John 4:5-42 (RCL, LFM)
John 4:5-15, 19b-26, 39a, 40-42 (LFM ALT.)

For background on the gospels for the Third, Fourth, and Fifth Sundays in Lent, please see the introduction to Lent, above.

The Text. Raymond Brown casts this story in two scenes and a conclusion:

Scene I (vv. 5-26): *Jesus' conversation with the Samaritan woman.* The enmity between Jews and Samaritans, though distant cousins, was longstanding and strong. Jews considered Samaritans ritually impure, which is why they used nothing in common (such as well ladles or buckets; v. 9). Samaritan women were considered especially untouchable. And this woman's immorality is shown in having had five husbands, and living with another man. The fact that she draws water at the sixth hour (noon), when water was typically drawn in the cool of the morning and evening, may also suggest moral stigma. It is thus outrageous that Jesus, a Jewish man, should be speaking with her.

But Jesus speaks with her of the most important thing: the water of life. In Greek, the same word means both "living water" and "flowing water." True to the foiling misunderstanding of many characters in John, when Jesus offers her living water, she replies (v. 11), "Sir … Where … are you going to get this flowing water?"[6] Jesus explains (vv. 13-14), describing "a spring of water gushing up to eternal life," or "a fountain of water leaping up unto eternal life."[7] Raymond Brown understands this living water to be Jesus' revelation, or Jesus' Spirit, both of which, when given and received, give life.[8] In a prolepsis of the reign of God, Jesus explains that those who worship the Father in Spirit and in truth can only do so if filled with the "Spirit that makes them God's children" and enables such heavenly worship of the Holy One.[9]

Scene 1 ends when Jesus reveals himself to the Samaritan woman as the Messiah.

Scene II (vv. 27-38): *Disciples return; the woman hurries to town to tell of Jesus, the Messiah.* The disciples, who had gone into town for food (v. 8), now return, utterly shocked to witness Jesus speaking with a Samaritan woman—although they seem more shocked to find him speaking with a woman than with a Samaritan (v. 27a). When she hurries off, the disciples offer Jesus some of the food they have brought. Jesus responds about deeper "food" (v. 32); they become the confused foils, wondering what food he means (v. 33). Jesus' discourse (vv. 34-38) seems to invite the disciples to participate in his work and ministry, which is food, "fruit for eternal life" (v. 36). The harvest imagery shows the ministry to be communal: one sows, another reaps; and Jesus invites the disciples to gather the harvest.

Meanwhile, the woman who had rushed home (leaving her water jar, v. 28), gives her personal testimony about Jesus, and invites townspeople to see this possible Messiah with the words, "Come and see."

Conclusion (vv. 39-42): *The townspeople come to believe.* By the eyewitness testimony of the woman, many come to believe that Jesus is the Messiah, and they invite him to stay. When they hear Jesus' revelation firsthand, they know Jesus as Christ "for we have heard for ourselves."

The Preaching. This dramatic story can serve as a sermon about Jesus' unconditional love and inclusiveness, "stooping" even to a tainted, outcast woman. A preacher might invite hearers to reexamine their own stereotypes, including ethnic or religious groups and the still-prevalent prejudice against women. Jesus knows (even if we don't) that the word might take root most deeply in those persons we consider unexpected or unworthy.

The story also lends itself to the communal nature of ministry and its relationship to thanksgiving: some will reap that for which they did not labor (v. 38a), while others will sow and labor and not get to see the fruits. Yet, in either position, the preacher might call the people to give thanks, recognizing and trusting in the larger salvific play of which they all are a part, though they may not know in which act they appear, nor who plays before or after them. But thanks be to God, the story of creation and redemption goes on, and each one is invited to play a small, though essential, part.

Further, a sermon on spiritual growth might let the woman serve as role model for the steps by which a person comes to believe in Jesus:
- being accepted and received in one's vulnerable, sinful or shameful state;
- being listened to and taken seriously, though the listener knows all the facts;
- having one's deepest hunger fed: being loved for who one is and invited to become greater;
- sharing one's experience with others (townspeople) who respond;
- becoming, then, part of a community of believers.

Because her heart was not hardened, her sin and pain did not ultimately get in her way.

Finally, the centrality of water to this story can hardly be ignored. It takes place at a well, and Jesus uses the immediate situation to draw a metaphor for what he gives that offers life: himself, his word, his Spirit, his ministry. The woman misses the metaphor and gets confused. The reader watches her begin to understand, as she asks for "this water," but again unclear, says, "so that I may never be thirsty or have to keep coming here to draw water." But by the end, her faith is shown—and she rushes off to share the good news. As soon as she does "get it," she wants it, and wants to share it.

She and her Samaritans stand in stark contrast to others who follow Jesus because they like his miracles (John 2:25), but are not interested in receiving the word of God, Christ's revelation, the living water. This is the water that saves, which is the ministry and purpose of Jesus: that the world might be saved through him (3:17).

The connection with baptism cannot be missed. While this living water is not directly the water of baptism but water Jesus gives to drink, the water imagery is profound. This story is placed following the Nicodemus account, which is about baptism, and scenes from the woman at the well are found in catacombs "as a symbol for Baptism."[10] Paul's statement in 1 Corinthians 12:13, "For in the one Spirit we were all baptized into one body … and we were all made to drink of one Spirit" suggests a spiritual metaphor for the drinking of living water.

Juxtaposing Exodus and John

In spite of the people's complaint and the Samaritan woman's (and the disciples') misunderstanding, God provides living water, water for life. Scripture says that if God's people do not keep covenant, and do not proclaim God's ethic of lovingkindness, even the stones will shout! (Luke 19:40). Here, through the very rock struck by Moses, God gives the means by which God's beloved will receive the water they need in order to live.

Many Christian interpretations understand the rock to be Christ, the source of living water (see Ps. 19:14; 78:35, NIV). One church has a baptismal font where the water trickles out of a large rock and into a bowl carved out of the rock itself, a strong symbol of Christ as source of life.[11]

A preacher might remind hearers that the stories and symbols in the New Testament begin in the First Testament, showing the continuity of God's lovingkindness of the body and of the spirit. God is the source of all good gifts, including physical life (water to drink) and holy, meaningful life (given by the Holy Spirit and Christ's revelation: living water). Particularly, as stated above, the story of the woman at the well was told on the third Sunday of the Lenten preparation of candidates for baptism. This story reveals God's work of ongoing creation and redemption through word and sacrament, which is the very pattern of Christian worship. Whether preparing for baptism or for baptismal renewal, hearers might be reminded that baptism connects them to Christ's death and resurrection (Rom. 6:3-5) and into Christ's work and ministry (John 4:31-38); and in baptism, one drinks of the same Spirit, through whom one is reborn a child of God (John 3), receiving and passing on Christ's living water.

Notes

1. John E. Huesman, "Exodus," in *The Jerome Biblical Commentary* (Englewood Cliffs, N.J.: Prentice-Hall, 1968), 55.
2. *An Inclusive-Language Psalter of the Christian People,* ed. Gail Ramshaw and Gordon Lathrop (Collegeville, Minn.: Liturgical Press, 1993).
3. As three examples: In the musical *Wicked,* the unappreciated, colored (green) Elphaba decides to quit trying to care, and just to become the "wicked" person people complain she is. The song leaders in the film *Paradise Road* enable prisoners to survive starvation and torture; and in the book version, *Song of Survival,* those in the lifeboats rant against the leaders, who, however, save their lives. Helen Colijn, *Song of Survival: Women Interned* (Ashland, Ore.: White Cloud, 1995).
4. Learning to trust God, however, can be a process. Psychologist Abraham Maslow showed that persons living at a basic survival level can be simply unable to turn from fear, even for God. According to his hierarchy of needs, persons need survival (food, water), safety, belonging, and self-esteem. Once these basic needs are met, persons seek learning, beauty, and self-actualization. See A. H. Maslow, "A Theory of Human Motivation," *Psychological Review* 50, no. 4 (1943): 370-96. Thanks to psychologist Sue Ellen McCalley, Avila University, for her interpretation of Maslow, adapted here.
5. Joseph A. Fitzmyer, "The Letter to the Romans," in *The Jerome Biblical Commentary*, 291-331; here, 305-06, §§50-51.
6. Translation from Raymond E. Brown, *The Gospel According to John (I–XII),* The Anchor Bible 29, 2d ed. (Garden City, N.Y.: Doubleday 1980), 166.
7. Translation in ibid.
8. Ibid., 178-79, passim.
9. Ibid., 180 (emphasis added).
10. Ibid.
11. St. Gregory of Nyssa Episcopal Church, San Francisco, California.

April 3, 2011
Fourth Sunday in Lent

First Reading
1 Samuel 16:1-13 (RCL)
1 Samuel 16:1b, 6-7, 10-13a (LFM)

The Text. Samuel, the priest, is grieving over but worried about Saul. This is Saul the king who disobeyed the Lord after a battle with the Amalekites, the same Saul to whom the Lord sent Samuel to inform that the spirit of the Lord was withdrawn from him (1 Samuel 15) and that he was rejected from being king (16:1). Samuel obediently informed Saul of his fall from grace (15:12-33). But here in the full drama of the RCL lection, Samuel continues to grieve over Saul's rejection (16:1a; cf. 15:34-35a), but also to fear Saul's retribution for his bearing the bad news and for having anointed Israel's second king, David (v. 13b).

The RCL also builds up suspense as to which of Jesse's sons is the one the Lord has chosen. The leaner story in the LFM keeps the focus on David, emphasizing that David was chosen (because "the Lord looks on the heart," v. 7), and David was anointed as a sign of God's call.

The Preaching. The RCL text shows the pain and poignancy of covenantal leadership when told from Samuel's perspective, and would lend itself to a sermon to church leaders, or in a sermon series on 1 Samuel.

Alternatively, in a story with the drama and suspense animating both lections, a preacher might ask, Who is the star of this story? Samuel might be it. He travels to

Bethlehem and examines each of the seven sons Jesse presents to him (v. 10). One by one, the Lord instructs Samuel to pass them over, which he does—but then he runs out of sons. A preacher could ask, What would you do in Samuel's situation? Assume you'd made a mistake? Go through the sons again, looking to make one of them fit, like Cinderella's glass slipper on one of the stepsisters? This, after all, was the task.

But verse 11a shows the listening obedience of Samuel, who has taken this on not as a job, or task to "get done," (i.e., "I'm not leaving here until I anoint one of Jesse's sons to be king of Israel. I didn't feel any tingle for any one of them—so let's try again."). In contrast, Samuel trusted what the Lord said ("I have provided for myself a king among his sons," v. 1), trusted his own "tuning in" to the Lord, and did not assume that "what he saw was what he would get." The fact that on the surface things didn't make sense did not stop Samuel. Therefore, Samuel asks an utterly strange, out-of-the-box question. "Jesse, you, er, uh, wouldn't happen to have any more sons, by any chance, would you?" Jesse does. Samuel's relationship with God is strong; he listens to receive God's word, and however difficult or strange it is, Samuel follows. He does not jump to a quick fix or forced outcome. Reminding us of our call to trust and obey like Samuel could be a sermon message.

So Samuel anoints David, another candidate for star of this story: David, the one least likely to be chosen. He's the youngest, dirty and smelly from spending his days out in the field with the sheep. He was less experienced (and more cocky, we learn later). Yet his pleasing appearance (v. 12) is an outward sign of his beauty within. We know proleptically that David will become Israel's hero, that the Lord's royal covenant will be made with David and his line, and that Jesus will be born in "the city of David." But for now, even before the Goliath story, David is the baby, the son whom Jesse never suspected would be the Lord's chosen.

Is this not true for every one of us? A preacher might capitalize on the reality that if the Spirit of the Lord rests upon us, we become able to accomplish more than we could alone. David is also a sinner (i.e., 2 Samuel 11-12), and thus a particularly good role model. May we all be as faithful to God, and as willing to repent when confronted with our sins, as David was.

A third candidate for star of this story is the relationship between God and God's chosen. It is God who chooses, and calls out the chosen through God's instrumental people (in this case, Samuel). There is a ritual action that makes the covenant real and assures persons of the intentional presence of God's spirit. In this case, the ritual sign of the mighty presence of God's spirit is Samuel's anointing of David with olive oil "in the presence of his brothers" (v. 13). Abundant oil is poured from a horn and "smeared"[1] on David before specifically identified witnesses. And not only David, but the witnesses, are aware of God's spirit upon the anointed one.

(For more preaching commentary on 1 Samuel, see below under the Psalm.)

Psalmody
Psalm 23 (RCL)
Psalm 23:1-3a, 3b-4, 5, 6 (LFM)

The Text. The whole of Psalm 23 is used on this Sunday in response to the first reading. The LFM suggests a way to divide it up for responsorial leadership, which might also be used for congregations proclaiming it antiphonally: side A (or the women, etc.) reading verses 1-3a and 5, alternating with side B (or the men, etc.) reading verses 3b-4, and 6.

Since the psalms are associated with David (to whom many are attributed), it is fitting after hearing of the anointing of David the shepherd to hear, in his voice as well as ours, "The LORD is my shepherd" (which would be a fitting congregational response to the four segments if a cantor or lector proclaims the whole psalm). Not only that, but verse 5 celebrates, "you have anointed my head with oil."[2] David's story is recapitulated in the psalm.

This psalm contains two distinct metaphors: that "I" am a *sheep* of the shepherd (23:1-4), and that "I" am a *guest* at the Lord's table (vv. 5-6). If holy communion is to be celebrated, a preacher may wish to link the banquet for the psalmist with the banquet of the kingdom in the eucharist. The abundance and promise of God's grace and forgiveness is suggested in "my cup is running over" (v. 5c).

Preaching 1 Samuel and Psalm 23. Anointing is the sign of the Spirit, used to make kings,[3] or priests, and in many Christian churches, the baptized. In baptism, persons become part of the "royal priesthood" (1 Pet. 2:9) through their union with Christ, the king. Thus, the sign of the Spirit's "coming upon" one being baptized has, from the early church, been *anointing.*[4]

Whether preparing candidates for Easter baptism or everyone for baptismal renewal, then, a preacher can remind hearers that the anointing imagery in 1 Samuel and Psalm 23 points not only to someone as great as David became, but to every one of us at baptism. At baptism, we become part of the body of Christ, anointed ones, *alter Christus.* It can be said of us, as Samuel prepared to say to God's chosen, "Surely the LORD's anointed is now before the LORD" (1 Sam. 16:6).

This is a great honor and a great responsibility, and a joyful privilege to be so loved and lifted. With this unspeakable grace comes humility in the paradox of God's greatness and our small, bumbling finitude. With this unspeakable identity comes a terrible responsibility to live into who we are as children of light, chosen and sent.

Yet how can we *not* live it when God's Spirit is with us? We are given the ability to respond to God's lovingkindness. The preaching might call the people to accept this response-ability. Whether a pastor will use actual oil or not, those baptized are anointed by the Spirit with grace and humility, the call to ethical living, and the partnership with the community of the faithful who are the *ecclesia* ("called out"), the body of Christ.

Stunningly, all who are baptized into Christ Jesus are called to participate in the prolepsis of the kingdom or reign of God, taking their share in the royal ministry of our Sovereign Lord. God smiles on the lowly, including the shepherd in Psalm 23, inviting us to the heavenly banquet where our cup will run over. The banquet, a sign of the fullness of God's reign in the end times, can be experienced now, and here, by those who trust in God and follow Christ, depending utterly, faithfully upon the Spirit for guidance, as Samuel did.

Second Reading
Ephesians 5:8-14 (RCL, LFM)

The Text. The imagery of darkness and light in Ephesians 5:8-14 recalls the psalmist's "valley of the shadow of death" (v. 4a) and points clearly to today's Gospel in which Jesus refers to himself as the light of the world. Followers of God in Christ by the Spirit are invited to live as children of light; and such lives will be manifest in ethical living. The fruit of living as children of the light is goodness and righteousness and truth (v. 9); and this is pleasing to the Lord (v. 10).

The Preaching. The baptized life in the early church was the fruit of a three-[5] to five-[6]year period of life-changing preparation in the areas of behavior, belief, and belonging.[7] Lives lived in holiness, purity, justice, and truth were lives of ethical behavior, at home, in private, at work, in community, and in the *civitas.* When Christianity became the state religion and thus dominant, these life-changing ethical standards were no longer expected of the baptized. A preacher might make a connection between ethics, justice, and living in the light (in Christ). Further, as North American culture moves further and further away from Christian predominance (a state called "Christendom"), a preacher might find it helpful to draw upon the experience of early Christians, for whom this epistle would be readily understandable, as a model for what intentional Christian living might look like today.

Gospel
John 9:1-41 (RCL, LFM)
John 9:1, 6-9, 13-17, 34-38 (LFM ALT.)

The Text. Raymond Brown sums up this story's plot: "As a sign that he is the light, Jesus gives sight to a man born blind."[8] This gospel is long, but is so dramatic and engaging, it is well worth proclaiming the whole chapter. The rich characterization of the several players lends itself to multiple voices proclaiming the different parts. The story itself can elicit rapt attention if, instead of reading in a monotone, the gospeler or readers vary voices when different characters speak: narrator, disciples, Jesus, neighbors, other witnesses, man born blind, Pharisees, and parents of the former blind man.

Signs of Jesus' glory and power reveal his identity. There are references in the Fourth Gospel to seven "signs"—miracles and healings—Jesus did which "revealed his glory" with the result that "his disciples believed in him" (2:11). Today's Gospel is the sixth sign, and next week's (the raising of Lazarus) is the seventh.[9]

The healing of the man born blind (and next week, Lazarus) is certainly a healing story, but it is also a miracle: while Jesus in other Gospel accounts[10] restores persons' lost sight, it was unheard of to heal a person *born* blind (9:32). Not only that, but stories of restoring sight usually begin with a request from the blind person (e.g., Bartimaeus, Mark 10:46-52). Bystanders and Pharisees are utterly challenged; they cannot believe what it is they are seeing. The question is, Who could do such extreme miracles? Howard Clark Kee calls these two miracles "test signs," since they are a kind of litmus test for the big question: *Who is Jesus?*

Jesus answers the question with one of the seven "I Am" statements in the Fourth Gospel: "I am the light of the world" (9:5b; cf. 8:12). The irony in John 9 is that the people who can see physically are blind spiritually, while the man born blind comes, through the scenes in the story, to see truly what matters most: that Jesus, the Son of Man, is the light of the world, the One who illuminates truth, who heals, who saves. Jesus is the One with power to bring light out of darkness.

Toward the end of this story, the young man, now with physical sight, is driven out by the Pharisees. Again, Jesus seeks him out. When he finds him, he poses the question, "Do you believe in the Son of Man?" (v. 35). Answering honestly, the man says he doesn't know who that is. But when Jesus reveals that it is he, the young man calls him *Kyrie* ("Sir," or "Lord") and proclaims, "Lord, I believe"—and worships him.

The Preaching. Two themes in particular are suggested by this story. The *first* offers a parallel between John's first-century minority believers and twenty-first-century believers within a culture where Christianity no longer has the status it once had (in some places Christianity is in the minority or even unaccepted), and Christendom is waning.

The audience of the Fourth Gospel was a community around the time of the Council of Jamnia (c. 90–93 C.E.), when the Jews were trying to sort out their identity. The Temple, locus of Jewish worship and symbol of the faith, had been destroyed in 70 C.E. There was a wide diversity of groups within Judaism, including Pharisees (who believed in resurrection from the dead), Sadducees (who did not), those who believed Kochba was the Messiah, those who believed Jesus was the Messiah, and those who believed the Messiah had not yet come. In the last decade of the first century (c. 90 C.E.), a prayer was added to the synagogue liturgy that said "… let Christians and heretics perish as in a moment, let them be blotted out of the book of the living… . Blessed art Thou, O Lord, who humblest the arrogant"—a prayer to which Jewish Christians could not attest.[11] This made it impossible for whose who believed in Jesus as the Messiah or *Christos* to worship any longer in the synagogue; they were now *aposynagogos*, excommunicated, put out of the synagogues (John 9:22; 12:42; 16:2).

Many stories in John's Gospel have Jesus predicting that his followers will be kicked out of the synagogue, showing John's congregation that they are in good company. The blind man's parents, for example, hesitate to speak up, and the story interprets their reticence as "fear of the Jews," a term that would not have been used in Jesus' time, but was used when the (formerly Jewish) Christians were separated from Jewish congregations. The author of this Gospel was a good pastor to the people, showing them that true sight is to recognize Jesus as the Anointed One, the Son of Man, the Savior. For those whose lives were lived in the light, Jesus would do for them what he had done for the man born blind: seek them out, ask for a profession of faith, and claim them for his own, granting healing and insight into the truth.

John continues to be a good pastor to today's congregations, who are beginning to feel the loss of Christianity's privileged status. Christianity is illegal in some countries, and the baptized may be put in jail (e.g., Pakistan). Even in the United States, there are various kinds of suffering endured by those whose lives or words witness (= *martyr*, Gk.) to Christ, the Son of God. Many businesses expect employees to work shifts around the clock every day, which means that people who assert their commitment to attend worship may put their jobs at risk. Schools schedule soccer games on the Sabbath or the Lord's Day (Sunday), so that young people and their families are faced with a "Sophie's choice" of an important team sport and their commitment as followers of Christ. A preacher might challenge and affirm today's believers as John did then.

But the primary comfort of this story is that the man gains both physical and spiritual sight—and, especially, the insight to know who Jesus is. The formerly blind man comes to *see* that Jesus is the Son of Man; and his response, even in the face of the Pharisees, is a bold profession of faith: "Lord, I believe" (v. 38). May it be so today.

2. The *second* theme is clearly the parallel between the baptismal process and the conversion (the growing faith and awareness) of the man with his profession of faith as he comes to recognize who Jesus is: healer, miracle worker, the light of the world, the One who saves, who frees from sin, the One who reveals God's work (v. 3b), who is from God (v. 33), who seeks out those in need. Those who are baptized are like the man born blind who come to see, be healed, and know Christ. In fact, "baptism was likened to the recovery of sight."[12] According to Justin Martyr (c. 100–165 C.E.), early baptizands were called the "enlightened ones," the "illuminated."

Because of this association, John 9 was one of the readings in the early church's Lenten preparation before candidates were baptized at Easter. As Raymond Brown notes, this "story of the man born blind appears seven times in early catacomb art, most frequently as an illustration of Christian Baptism. Chapter [9] served as a reading in preparing converts for Baptism …"[13] One comes to see, and know. This "knowing," setting one's heart on a hopeful certainty toward which one's life turns, is called "belief." The confession of the formerly blind man was a climax in the reading: "I do believe, Lord." Having heard the faith profession of the one Jesus sought out and healed, who was born in original blindness but had come to see and recognize the Lord, it is likely that the candidates for baptism would then have recited the creed in their own profession of faith.[14]

In addition to identifying the man born blind to baptismal candidates, the means Jesus uses to heal this man is *water*. He anoints him with mud and spittle, and then *sends him to the pool at Siloam,* where he washes and is healed. It is the washing in the water that effects his healing, that washes away his blindness from birth.

And a third parallel to baptism is that the name of the pool means "sent"—a tantalizing sermon topic. Who is sent? Jesus is sent from the Father. And every one who is baptized into Christ Jesus is also sent forth into the world, radiant with the light of Christ, to shine into the dark places, bringing love and forgiveness, healing and words of grace. Whether preparing for baptism or renewal of one's baptismal identity in Christ, this story invites hearers to pay attention, that they may see what God is doing in their very midst; and believing on the One who is the light of the world, to live as children of God and bear witness to Christ in the power of the Spirit.

Lent follows Jesus from his water baptism to his baptism on the cross. Whether or not the preacher is preparing hearers for baptism or baptismal renewal, this is a good week to remind the people of the meaning of baptismal identity: the baptized are washed and sent. Baptism connects us to the Lord who is light so that seeing we might be light to the world.

Notes

1. While NRSV translates "spread," Raymond Brown prefers "smeared": *epichriein* = "smearing" in John 9:6, 11. See *The Gospel According to John (I–XII)*, The Anchor Bible 29, 2d ed. (Garden City, N.Y.: Doubleday 1980), 370-82; here, 369, 381. In either case, enough oil to spread or smear is suggestive for Christian liturgy, which often uses but a thin film.

2. Translation from the psalter in *The Book of Common Prayer* (New York: Church Publishing, 1979), 613.

3. Sometimes priests (Exod. 29:7) and prophets (1 Kings 19:16) were also anointed, though the sign-act was most strongly associated with kingship. The king was then called "the Lord's anointed" (e.g., 1 Sam. 16:6) or "the anointed one" (= Messiah, *Christos*). William F. Stinespring, annotations for 1 Samuel, *New Revised Standard Version,* Oxford Annotated Ed. (New York: Oxford University Press, 1991), note on 1 Sam. 10:1.

4. In the West, laying on of hands became the predominant sign of the Spirit's presence, while anointing was retained in the East. Since the liturgical reform of the late twentieth century, anointing has found its way back into the Western church. For a historic study of anointing, see G. W. H. Lampe, *The Seal of the Spirit: A Study in the Doctrine of Baptism and Confirmation in the New Testament and the Fathers* (New York: Longmans, Green, 1951).

5. Three years was the typical preparation time in Rome according to *Apostolic Tradition*, a "church order" or description of practices in Rome c. 215 C.E. See Geoffrey J. Cuming, *Hippolytus: A Text for Students* (Bramcote Notts, UK: Grove, 1976), §17.

6. Mandated by the Council of Elvira, Spain (305 C.E.): *Canons of Elvira* 11, in Adalbert Hamman, "Catechumen, Catechumenate," in *Encyclopedia of the Early Church*, ed. Angelo diBerardino, I (Cambridge: James Clarke), 151-52. Cited in Alan Kreider, *The Change of Conversion and the Origin of Christendom* (Harrisburg, Penn.: Trinity Press, 1999), 24.

7. Kreider, *The Change in Conversion*, xv-xvii.

8. Brown, *The Gospel According to John,* 369.

9. Some have speculated that the evangelist drew upon a "signs source," though there is no consensus as to what it may have included. On signs, I'm following Howard Clark Kee, *Understanding the New Testament,* 4th ed. (Englewood Cliffs, N.J.: Prentice-Hall, 1983) 155-56, 158-62. The first is turning water into wine (John 2:1-11); then healing the son of a Gentile military officer in Capernaum (4:54), healing the lame man (5:1-18), feeding the five thousand (6:1-14), and walking on water (6:16-21).

10. Raymond Brown notes the following other healings of the blind (*The Gospel According to John,* 378): "a) Healing of Bartimaeus (Mk 10:46-52; Luke 18:35-43; Mt 20:29-34 [two blind men]).
    b) Two blind men in Galilee (Mt 9:27-31—a doublet of the preceding?).
    c) A blind mute in Galilee (Capernaum?)—this is according to Mt 12:22-23; but Luke 11:14 mentions only a mute and places the scene on the way to Jerusalem.
    d) A blind man healed in stages with the use of spittle at Bethsaida (Mark 8:22-26). In similar circumstances Mt 15:30 gives a summary which mentions healing the blind.
    e) At Jerusalem, in a summary connected with the cleansing of the Temple, Jesus is said to have healed the blind (Mt 21:14)."

11. In 90–117 C.E., an additional prayer was added to the 18 Benedictions, making them 19. Inserted as #12, the Palestinian prayer read, "For apostates, let there be no hope, and the dominion of arrogance do Thou speedily root out in our days; and let Christians and heretics perish as in a moment, let them be blotted out of the book of the living, and let them not be written with the righteous. Blessed art Thou, O Lord, who humblest the arrogant." C. W. Dugmore, *The Influence of the Synagogue Upon the Divine Office* (Westminster, UK: Faith Press, 1964), Appendix, 120.

12. Laurence Hull Stookey, *Calendar: Christ's Time for the Church* (Nashville: Abingdon, 1996), 51.

13. Brown, *The Gospel According to John,* 380. He cites F.-M. Braun, *Jean le Théologien et son Evangile dans l'Eglise ancienne* (Paris: Gabalda, 1959), 149ff.; E. Hoskyns, *The Fourth Gospel,* ed. F. N. Davey, 2d ed. (London: Faber, 1947), 363-65.

14. Brown, *The Gospel According to John,* 380-81. He cites Braun, *Jean le Théologien,* 149ff ; Hoskyns, *The Fourth Gospel,* 363-65; and Braun again, 158-59.

April 10, 2011
Fifth Sunday in Lent

First Reading
Ezekiel 37:1-14 (RCL)
Ezekiel 37:12-14 (LFM)

The Text. Ezekiel, not only prophet but priest, proclaimed during the disheartening fifty-year period of the Babylonian exile and captivity. His prophecy leans toward apocalyptic in the vibrancy of his visions, his enacted metaphors, and his rich symbology—like this vision of the Valley of Dry Bones.

Ezekiel's metaphoric vision occurs in Babylon, where perhaps inspired by a desert plain where fallen soldiers lay unburied, he sees "the whole house of Israel" (v. 11) like dry bones—lifeless, hopeless, "cut off completely" (v. 12). They were severed from Jerusalem and their homeland like bones from each other.

So the Lord gives to Ezekiel this vision of the bones reconnecting with each other, becoming juicy with flesh, and finally being filled with the wind, the breath, the spirit of life (*ruach* means all of these—a Hebrew pun). This is a vision of hope for restoration to their home, the land God had given them. The word of the Lord gives hope now for the new life God is even now bringing into being.

But there is a turning point in the story at verse 12 where the LFM reading begins: the image switches from dry bones to graves: "I am going to open your graves … O my people." In effect, God announces, "Not only will I restore you to yourselves and your homeland, but I will give life to the dead!"

Our God is a God of life: life in contrast to the death and separation of exile, and life in contrast to physical death. Both require the Spirit of the Lord, who animates persons and communities, breathing life into all things. And when this occurs, "'then you shall know that I, the LORD, have spoken and will act,' says the LORD" (v. 14).

The Preaching. The sequence for the bones is in many ways the sequence for all life, from building community or starting an organization to forgiving or creating reconciliation: first, *connection* (one remembers the old spiritual, "Dem Bones": "the foot bone's connected to the ankle bone, … Now hear the word of the Lord!"). Linking, attachment, relationship comes first. Then, *juicy flesh.* Meat. Substance. Structure. Finally, the breath and animating Spirit of the Lord!

Donald Jackson, the calligrapher of the contemporary hand-written *St. John's Bible* (and also the calligrapher for the queen of England), painted an illustration of the valley of dry bones with contemporary images of blight and death: junkyards stacked with old cars, neighborhoods where latchkey kids and homeless are not safe, piles of eyeglasses left from the Holocaust. The question now, as then, is: *Can these bones live?*

The answer comes in spite of logic, all evidence to the contrary. The word of the Lord *is* action. The word of the Lord is powerful, and will not return empty, but effects or accomplishes that which it proclaims. These bones (relationships, situations, death-dealing worry, the church, etc.) will not just survive: they will *live.* And not only will they be restored, but they will be called up from the grave to live again, and thrive!

And the answer comes with the unexpected twist that the human family is part of the new life. The Lord calls upon Ezekiel, the mortal, to prophesy, to speak God's word, obediently and with utter faith. Not only is the prophet-priest called to proclaim hope and power and life to the hearers, but the church, God's priestly people (1 Pet. 2:9-10), are called to proclaim to the world. In spite of our expectations, or what seems impossible to us, or what anyone else says, the Lord is the Lord of restoration and life! A preacher could call the people to Ezekiel's faith and obedience—a word (*obey*) that comes from "listen," a deep, faithful, trusting, open-heart listening attentively to the Lord. Now hear the word of the Lord!

Psalmody
Psalm 130 (RCL)
Psalm 130:1-2, 3-4, 5-6, 7-8 (LFM)

Though Psalm 130 is considered one of the seven penitential psalms, its expressed hope and trust in the Lord (vv. 5, 7) makes it a fitting response to the Valley of Dry Bones. The psalmist trusts in God's love and power (v. 7), and especially in God's word (v. 5b). These words are spoken out of the valley, the "depths," out of the death of sin and guilt and other soul-searing pain. As the people pray all eight verses, they express trust that God "will redeem Israel" and liberate the worshiping congregation and everyone they represent from "all its iniquities." "My soul waits for the Lord" "and in his word I hope" (vv. 6a, 5b).

Second Reading
Romans 8:6-11 (RCL)
Romans 8:8-11 (LFM)

The Text. In this section of the letter to the Romans, Paul continues his discussion of the tension between law and gospel, flesh and Spirit. In particular, Paul is here trying to show how the Spirit of God, made available through the resurrection of Christ, enables a person to transcend selfish instincts in order to live for God, beyond sin, in peace, reconciliation, and freedom for ethical love of neighbor. Followers of Christ live in the Spirit. The Christian life is lived by the Spirit, through the Spirit, because of the Spirit. In fact, there are twenty-nine occurrences of the word *spirit* in Romans 8, but only five in all of Romans 1–7.[1] This reading is about the Spirit.

The Spirit is interchangeably the Spirit of God and the Spirit of Christ. It is this Holy Spirit that empowers Christian living, which is a sharing in the risen life of Christ. Only in this Spirit is right living and right relationship—"righteousness"—possible. The law shows the way to live, but does not give the power to do so. It is the Spirit of Christ that makes possible this holy living, this participation in the divine life (cf. 2 Pet. 1:4).

The RCL begins in the midst of the "flesh vs. Spirit" discussion. The LFM begins right at the end of this section with "those who are in the flesh cannot please God." It is indeed the purpose of the human life (at least by the peoples of the Book) to please God—but we of ourselves are not capable of doing so. It is God's Spirit who initiates the desire to please God, and who turns the heart away from self to see what God desires, and who enables thoughts, actions, and intentions that would actually be pleasing to the Holy One. Verses 9-11, then, show that a God-pleasing, ethical, holy, righteous and nonsinful life is one lived in and by the Spirit of the risen Christ.

The Preaching. The epistle, like Ezekiel and John, refers to resurrection living, which is life in the Spirit, the one way to true life. This passage can easily be preached in juxtaposition with either or both of the other passages.

The inference can be drawn that those who are baptized into the death and resurrection of Jesus Christ and anointed by the Spirit, begin their resurrected living at baptism. The story is told of a Lutheran bishop during World War II in occupied Denmark, who was working with people to help Jews and other hunted persons hide and escape. The occupying Nazi officer got wind of the activity and called in the bishop. "I know what you're up to—and you must stop this activity at once!" he shouted. "Do you not know that I have the power of life and death over you?"

"I died at my baptism," the bishop replied. "You have *no* power over me."[2]

This is the freedom begun at baptism, which, by the power of the Spirit, may be cultivated throughout the Christian life.

Gospel
John 11:1-45 (RCL)
John 11:1-45 or 11:3-7, 17, 20-27, 33b-45 (LFM)

The Text. The raising of Lazarus takes place just before Jesus enters Jerusalem (12:9-19). In contrast to the synoptic gospels, which present Jesus' cleansing of the Temple (and the reaction it inspired) as precipitating the events leading to the crucifixion, the author of the Fourth Gospel identifies this exceptional miracle, resuscitating someone who was buried and had been dead four days, as the impetus. The narrative tension toward the cross has been building to this dramatic apex, so that Jesus' self-proclamation, "I am the resurrection and the life," at the raising of Lazarus sets in motion the passion of Jesus. This very act poses the same question raised in the miracle of last week's gospel, the healing of a man born blind, namely, *Who is Jesus?*

This story not only states that Jesus is the resurrection and the life (v. 25), but it shows that Jesus is the resurrection and the life. While Lazarus is not resurrected but resuscitated,[3] it is unthinkable that someone could bring to life someone dead, especially someone who was assumed to be already deteriorating. The burial practice in such a hot climate, given that the Israelites did not embalm like the Egyptians did, was to bury on the same day the person died. Preparing the body, mourning, and other events took place after the burial, such as bringing spices to care for the body and mitigate the stench. When Jesus arrived the fourth day after Lazarus died, people had already come to support Mary and Martha and to grieve his loss (vv. 19, 31; also 33, 36-37), so there was a large number of people there who witnessed Jesus' miracle.[4]

When the blind receive their sight and the dead are raised, it is a sign that the Messiah has come (Matt. 11:5). Yet as sufficient as raising Lazarus is to demonstrate that Jesus is the Messiah, the story's evidence is even more stark when compared with the timing of Synoptic accounts of Jesus raising the dead: Jairus's daughter had just died when Jesus healed her (Mark 5:22-43; Luke 8:41-55); and the dead body of the son of the widow of Nain was being carried out of the city for burial when Jesus raised him (Luke 7:11-16), indicating he had died earlier that day. Here, Lazarus was dead four days (it took a day for the message to get to Jesus; he stayed where he was for two more days [vv. 5-6], and then it took a day for him to get to Bethany).[5] This is no rumor, no coincidence. Before numerous witnesses, Jesus called Lazarus forth from the grave, dramatically dead four days. No one can doubt what this means: *Jesus is the Messiah.*

Why four days? This is a question especially because translations make Jesus sound heartless. The NRSV (vv. 5-6) is an improvement on the earlier RSV ("Now, Jesus loved Martha and her sister and Lazarus. So when he heard that he was ill, he stayed two days longer in the place where he was," RSV). Raymond Brown considers verse 5 a parenthetical insertion, letting verse 6 follow from verse 4's claim that Lazarus would not die but that the event was for God's glory: "Jesus … said, 'This sickness is not to end in death; rather it is for God's glory, that the Son [of God] may be glorified through it.' (Yet Jesus really loved Martha and her sister and Lazarus.) And so, even when he heard that Lazarus was sick, he stayed on where he was two days longer."[6] The delay, then, creates suspense in this story of a shocking, dramatic, unheard-of miracle, in which the raising of a man dead four days (leaving no doubt that Lazarus was really dead) unequivocally demonstrates that Jesus is the Messiah and the Son of God.

The sharp relief caused by the delay makes all the more real other results of this miracle:

1. This healing miracle glorifies God who is loving and powerful.
2. This miracle also enables Jesus, God's Son, to be glorified, not as a great guy, but because it leads to his death—which, in the Fourth Gospel, is part of ("a stage in") his glorification.[7]
3. The promise of John 5:28-29 is fulfilled and realized, which says, "the hour is coming when all who are *in their graves* will hear his *voice* and will *come out*—those who have done good, to the *resurrection of life*." Note the parallel in chapter 11:
    v. 17: Lazarus is *in the tomb.*
    v. 43: "Jesus shouts in a loud *voice*, 'Lazarus, *come out!*'"
    v. 25: I am the *resurrection* and the *life*.[8]
4. Martha and the witnessing crowd come to believe who Jesus is (vv. 23-27, 45).

Jesus *is* the resurrection and the life, and those who believe in him, even though they die, will live—on the last day, and in the present day, here, now, today.

The Preaching. This story contains several dramatic contrasts between death and life. As Reginald Fuller has described it, "Jesus goes to his death as the one who is the resurrection and the life and who will die to inaugurate the resurrection of all" (vv. 25-26).[9] Further, Jesus gives life to Lazarus, yet this miracle instigates Jesus' death. Not only that, look at the irony that Jesus gives life to people, and people give death to Jesus. And most of all, through all the healings climaxed in this ultimate healing, Jesus demonstrates over and over that he mediates life, and that believing in him *is* life. Jesus' presence enables eternal life, both at the *end times* (final eschatology: "I will raise them up on the last day," 6:40, 54)[10] and *now* (realized eschatology: 5:24-25). Here are several approaches to preaching life and preparing hearers for resurrection.

1. *Believe: Jesus is the Christ.* Martha and Mary both know Jesus not only as friend but as healer, for each of them says to him, "Lord, if you had been here, my brother would not have died" (vv. 21, 32). Martha goes on to say, "But even now I know that God will give you whatever you ask of him" (v. 22). But when Jesus says, "Your brother will rise again" (v. 23), Martha's imagination cannot stretch to giving life after four days dead (v. 24).

Even his closest, most trusting friends, have a difficult time fathoming that this man is the Son of God: and that a *new world,* and a *new humanity,* is beginning. Martha and Mary do not comprehend who Jesus is until this miracle is complete—because they witnessed it firsthand.

What about the people today who are not witnesses of this miracle, and who may not be intimates of Jesus? Do they know, grasp, believe that Jesus is the Christ, the Son of God? How will the resurrection connect with their lives? How will Easter, two weeks from today, have meaning for them? A preacher may want to confront the congregation with the challenging questions, *Who is Jesus?* and, *Who is Jesus for you?*

Preaching from the perspective of Martha and Mary in order for the congregation to identify with them—knowing Jesus but not knowing him as the Christ—gives a chance to awaken hearers to God's intention: to raise the dead! Resurrection is the center of the Christian faith because God calls and enables people to be fully human and fully alive. Whether the physically dead, who will be raised with Christ on the last day; or the spiritually dead now, who are not living but merely surviving; or the communally dead, stuck in individualism and isolation, Christians are called to live fully, abundantly, truly, lovingly, deeply—starting *now.* Jesus does not say "I *will be* the resurrection and the life," but I *am.* Today. Tomorrow. Every day. Eternal life is *now.* A preacher may do what Jesus did: pointedly asking, "Do you believe this?" (vv. 25-26). The Apostles' Creed, "I believe," is and was (in its various forms[11]) the "symbol of the faith," a profession of faith in Jesus as the Christ, always the preliminary to baptism in the early church. The question to Martha is the question to us, at baptism and every day thereafter.

2. *The raising of Lazarus, paired with the coming resurrection of Jesus, signals eternal life.* Raising the dead, including Lazarus today and Jesus in two weeks, is a sign of *eternal life.* What people fear most is *not-being:* nihilism or self-obliteration. What is profound and life giving about the Christian word is that death does not take away our being. When we die, we are still ourselves. Resurrection makes us different, but shows that we are not gone. Christians know that even though we die, we are alive in Christ, in whatever mysterious way that will be. But we still are. In death, we are in the nearer presence of God, and some believe that we continue to grow and become more real (e.g., C. S. Lewis, *The Great Divorce*). With this knowledge, then, the sting of death is truly taken away. The raising of Lazarus prepares the people of God for the wondrous truth of the resurrection of Jesus and its implication for us: they who believe will never die; it is death that has died; and we are an *Alleluia!* people who, even at the grave, can sing.

3. *The baptismal life is life together in Christ, participating in his ministry and holiness.* Baptism is initiation into Christ's death and resurrection (Rom. 6:3-5), and into Christ's ministry (including teaching, healing, and controversy). But baptism is also anointing by thc Holy Spirit and initiation into eternal life, not only on the last day, but beginning now, in the sacramental *kairos* moment at baptism.

How powerful it must have been for the early church candidates in the last weeks before baptism, to be confronted with Jesus Christ with the same revelation as the woman at the well, the man born blind, and Lazarus. For they, too, had secrets about which they were ashamed, and had been ostracized and misunderstood. They, too, had looked in the wrong wells for the quenching of their life thirsts. They, too, had been sinners from their birth, blind to the healing light that comes from love, forgiveness, and gratitude. They, too, had been dead—and were now getting ready to be called forth from the tombs of their former lives into eternal life with Christ and his body of disciples. So it is for us. We are like dry bones made juicy with flesh and anointed by the Spirit. We are liberated like the children of Israel crossing the Red Sea; we, like Lazarus, are unbound and set free.

There is no better prototype for what it means to be baptized into the crucified and risen Christ than the raising of Lazarus. This is a day to preach to the church, to insiders, to the baptized and those preparing for baptism. This is a day for guests and visitors to overhear an insider's view of what it means to be Christian today. For Christianity in the twenty-first century is more like in the first century: *Christian* is not the same "good citizen" or "nice person."[12] In contrast to the Holy Roman Empire, Calvin's Geneva, or the seventeenth-century Congregational Commonwealth of Massachusetts, the *civitas* and the *ecclesia* are not the same. To be Christian is something very specific, made plain during Lent, especially today.

4. *Be an Easter people: practice resurrection daily.* The Fourth Evangelist wrote to assure a people who, like Thomas, may have had their doubts, especially when they weren't there to witness Lazarus's coming out. But John asserts that as blessed as they were who had seen Jesus face to face, yet more blessed are "those who have not seen and yet have come to believe" (20:29b). It is not the eyewitness that matters most. It is knowing that Jesus is the Christ, the Son of God, so that "believing you may have life in his name" (20:31). And, as Raymond Brown points out, "Just as Jesus gives life to his beloved Lazarus, so will he give life to his beloved Christians."[13]

In John, Christ is glorified on the cross, which is where his work on earth was finished (19:30). Out of his side come blood and water (19:34), elements of the sacraments (ordinances) of holy communion and holy baptism. Christ is the sacrament of God.[14]

And the baptized are called to live into this glory, this life, this self-giving ministry. Can we drink in the truth that Jesus is the living water? Can we see that Jesus is the light of the world? Can we live freely, taking risks in the sure and certain knowledge that Jesus is the resurrection and the life? Are we willing to unbind each other, as odd or unacceptable as that may be? Believing, will we recognize the power and the glory of Jesus' presence among us?

Tuning into this glory, and the state of our lives, has been the purpose of Lenten practice and of the preaching of these lections. Now the preacher may put the question clearly: Are we open to the gift of life? To utterly spend ourselves, knowing that even death cannot overcome this life God gives in Christ Jesus? Living such foolishness in spite of the stench, the improbability, the doubt of our best friends and the hiddenness of the One inside us is our call. As Wendell Berry writes, living such foolishness is exactly the way to "practice resurrection."[15]

Notes

1. Joseph A. Fitzmyer, "The Letter to the Romans," in *The Jerome Biblical Commentary* (Englewood Cliffs, N.J.: Prentice-Hall, 1968), 314, §80. I follow Fitzmyer on the Spirit.
2. With thanks to the Rev. Prof. Louis Weil for telling this story.
3. Raymond Brown notes that there may be a theological reason for the evangelist's vivid description of Lazarus emerging bound in the linen strips of his burial garment, for Lazarus will die again. In contrast to Lazarus, when Jesus is resurrected (and will never die again), his burial clothes remain in the tomb (20:6-7). See *The Gospel According to John (I–XII),* The Anchor Bible 29, 2d ed. (Garden City, N.Y.: Doubleday, 1980), 427 n. on v. 44.
4. Whereas "the Jews" is a pejorative term earlier in John's Gospel (e.g., 9:22), here it refers to sympathetic persons, including Lazarus' mourners. Ibid., 424 n.19.
5. Brown suggests that Jesus "would be of more help to Lazarus when Lazarus was dead" (ibid., 431).
6. Ibid., 420. See also 431: Lazarus' sickness "is for God's glory … as a sign of eternal life."
7. Ibid., 431. On Jesus' glorification, he points to John 12:23-24; 17:1.
8. On this parallel, I follow Brown, and use his translation of v. 43 (ibid., 437).
9. Reginald Fuller, *Preaching the Lectionary* (Collegeville, Minn.: Liturgical Press, 1984), 51.
10. Suzanne Toolan's hymn "I am the bread of life," found in many hymnbooks, quotes John 11 in stanzas 4, 5 (e.g., "I am the resurrection," 11:25).
11. See J. N. D. Kelly, *Early Christian Creeds* (New York: Longman, 1991).
12. See the introduction to C. S. Lewis, *Mere Christianity* (New York: Macmillan, 1952).
13. Brown, *The Gospel According to John,* 431.
14. See also Edward Schillebeeckx, *Christ: The Sacrament of the Encounter with God,* trans. Paul Barrett (New York: Sheed and Ward, 1963).
15. From Wendell Berry," Manifesto: The Mad Farmer Liberation Front,"in *The Selected Poems of Wendell Berry* (Washington, D.C.: Counterpoint, 1998), or see http://www.context.org/ICLIB/IC30/Berry.htm, accessed January 5, 2010.

Holy Week

Craig A. Satterlee

As we consider the readings appointed for Holy Week, we will see that the gospel writers used the language and images of Passover to present and interpret Jesus' passion, death, and resurrection. It is not surprising, then, that the Passover, the center of the Jewish year as commemoration of their release from slavery, became equally important for Christians. In 1 Corinthians 5:7-8, for example, Paul deliberately takes over the language of the Jewish Feast of Unleavened Bread and calls Christ our paschal lamb, which has been sacrificed for us. Over time, the church came to understand the Passover themes of slavery and redemption as the release from sin and death through Christ's death and resurrection. Christ's passion, death, and resurrection were all commemorated together at the Christian Pascha with services signifying the making of new Christians through baptism, laying on of hands, and first communion.

In the fourth century, as throngs of pilgrims from all over the world arrived in Jerusalem—the place of Jesus' passion, death, and resurrection—the church in Jerusalem determined to divide the celebration of Jesus' passion, death, and resurrection into distinct commemorations and hold a special service at the holy place where each event occurred. The Jerusalem church combed the Bible for hints of days and places and thus Holy Week was born. In addition to the crowds of pilgrims that provided the assembly and the sacred sites of the culminating days of Jesus' life and ministry, which offered a context for each service, the end of persecution brought the construction of church buildings on the holy places where unique services could be held. All these factors contributed to the Holy Week services that shape the church's observance of Jesus' passion, death, and resurrection today.

Egeria (383 c.e.), a Spanish pilgrim, described the services in detail because they were novel.[1] Palm Sunday was the beginning of "the Great Week." People gathered at the Mount of Olives and went before the bishop carrying palms and branches and singing psalms and antiphons, repeating, "Blessed is he who comes in the name of the Lord." Minor services were held the next three days, except on Wednesday when the presbyter read about Judas's plot to betray Jesus and the people would groan and lament at this reading. Thursday included communion and a trip to Gethsemane. Following services throughout Thursday night, the assembly processed from

Gethsemane to the Sanctuary of the Cross, where the account of Jesus' trial before Pilate was read. The procession then moved to the column where Jesus was flogged. After going home to rest, the people returned to the Sanctuary of the Cross, where a casket holding a relic containing what was believed to be wood from the cross was placed before the bishop on a linen-covered table. The people filed past, touching the cross and kissing the wood. From noon until three o'clock, Scripture about the Passion from the Psalms and the Prophets, Acts or the Epistles, as well as the Gospels was read. Prayers appropriate to the day were said between the readings. At three o'clock, John's account of Jesus' death was read and the service ended shortly thereafter. In the evening, the assembly reconvened in the Sanctuary of the Resurrection, where the account of Jesus' burial was read. All who were able maintained a vigil there throughout the night. Pilgrims like Egeria took these experiences home with them. While it was necessary to modify these services as they moved beyond Jerusalem, since complete realism was only possible there, by the end of the fourth century these days were accepted as required observances throughout the church. Particularly after the Second Vatican Council, the ceremonies held in fourth-century Jerusalem became the model of the church's Holy Week observances.

The history of Holy Week reveals that preaching is coupled with powerful liturgical acts. In addition to responding to the narrative of Christ's final work through sermons, the church waves palms, washes feet, venerates the cross, lights a new fire, follows the light of the paschal candle, sings, baptizes, and proclaims Christ by eating the bread and drinking the cup. At its best, preaching complements and empowers these liturgical acts, rather than competing with or overshadowing them.

Holy Week is about Jesus. It is the week when the church remembers and commemorates Jesus' passion, death, and resurrection. Preaching, therefore, is about Jesus; it is not about us. This is not the time to tell people to be like Jesus because we cannot possibly do what Jesus does for us this week. If we need to place ourselves in this week, be clear that on Sunday we crucify, on Monday we protest with Judas, on Tuesday we wish to see Jesus, on Wednesday we betray, on Thursday we resist having our feet washed and join in stripping Jesus, and on Friday we are anyone at the cross, so that on Saturday we might be raised with Christ. Moreover, since this week is about Jesus, preachers rightfully use scriptural images and language, rather than searching for appropriate material from experience and culture. If the Christian story is not compelling during this Holy Week, the gospel is somehow wanting.

Finally, since the nature of Holy Week worship invites shorter homilies, it is essential both that Scripture is read well and that preachers not try to say everything. Traditionally, in the lectionaries of the church, the Gospel of John is used during Holy Week and therefore gives the final word on the events of Jesus' passion. While the synoptic gospels may provide the "history," the Gospel of John provides the "theology." Except for Palm/Passion Sunday, the gospel readings for Holy Week (Monday-Wednesday) are from John. During the Three Days, John interprets the

Paschal Mystery both in lectionary and liturgy—Maundy Thursday foot washing (John 13:1-17, 31-35b), Good Friday adoration of the cross (John 18:1—19:32), and, while the synoptic gospels are appointed for the Vigil in most resources, John 20:1-18 is the Vigil gosgel in Evangelical Lutheran Worship and is the appointed gospel reading for Easter Day in all three cycles. In addition to reading the pericopes themselves prayerfully, reviewing Johannine images and emphases is a helpful way to prepare to preach.

Several themes emerge from the readings taken as a whole. First, Jesus' passion is the fulfillment of Scripture and therefore God's plan. Second, Jesus is the humble, meek, suffering king destined for defeat, disgrace, and death, and totally dependent upon God for vindication and exaltation. Third, Jesus knows what will befall him, controls every event, and willingly and obediently goes to the cross. Finally, Jesus understands the significance of his suffering and death—making God known, revealing God's glory, and drawing all people to himself.

Note

1. Egeria, *Travels,* 30-38, trans. John Wilkinson (London: SPCK, 1971), 132-38.

April 17, 2011
Sunday of the Passion / Palm Sunday

Revised Common Lectionary (RCL)	Lectionary for Mass (LFM)
Liturgy of the Palms	*Processional Gospel*
Psalm 118:1-2, 19-29	Matthew 21:1-11
Matthew 21:1-11	
Liturgy of the Passion	*Palm Sunday: At the Mass*
Isaiah 50:4-9a	Isaiah 50:4-7
Psalm 31:9-16	Psalm 22:8-9, 17-18, 19-20, 23-24
Philippians 2:5-11	Philippians 2:6-11
Matthew 26:14—27:66 or 27:11-54	Matthew 26:14—27:66 or 27:11-54

With Jesus, we begin Holy Week by entering Jerusalem. In fourth-century Jerusalem, the assembly went to the Mount of Olives in the early afternoon of the Sunday that began Holy Week. At about five o'clock, the gospel account of Jesus' entry into Jerusalem was read and the people processed on foot from the summit of the Mount of Olives into the city. Children participated in the procession and everyone carried branches of palm or olive. Over time, this way of observing the first Sunday of Holy Week spread from Jerusalem, and the blessing and distribution of palms, procession, and appropriate gospel narrative became the way this day was celebrated.

Today, the first day of Holy Week is called different names in different places. But less frequently is it still simply referred to as "Palm Sunday." Not only has the name changed, the way the day is celebrated has changed as well. In addition to following Jesus into the city, the church follows Jesus as he makes his way to the cross. Jesus' entrance into Jerusalem, the traditional Palm Sunday narrative, is read as a processional gospel. The waving of palms and singing of "All glory, laud, and honor" quickly give way to the account of our Lord's passion, this year from Matthew. Although we have been doing it this way for many years now, many in worship are still trying to figure out why.

The reason we celebrate the first day of Holy Week as both Palm and Passion Sunday is simple. The church has come to recognize that allowing Jesus' entry into Jerusalem to stand alone and interpreting it as an utterly joyous and victorious occasion misrepresents the gospel. The label "triumphal entry" is, in fact, a misnomer. Jesus' entry into Jerusalem is charged not with victory but with irony. The New Testament writers knew fully well that the "Hosanna!" cries of Sunday would by Friday turn into calls for crucifixion. And this is as true for us as it is for the people of ancient Jerusalem. Our faith, too, is fickle. We are the crucifiers of the One whose coming we have called "blessed." We acknowledge this truth as we burn the palms that we waved on this day to mark our foreheads come Ash Wednesday. There is only one reason that Jesus enters Jerusalem: to die. The gospel writers are clear about this, and "Palm Sunday" observances that are a happy parade for Jesus forfeit biblical integrity.

More than this, if there ever was a time when the entire assembly in worship on Palm Sunday could be counted on to make the pilgrimage through Holy Week by returning to church on Maundy Thursday and Good Friday to hear the rest of the story, that time is long gone. For many if not most worshiping on Palm Sunday, the next time they worship is Easter morning. The Easter liturgy is rightfully a triumphal, celebratory event. If Palm Sunday worship has this same tone, those who only come on Sundays will receive a very distorted view of gospel reality. The church is obliged to insist that there is no route to an empty tomb except by way of the cross. And so we read the Passion on Palm Sunday.

Perhaps the most important issue preachers need to consider is whether we will, in fact, preach on Palm/Passion Sunday. Yes, the reading of Christ's Passion is long and a sermon will make worship even longer. Yet, more than this, there is wisdom in letting the word of God have the last word on this day. Perhaps the best thing we can do is to devote our time of sermon preparation to making sure the Passion narrative is read well, with care and cadence, with discipline and maturity. Rather than explaining this reading, we might better invite our congregations to savor the story, to meditate on the mystery, to allow it to wash over us and seep into our pores. Instead of calling our people to think, why not encourage our people to feel our Lord's passion and death.

Worship planners will spend time carefully considering how the Passion will be read. One option is to present it as a play, with a different reader assigned to each character. Another option is to divide the Passion into scenes—the anointing, the supper, the garden, the trial, the cross, the burial—with different readers reading each scene. A third option is for a single voice to proclaim it all.

However the Passion is read, the readers will need to spend time with the story, deciding how each word will be said by considering how each word will be heard. In Gethsemane, for example, the emphasis is not placed on "If it is possible, take this cup from me." The emphasis is placed on "Nevertheless, not what I want but what you want" (Matt. 26:39). Jesus' response to Judas's greeting and kiss in the garden (Matt. 26:50) should be read as a challenge or command and not as a surprise. We need to figure out how to speak of the Jews about whom Matthew was writing without vilifying Jewish people today. We need to ask how our tone will portray Jesus, Caiaphas, Peter, and Pilate. The decisions we make are themselves powerful proclamations of what the Lord's passion means for us and for the world.

Yet, having said all this, I must confess that I generally preach on this Sunday. The preaching is always a short homily as opposed to a sermon. The homily does not overshadow or diminish the Passion. This is not a time for "illustrative material." If the story of Christ's passion and death is not compelling on its own, our preaching is in vain. Rather then explaining or illustrating the story, I offer a lens with which we might meditate on the Passion. It might be a piece of the story, one scene from the entire play. It might be a thread that runs through the entire narrative. I always lift up the movement of the day, from *Hosanna!* to *Crucify!* To say it again: our faith, too, is fickle. We are the crucifiers of the One whose coming we have called "blessed." If you choose to preach, spend considerable time reading the Passion yourself.

Liturgy of the Palms

Gospel
Matthew 21:1-11 (RCL, LFM)

Matthew's account of Jesus entering the city of Jerusalem highlights the motif of the fulfillment of Scripture in several ways. First, Matthew makes explicit what is only implicit in Mark; namely, that Jesus' mode of entry as the "meek and humble king" fulfills Zechariah 9:9. "Lo, your king comes to you; triumphant and victorious is he, humble and riding on a donkey, on a colt, the foal of a donkey." That Jesus rides two animals—a donkey and her colt—is an indication of Matthew's literal reading of Zechariah. Jesus rides a donkey rather than a warhorse, a symbol of power and might, indicating his humility. Matthew eliminates the words "triumphant and victorious is he" from Zechariah to emphasize further that Jesus is the meek or humble king. Jesus enters Jerusalem from Bethphage, a small village east of Jerusalem, by way of the Mount of Olives. According to Zechariah 14:4, on "the day of the LORD," which was understood as the eschaton in Jesus' time, "on that day [the LORD's] feet shall stand on the Mount of Olives, which lies before Jerusalem on the east." Matthew indicates that Jesus' entrance into Jerusalem has eschatological implications. The crowd greets Jesus with Psalm 118:26: "Blessed is the one who comes in the name of the LORD" (Matt. 21:9). The whole city was "shaken" or in turmoil and wonders about the "prophet" (Matt 21:10-11; cf. Deut. 18:15, 18).

Everything Jesus does fulfills the Scriptures. Yet, Jesus fulfills the Scripture in unanticipated ways. Jesus comes in the biblical role of the meek and humble, rather than the triumphant and victorious, king. In fact, the crowd does not even acclaim Jesus as king, but instead hails Jesus as Son of David and the One who comes in the name of the Lord. As the meek and humble king, Jesus is among those blessed by God; he is one of the suffering righteous of the Psalms (cf. Matt. 5:5; 27:43). In fulfilling the Scriptures, Jesus reinterprets them to show that Jerusalem's king and ours is the One destined for defeat, disgrace, death, and complete dependence on God for vindication.

As a foreshadowing of Matthew's account of Jesus' passion, Jesus' entrance into Jerusalem highlights some of this evangelist's perspectives on the events of Holy Week. As we have seen, everything takes place according to the Scriptures. Moreover, Jesus controls every event. While it is not clear whether Jesus' instructions to the disciples concerning the donkey and her colt (vv. 2-3) reflect an arrangement Jesus made with the owner or indicate divine foreknowledge, it is clear that Jesus is in control. Finally, as the meek and humble king, Jesus maintains his identity as Lord and Son of David even as he suffers. Any of these themes provide rich possibilities for connecting the processional gospel and passion narrative homiletically. The preacher might also effectively contrast the way Jesus enters the city of Jerusalem with the way that Jesus leaves it—alone, rejected, and mocked (Matt. 27:32-44).

Psalmody
Psalm 118:1-2, 19-29 (RCL)

Psalm 118 suggests a thanksgiving liturgy on the occasion or anniversary of a major victory or deliverance. In verses 1-2, the assembly is called to give thanks to and praise God for God's enduring mercy. While not written as a response to the gospel reading for the Procession with Palms, images in verses 19-29 suggest that Palm/Passion Sunday is the occasion for victory, deliverance, and praise. These images include the righteous entering through the gate of the Lord (v. 20); the stone that the builders rejected becoming the chief cornerstone (v. 22); cries of "Hosanna!" and "Blessed is the one who comes in the name of the LORD" (vv. 25-26); and a procession with branches (v. 27). In fact, in all four gospels, Psalm 118:26 is used by the crowds to praise and hail Jesus on his entry into Jerusalem. Though the occasion for celebration has changed since the psalm was originally used liturgically, the psalm's purpose remains the same. The assembly acknowledges salvation as God's wondrous act (vv. 22-24), prays for salvation—"Hosanna" or "Save us" (v. 25)—and blesses the victor (cf. vv. 10-12) who enters in God's name.

Liturgy of the Passion (RCL) / Palm Sunday: At the Mass (LFM)

First Reading
Isaiah 50:4-9a (RCL)
Isaiah 50:4-7 (LFM)

The first reading for the Sunday of the Passion is the poignant third servant song, which describes the servant's suffering and affliction. Read on this day, one might gravitate to the servant not rebelling, giving his back to those who strike and his cheeks to those who pull out the beard, and not hiding his face from insults and spitting. We cannot help but think of Jesus' treatment at the hands of the soldiers (Matt. 27:27-31). The words *vindicate, adversaries,* and *declare me guilty* (vv. 7-9) certainly suggest a trial. Yet, the description of affliction is not as important as the servant's declaration of confidence in God.

The servant proclaims what the Lord God has done for him four times (vv. 4, 5, 7, 9). The Lord God gave the servant the tongue of a teacher. The Lord God awakens and opens the servant's ear, and (twice) the Lord God helps the servant. This is not a song of lament but a song of confidence in God. "… I know that I shall not be put to shame; the one who vindicates me is near" (vv. 7-8). So the servant is unwavering in his obedience to God, even in the face of opposition and abuse. The servant sets his face like flint and summons his adversaries to confront him.

The song further indicates that the reason the servant is afflicted is because the servant spoke what he heard the Lord God saying. In the words of the song, the servant "sustain[ed] the weary with a word" (v. 4). The servant sustains the faint, the powerless, the weary, and the exhausted (cf. Isa. 40:29-31). This is more than a word of comfort. The servant speaks a word of "insistence that the truth of Yahweh contradicts and denies the power and erodes the authority of Babylon … energizing the exiles to their distinctive identity in a context where that identity is at risk."[1]

And God sustains the servant. The servant can bear assaults because God helps him. So the servant rejects the conclusion that those who see his affliction might draw—that the servant is being put to shame because he is guilty in God's eyes. Instead, the servant assents to and accepts affliction as the consequence of faithfully speaking the word he received from God.

On the Sunday of the Passion, the church identifies the servant as Jesus. In these words from Isaiah, the church finds Jesus' own commentary on his passion. The Lord God opened Jesus' ear to understand the significance of his crucifixion. Jesus knew the righteousness of his obedience. Jesus loved the weary and sought not only to sustain them, but also to deliver them from evil. Rather than shaming and punishing, the Lord God helped Jesus. While the Lord God did not remove Jesus' anguish, God gave Jesus confidence and strength to enter Jerusalem and make his way to the cross.

Psalmody
Psalm 31:9-16 (RCL)

As a response to Isaiah, Psalm 31:9-16 speaks more to suffering than to confidence in God. The psalmist pleads to the Lord for help (v. 9), describes his serious plight (vv. 10-13), expresses confidence in God (vv. 14-15), and asks for deliverance (v. 16). The affliction is physical, psychological, and social (vv. 9-13); the psalmist feels sick, isolated, and disgraced. Enemies ridicule, neighbors mock, and acquaintances avoid as they would a corpse or discard like a shattered dish. If this is to be a portrait of Jesus, it is that of an innocent, unjustly persecuted, accused, and condemned person who seeks refuge in God. Alternatively, this psalm may be the plea of the weary that Jesus sustains with a word, the cry for help from those that Jesus delivers on the cross.

Psalm 22:8-9, 17-18, 19-20, 23-24 (LFM)

Psalm 22 is the primary Old Testament passage used by the gospel writers to present and interpret Jesus' passion. Like Psalm 31, Psalm 22 is a prayer for help by one who suffers. The best-known connection between this psalm and Jesus' passion is the psalm's first sentence: "My God, my God, why have you forsaken me?" (cf. Matt. 27:46). Features of the psalmist's experience also appear in Matthew's account of Jesus' suffering: verse 7 in Matthew 27:39; verse 8 in 27:43; and verse 18 in 27:35. By using the experiences of the one who prays in the psalm, the gospels connect Jesus and the psalmist. In this way, the passion of Jesus is set within the established faith tradition. Jesus' suffering and death fulfills the Scriptures.

Second Reading
Philippians 2:5-11 (RCL)
Philippians 2:6-11 (LFM)

This is not the day to preach, "Let the same mind be among you that was in Christ Jesus" (v. 5). Paul seems to know that exhorting our hearers to have the same disposition that Christ had or to embrace Christ Jesus as their example is an unrealistic challenge. Paul begins by telling what Jesus did *not* do. Unlike Adam (cf. Gen. 3:5, 22) and us, Christ did not desire to be like God. What Adam and we desire, Christ is content to forgo. This distance between Jesus and us is particularly striking on Passion Sunday. Perhaps this is why *Lectionary for Mass* does not include verse 5 in the pericope.

Since we cannot be like Christ, we might understand Paul's command to mean, "Let the same mind be among you that you have in Christ Jesus."[2] Paul commands his hearers to have the attitude that belongs to those who are in Christ. Paul then proclaims both Jesus' attitude and the gospel events that make us "in Christ Jesus." As such, this "christological hymn" provides a way of poetically describing, interpreting, and understanding Christ's passion in terms of Christ's voluntary, self-giving humiliation and his exaltation by God. Humiliation is Christ's action, rather than something that happened to Christ or that someone did to Christ. Exaltation is God's work.

Philippians makes plain that the One who suffers and dies is none other than God. Christ was in the form of God; Jesus made God visible. Though Christ possessed equality with God, Christ chose not to use it for his own advantage. Instead, Jesus emptied himself and became human. Rather than claiming the form of the Lord, Jesus took the form of a slave. Christ's obedience unto death is a continuation or deepening of his self-giving. In his self-giving and humiliation, Christ reveals what God is like; we see "the form of God." Thus, Philippians declares that Christ's self-emptying is part of God's plan.

The use of the word *therefore* in verse 9 indicates that, because Christ emptied himself, God has "highly exalted" him. God bestowed on Christ the status and honor that Christ did not claim for himself. Jesus is given the name "that is above every name" (v. 9), and every creature "in heaven and on earth and under the earth" (v. 10) acknowledges that Jesus is Lord. Jesus is now exalted to the highest place possible— universally acknowledged as equal with God. On the Sunday when we read Christ's Passion, this hymn proclaims how it is that we are in Christ Jesus.

Gospel
Matthew 26:14—27:66 or 27:11-54 (RCL, LFM)

The gospel reading opens with Judas offering to betray Jesus for money (Matt. 26:14-16), a sharp contrast to the unnamed woman who lavished Jesus' head with an alabaster jar of expensive ointment (Matt. 26:6-13). While the woman prepares for Jesus' burial by spending extravagantly, Judas prepares for Jesus' burial by naming the price of betrayal—thirty pieces of silver, the price of a slave gored by an ox (cf. Exod. 21:32). At his last Passover, Jesus makes clear that he is aware of Judas's betrayal, which will take place according to the Scriptures (26:20-25). In this way, Matthew quickly makes evident that Jesus knows what is happening to him and why it must happen. In fact, Matthew's account of the arrangements to celebrate Passover (26:17-19) emphasizes Jesus' taking charge of the situation and willingly meeting his fate. While Judas and his conspirators seek "an opportune time" to seize Jesus (26:16), Jesus announces, "My time [*kairos*] is near" (26:18). That the disciples "did as Jesus directed them" (26:19) suggests that Jesus has carefully orchestrated the events of his passion.

At the Passover table, Jesus performs the actions that would have been familiar at Sabbath and holiday meals; Jesus' "blessing" (26:26) is not so much a consecration as a thanksgiving. Yet, Jesus gives new meaning to the familiar actions: sharing in Jesus' bread means sharing in his death. Jesus' description of the cup as "my blood of the covenant" (26:28) echoes Moses' sealing God's covenant with Israel by sprinkling the people with animal's blood (Exod. 24:8). The phrase "for the forgiveness of sins" (26:28) is Matthew's distinctive contribution to New Testament accounts of the Eucharist, and is the climax of the Matthean theme of Jesus' power to forgive sins (see Matt. 1:21; 5:23-24; 6:12, 14, 15; 9:6; 18:21-35). That Jesus tells the disciples to eat and drink contributes to the theme of Jesus controlling events in the Passion. Jesus also knows in advance that Judas will betray him, that the disciples will all desert him, and when Peter will deny him.

Jesus then brings the disciples to Gethsemane, where he prays and is arrested (26:36-56). The place is packed as pilgrims unable to find lodging in Jerusalem are camping out. Amid this chaos, Jesus prays three times, first that this cup or fate might pass from him and then that God's will be done (26:39, 42, 44). The attentive listener will hear echoes of the Lord's Prayer: "My Father, your will be done." When Jesus finishes praying, he announces that the time of his passion and death is at hand (26:45). Jesus has made himself available to be arrested by remaining in Gethsemane because he is convinced, through prayer, that it is God's will. On cue,

Judas arrives with a crowd. Aware of the crowds in Gethsemane and the possibility of a riot, Judas and his co-conspirators arranged for a signal. Yet, Jesus seems to give Judas permission to seize him (26:50). The cutting off of the ear of the high priest's slave provides Jesus with the occasion to explain why Jesus—and his heavenly Father—permits Jesus to be arrested: so that the Scriptures might be fulfilled (26:54). Jesus asks whether the crowd came to seize him as a *bandit* (26:55); the word has connotations of a political revolutionary or even a terrorist as opposed to a robber. The point is that the crowd comes after Jesus as if he was a suicide bomber about to carry out his mission in the Temple during Passover, or at least at the place where innocent pilgrims were camping out. Jesus rebukes these charges by telling his companion to put his sword back into its place and by not calling upon his Father to send him twelve legions of angels.

Those who seized Jesus take him to Caiaphas. Following Mark, Matthew juxtaposes Jesus' "trial" before the high priest and Peter's denial (26:57-75), highlighting the contrast between Jesus' faithfulness and Peter's (and our) cowardice. Jesus is accused of threatening to destroy the Temple (26:61). This talk would have threatened the chief priests and elders, who were in charge of and controlled the Temple. Threatening to destroy the Temple would also have threatened the common folk because the rebuilding and upkeep of the Temple was the major industry of Jerusalem. The chief priest then orders Jesus to state under oath before God whether he is "the Messiah, the Son of God" (26:63). By "Messiah," the chief priest means a political revolutionary. For Matthew, the false testimony against Jesus is that he said he was able to destroy and rebuild the Temple; Jesus did not threaten the Temple. Also, Jesus does not describe himself as Messiah in political or revolutionary terms. So, while the charges against Jesus are serious, the trial is a sham. That the trial is a charade becomes obvious as the judges spit at, strike, and slap Jesus. Still, Jesus remains faithful to God's will. At a morning proceeding, the chief priests and elders condemn Jesus to death, bind him, and hand Jesus over to Pilate (27:1-2).

Judas's death (27:3-10) has no parallel in the other gospels (cf. Acts 1:18-19). In Matthew, Judas commits suicide because he betrayed innocent blood. The priests purchase a field to bury foreigners, which is known as the Field of Blood because it was purchased with "blood money." Judas's death both confirms Jesus' warning at the Last Supper and fulfills the Scripture (Matt. 26:24; Zech. 11:13, with elements of Jer. 18:2-3; 32:7-9). Again, we have evidence that Jesus knew what was to happen, and that what happened was according to God's plan.

Jesus stands before the governor (27:11-26). As the Roman governor, Pilate came to Jerusalem at Passover to supervise the large crowds of pilgrims who converged to celebrate liberation from slavery. Since this was a tense and potentially explosive time, Pilate stood ready to immediately put down any uprising among the people. When Pilate asks Jesus if he is "King of the Jews," Pilate wants to know if Jesus is a political danger connected with popular uprisings. Jesus is executed for being such a threat

(27:29, 37). Pilate's wife warns her husband to "have nothing to do with that just man" (27:19), so Pilate gives the crowds a choice between Jesus and Barabbas. The people, persuaded by their leaders, choose against Jesus. Pilate publicly distances himself from responsibility for Jesus' death (27:24-25) and "all the people" take responsibility for Jesus' execution. Though "all the people" was, in reality, a small number of people and despite the fact that Matthew intended them to represent all Jews opposed to Christianity, on this day, preachers do best to clearly identify "all the people" with all God's people, rather than working through the historical realities of this text or the fact that Matthew treats Pilate sympathetically. Jesus' blood is on *our* hands, not the hands of the Jews.

Matthew's account of Jesus' crucifixion (27:27-44) consists of three scenes: Jesus is mocked as "King of the Jews" (27:27-32); the crucifixion (27:33-37); and Jesus is derided (27:38-44). The soldiers mockingly dress Jesus as a caricature of a king and salute him as they would the emperor. They kneel before Jesus and hail him as king. In so doing, the soldiers ironically and unwittingly speak and act truthfully. The irony continues in the crucifixion. The death sentence nailed on Jesus' cross names him "King of the Jews" (27:37). While Romans interpret it to mean "Jewish revolutionary" and the chief priests and elders dismiss it as false claims made by Jesus' followers and even the people, the truth of Jesus' identity as Messiah is ironically proclaimed by his opponents.

Again, Matthew stresses that Jesus' crucifixion fulfills the Scriptures. That his garments are divided (27:35) echoes Psalm 22:18, and the wine mixed with gall (27:34) echoes Psalm 69:21. Matthew also introduces the theme that the guard watched over Jesus from crucifixion through resurrection. Scripture continues to be fulfilled as the passers-by "shake their heads " at Jesus (27:39), and the bandits insult Jesus (27:44; cf. Pss. 22:7; 69:9; Isa. 53:12).

Matthew narrates Jesus' death (27:45-56) in three scenes: Jesus dies on the cross (27:45-50); the signs of the significance of Jesus' death (27:51-54); and the women who stand as witnesses (27:55-56). Like Mark, Matthew assumes Jesus' physical suffering and focuses on the significance of Jesus' death. Jesus "breathed his last" (27:50) or gave up his spirit, and died according to the Scriptures. Matthew alludes to several passages to make this case. The darkness at noon (27:45) suggests Amos 8:9, and the vinegar-filled sponge Psalm 69:21. Jesus' words from the cross are the first words of Psalm 22, and suggest the righteous sufferer who laments his suffering but places his fate in God's hands. The verb "cry out" with the adverb "again" (27:50) suggests that Jesus repeated Psalm 22 before dying.

Matthew describes signs, including the resurrection of the saints in Jerusalem, which point to the significance of Jesus' death. Matthew's description is based on Ezekiel 37:1-14—Ezekiel's vision of the dry bones returning to life. By using this passage, Matthew shows that Jesus' death marks a turning point in God's relationship with humanity because it makes the resurrection of human beings possible. The curtain of the Temple is torn in two. The earth shakes and rocks are split. The tombs of the saints are opened and they are raised. After Jesus' resurrection, which Matthew anticipates while describing Jesus' death, the raised saints come out of their tombs and appear to many in Jerusalem. According to Ezekiel's vision, the resurrection of the dead signifies the restoration of Israel. When the centurion and the guard who had overseen Jesus since his arrest witnessed these signs, they confess that Jesus is "Son of God." Rather than the execution of a revolutionary, Jesus' death was willed by God, in accordance with the Scriptures, as central to God's plan of salvation. Jesus' body is placed in the tomb (27:57-61) and a guard of soldiers is posted there (27:62-66). Jesus is dead and both friends—including Joseph of Arimathea, Mary Magdalene, and the other Mary—and enemies represented by the Roman guard know where he was buried.

One thread running throughout Matthew's account of the Passion is that Jesus dies willingly. Tying together Jesus' entry into Jerusalem, where Jesus obtains the donkey and colt by the statement, "The Lord has need of them" (21:3), and the Last Supper, where Jesus obtains the upper room with the statement, "I will keep the Passover at your house with my disciples" (26:18), makes clear that, in Matthew, at every step of the journey, Jesus is in far more control, both of himself and the situation, than his captors are. Jesus is not a victim. He rejects the sword and refuses to call an army of angels. Jesus does not have to die. Jesus chooses to die.

Jesus chooses to die because this is Jesus' *kairos*, his time of fulfillment of the Scriptures. Jesus enters into this time willingly, in trust and obedience to God. In this way Jesus is revealed as God's Son. In fact, Jesus is killed for being who he truly is. At his trial, Jesus is condemned for being God's Son. At the cross, the onlookers and bandits mock Jesus for being the Son of God. And after his death, the soldiers confess that Jesus is truly the Son of God. The curtain of the Temple tears in two, declaring that the God of Jesus will allow nothing to keep us from God.

The good news is that we know God in Jesus' willing and obedient suffering and death. This Passion account declares all that Jesus was willing to do, the price that Jesus was willing to pay, the depth of love that Jesus was willing to express for us who praise him one moment and condemn him the next. Why did Jesus have to die? Jesus did not have to die. Jesus chose to die for us because that's who God is.

Notes

1. Walter Brueggemann, *Isaiah 40–66*, Interpretation: A Bible Commentary for Teaching and Preaching (Louisville: Westminster John Knox, 1998), 122.
2. *The New Interpreter's Bible* (Nashville: Abingdon, 2000), 11:507.

April 18, 2011
Monday in Holy Week

Revised Common Lectionary (RCL)
Isaiah 42:1-9
Psalm 36:5-11
Hebrews 9:11-15
John 12:1-11

Lectionary for Mass (LFM)
Isaiah 42:1-7
Psalm 27:1, 2, 3, 13-14

John 12:1-11

From the inception of Holy Week in fourth-century Jerusalem, Monday, Tuesday, and Wednesday were celebrated with the established order of office and eucharist, rather than with special services. Today, congregations might observe these days with morning or evening prayer, a contemplative eucharist, or a service that includes a ritual action appropriate to the appointed readings. On Monday, for example, that might be anointing. One important function of these three days is to turn worshipers' attention from themselves to Jesus, since the readings appointed for these days are related to Jesus' passion and crucifixion. This is the time for Christians to reflect upon and bring to a close their personal journey from the ash of Lent's first Wednesday through six weeks of self-examination and disciplined devotion. By the time that we enter into the Great Three Days, we are to be free to fully attend to the church's celebration of Jesus' death and resurrection, rather than focusing on our own sin and death. Preachers might approach these three days as moves in a continuing sermon or as a sermon series by using a common approach, such as contemplating a different scriptural image each day, identifying with a biblical character, or reinforcing the common purpose of slowing our lives and enlivening our spirits as we anticipate the Great Three Days. Most important, these sermons are about Jesus, not about us. Rather than providing exegetical commentary, I attempt to demonstrate how these sermons might connect by relating the Old Testament and gospel readings across these three days.

First Reading
Isaiah 42:1-9 (RCL)
Isaiah 42:1-7 (LFM)

I cannot help but hear these words from the prophet Isaiah as *God's call to Jesus:* "Here is my servant, whom I uphold, my chosen, in whom my soul delights; I have put my spirit upon him" (42:1). How can we hear these words and not think of Jesus at the Jordan—when "the heavens were opened to him and he saw the Spirit of God descending like a dove and alighting on him. And a voice from heaven said, 'This is my Son, the Beloved, with whom I am well pleased'" (Matt. 3:16-17).

We, like Isaiah's coastlands, "wait for [Jesus'] teaching" (42:4). Recall the Sermon on the Mount (Matt. 5:1-48; 6:24-34), which we heard on those Sundays after the Epiphany. Or, closer to where we are, remember Jesus' conversation with Nicodemus (John 3:1-17). We look to Jesus to "bring forth justice to the nations" (42:1). Perhaps that's what a woman of Samaria was looking for when Jesus encountered her at a well (John 4:5-42). And I cannot hear Isaiah speak of "open[ing] the eyes that are blind" (42:7) without thinking of the man born blind whom Jesus healed and the faith community expelled because of its own blindness (John 9:1-41). And when it comes to "bring[ing] out the prisoners from the dungeon, from the prison those who sit in darkness" (42:7), is there any cell stronger than the cell that held Lazarus (John 11:1-45), the cell that awaits us all?

How wonderful to see God give glory to Jesus. How amazing to witness as the former things pass away, and God in Christ now declares new things. I think it's safe to say that we all want to be part of that. But Isaiah and this Holy Week remind us that there is more to God's call for Jesus than teaching, signs, and the assurance of being the one in whom God is well pleased. Isaiah clues us to what God calls Jesus to do this week: "He will not cry or lift up his voice, or make it heard in the street" (42:2). And Jesus stood silent before Caiaphas and would not answer Pilate (Matt. 26:63; 27:14). Only God heard Jesus' distress in Gethsemane, and even then Jesus subordinated his distress to God's will (Matt. 26:39-44).

"A bruised reed he will not break," Isaiah declares, "a dimly burning wick he will not quench" (42:3). With scarlet robe on his back and crown of thorns on his head, Jesus held a reed in his right hand, even as they knelt before him and mocked him (Matt. 27:27-30). If we are looking for our place in the story this week, we are right there. We are the reed in Jesus' right hand. When it comes to considering God's call, the call that God extends to Jesus and to us, of ourselves we are little more than bruised reeds and dimly burning wicks. But rather than breaking us and quenching us, Jesus goes to the cross for us. There his body is broken for us bruised reeds. There his life is quenched for us dimly burning wicks. Considering God's call, Jesus faithfully brings forth God's justice. He does not grow faint and is not crushed until he has established justice in the earth. Only then does Jesus cry again with a loud voice and breathe his last (cf. Matt. 27:50).

Psalmody
Psalm 36:5-11 (RCL)
Psalm 27:1, 2, 3, 13-14 (LFM)

Psalm 36 provides a vision of God's love (vv. 5-9) and a request for God's continued lovingkindness, favor, and protection (vv. 10-11). God's love stretches from the heavens to the great deep. It fills the whole house (cf. John 12:3). Psalm 22 is the primary Old Testament passage used by the gospel writers to present and interpret Jesus' passion. (For more commentary, see the Psalm for Palm/Passion Sunday, p. 198.)

Second Reading
Hebrews 9:11-15 (RCL)

The preacher can use the reading from Hebrews to provide an explanation of Jesus' death on the cross. While these verses contrast Jesus' sacrifice with those of the Old Testament, preachers are careful not to discount or dismiss those people of faith. The people of the Old Testament "clung to the promises of God even when they could not see how these promises would be fulfilled. They were, then, people in waiting, people on a journey toward a land they could not see, and everything about their approach toward God carried the symbolism of the transitory.... . They were reaching forward to a God they could not grasp, and now God has reached back to take their hands."[1]

These verses present Christ's high priestly offering of himself as a new sacrifice. Following the structure of verses 1-10, where the place and ritual of the earthly tabernacle are described, Christ is presented as improving on the old sacrifice and accomplishing the "good things"—access to God and the perfecting of the conscience (vv. 8-9)—once for all. Hebrews invites us to understand the crucifixion not only as Jesus dying but also as Jesus entering God's very presence once and for all. There, Christ offered his own blood to establish the new covenant for all. Christ offered his own life to relate us fully and finally to God. In so doing, Christ secures for us freedom—from sin, from death, from all that enslaves us—that is eternal.

Gospel
John 12:1-11 (RCL, LFM)

There was so much going on at Mary and Martha's house the night of that dinner party. Lazarus had come home from the dead, and a great crowd had shown up to see him. The chief priests dropped by. And you know how nervous folks get when the clergy show up at a party. And then Mary did that thing with the oil—anointing Jesus' feet and wiping them with her hair. Right in front of God and everyone. Mary used so much oil that the whole house stunk of perfume. No wonder a fight broke out. It seems the dispute was about the oil. Judas claimed he wanted to use the oil to liberate the poor; but really, Judas wanted to use the oil to make himself rich.

There is so much going on at our eucharistic dinner party on Monday of Holy Week. We who by baptism have come home from the dead are here. As in Bethany, our house is full of crowds abuzz about the latest news. There's the war(s) and the economy, of course. Then there are the daily battles of school, work, career, church, family, friendship, relationship … and getting ready for the Great Three Days and Easter.

Wouldn't it be great if someone would do something outrageous, like Mary did? Wouldn't it be wonderful if someone would do something that would shock this house into stopping? Amidst all the busyness of that dinner party, Mary sees it. Jesus said, "Leave her alone. She bought it so that she might keep it for the day of my burial." How long had Mary kept that oil? And how did Mary know that this was the time to bring it out? While these things are fun to think about, they really don't matter. Mary sees that the day of Jesus' burial is drawing near, and that nothing else matters. And moved by love or gratitude or devotion or faith, Mary pours her oil, Mary pours herself, out in extravagance.

We know that our remembrance of the day of Jesus' burial draws near. It's less than a week away. On the cross Jesus brings war-torn nations, cumbersome ecclesial processes, questionable public policies, departed loved ones, unreconciled relationships, and a dying creation home from death. In the midst of our busyness, how will we prepare for that day?

What if we make today about wasting costly oil? What if, aware of the coming day of Jesus' burial, and moved by love or gratitude or devotion or faith, we make today about doing something for someone else that is so wonderfully wasteful, so shockingly extravagant, so pleasingly provocative that this whole house stops to smell the fragrance of Jesus' burial?

Okay, it's fun to think about, but we'll never do it. We're just too busy. Or, we will feel foolish. Or, it will seem like such a waste. So maybe we can carry the image of wasting costly oil for others with us as we unite in prayer, as we share Christ's peace, as we make our way to the table, and return to the busyness of our day. And maybe, as we carry out our busyness, we can try real hard to smell the fragrance of Jesus' burial. For it does fill this whole house.

Note

1. Thomas G. Long, *Hebrews*, Interpretation: A Bible Commentary for Teaching and Preaching (Louisville: John Knox, 1997), 98.

April 19, 2011
Tuesday in Holy Week

<table>
<tr><td>**Revised Common Lectionary (RCL)**</td><td>**Lectionary for Mass (LFM)**</td></tr>
<tr><td>Isaiah 49:1-7</td><td>Isaiah 49:1-6</td></tr>
<tr><td>Psalm 71:1-14</td><td>Psalm 71:1-2, 3-4a, 5-6ab, 15, 17</td></tr>
<tr><td>1 Corinthians 1:18-31</td><td></td></tr>
<tr><td>John 12:20-36</td><td>John 13:21-33, 36-38</td></tr>
</table>

The readings appointed for Tuesday in Holy Week celebrate the global ramifications and world-changing implications of Jesus' death on the cross. God expands Jesus' mission from bringing back Jacob and gathering Israel to bringing salvation to the end of the earth. Thus, Jesus declares that, when he is lifted up from the earth, he will draw all people to himself. Paul provides an extended meditation on the meaning of the cross: as the power and wisdom of God, which turns the way humanity views and understands the world on its head. Since the cross is so central in these readings, worship leaders might consider ways of making the cross central in worship.

First Reading
Isaiah 49:1-7 (RCL)
Isaiah 49:1-6 (LFM)

Isaiah 49:1-6 is a servant song with a word of elaboration appended to the end (v. 7). Some scholars understand the servant song as a thanksgiving hymn from an individual (see vv. 4-6), others as the commissioning of a prophet (see vv. 1-3). The first four verses constitute the servant's reflection on his vocation and include a note of dejection: "I have labored in vain, I have spent my strength for nothing and vanity" (v. 4). God commissions the servant against the backdrop of prior activity. The Lord formed the servant from the womb, to bring Jacob back to God and to gather Israel to the Lord (v. 5). Though the servant feels dejected, God counts his mission as "too light a thing" and recommissions the servant to bring God's salvation to the end of the earth (v. 6). In verse 7, the Lord assures that, though the servant is presently deeply despised, abhorred by the nations, and the slave of rulers, the servant will succeed in binging salvation to God's people everywhere. So, the servant addresses this song to the "coastlands, [to] peoples from far away" (v. 1).

If we join the church and approach Isaiah's servant songs as speaking of Jesus, we hear the Lord say to Jesus, "It is too light a thing that you should be my servant to raise up the tribes of Jacob and to restore the survivors of Israel; I will give you as a light to the nations, that my salvation may reach to the end of the earth" (Isa. 49:6). God gives Jesus as a light to the nations, so that God's salvation may reach to the end of the earth. This theme is echoed in the gospel reading where some Greeks, representing "peoples from far away," wish to see Jesus. Jesus refers to himself as the light, saying, "The light is with you for a little longer," and declares, "And I, when I am lifted up from the earth, will draw all people to myself" (John 12:35, 32). This servant song is Jesus' declaration to God's people everywhere that his death on the cross will bring them God's salvation.

Psalmody
Psalm 71:1-14 (RCL)
Psalm 71:1-2, 3-4a, 5-6ab, 15, 17 (LFM)

Psalm 71 includes sentences and motifs found both in Psalms 22 and 31, which are used in telling the passion story, and the reading from Isaiah appointed for this day (cf. v. 6). The psalm is a prayer for help, which is prayed as a way of seeking refuge in the Lord. Petitions for help are interwoven with declarations of trust and descriptions of trouble. Confidence in God outweighs concern over trouble (v. 5). Read during Holy Week, the words, "I have become a portent to many" (v. 7), declare that Jesus' suffering is a sign that calls for understanding and response.

Second Reading
I Corinthians 1:18-31 (RCL)

Paul explains Jesus' death on the cross as the wisdom and power of God. The cross is God's shocking intervention in history to save and transform the world. Paul uses Old Testament passages in verses 19 and 31 to show that God judges and saves in ways that defy human expectations. Paul also names the gospel's divisiveness; since the cross defies human notions of wisdom and power, some will consider the message of the cross to be foolishness and others will regard it as power. Those who regard the message of the cross as foolishness perish; those who receive it as a manifestation of God's power are saved.

Wisdom is the theme of verses 18-24; quoting Isaiah 29:14, Paul declares that, on the cross God destroys human wisdom, rendering it null and void. Power is the theme of verses 26-31. God chooses to demonstrate divine power through the shameful and powerless death of a crucified Messiah. Ethnicity provides the social framework for the discussion of wisdom (Jews); social division provides the backdrop for Paul's discussion of power (Greeks). Verse 25 summarizes the passage: even while saving us, God turns our ways of seeing and understanding the world upside down.

Paul also makes clear that the message of the cross is for all people. In verses 22-24, Paul presents the message about Christ crucified in the presence of all humanity, which Paul describes in common Jewish categories—the people (Jews) and the nations (Greeks). Though the two groups demand different things (signs, wisdom), they are a common humanity in their unresponsiveness to the gospel.

While a crucified Messiah may not surprise us, we nevertheless trust our notions of wisdom and power more than the message of the cross. We sometimes dismiss preaching Christ crucified as impotent. We feel that we need to tell people what to do. Better yet, we need to do something ourselves. Unsure of the power of the gospel, we seek to exercise power of our own. In Paul's language, we find other things to boast about (v. 29). On this day, Paul makes clear that Christ Jesus became for us God's wisdom and our righteousness, sanctification, and redemption (v. 30). A sermon based on this passage boasts of the world-changing power of Jesus' death on the cross.

Gospel
John 12:20-36 (RCL)

Today Jesus concludes his public ministry. Some Greeks say, "We wish to see Jesus" (vv. 20-22). These Gentiles want to accept Jesus as the One who reveals God. Their presence and desire shows that the Pharisees' statement has come true: "The world has gone after him" (12:19). Jesus responds that the hour has come and explains what this means for him, for his followers, and for "the Jews." Jesus bids farewell in terms of grains of wheat. Jesus speaks of his death on a cross. And after Jesus says this, Jesus departs and hides from the crowd. The next time the world sees Jesus, Jesus will be lifted up from the earth, dying on a cross, driving out the ruler of this world, drawing all people to himself.

We, too, wish to see Jesus. We who know the story so well honestly, desperately, wish to see Jesus. We who hear the word, wash the feet, strip the altar, adore the cross, light the new fire, splash the water, eat the bread, and drink the cup, we want nothing more than that Jesus will not be hidden from us.

Jesus tells us where to look. Jesus tells us to look to the cross. But even as we make the sign of the cross, even as we carry the cross, even as we mark newly baptized and newly absolved Christians with the cross, these are but hints, echoes, images, reminders of the cross on which Jesus died for us. We cannot go to Golgotha and see our Savior strung out on the cross.

So how do we really, truly, honestly see Jesus during this Holy Week? If we cannot see Jesus, perhaps we should look for those who follow him. If we cannot see the cross, we can see the grains of wheat. We can see those who by dying to themselves bear much fruit. We can see those who follow by serving. We can see those who by losing their life in this world give a glimpse of eternal life. They are right here. They surround us right now. Somewhere in an arm's-length or a phone-call's reach are those grains of wheat who choose to follow Jesus by losing their life for us.

So often we get overwhelmed by all that the gospel calls us to be. So often we get angry because we're doing such a bad job of being it. We get impatient that the inclusive reign of God is coming so slowly. We become demoralized because expressions of justice and mercy feel so unfair.

But you know, when you dig around in the dirt of the church, you find that it is filled with grains of wheat. Everywhere you touch you find followers of Jesus who in some way have chosen to fall into the dirt of the church and die to themselves, rather than remain alone. The church's dirt is filled with grains of wheat who give a glimpse of eternal life in the way they choose to lose their life. And sometimes they do that for us.

Perhaps we can keep these grains of wheat in mind this week as we unite in prayer, share Christ's peace, make our way to the table, and return to the dirt of our lives and the world. Maybe we can try real hard to reach out and touch one of those grains of wheat. Or, better yet, maybe we could allow one of those grains of wheat to take root in the dirt that surrounds us. Who knows, we may end up seeing Jesus.

John 13:21-33, 36-38 (LFM)

See commentary on the gospel for Wednesday in Holy Week, p. 214.

April 20, 2011
Wednesday in Holy Week

In Western Christianity, Wednesday in Holy Week is sometimes known as "Spy Wednesday," indicating that it is the day that Judas Iscariot first conspired with the Sanhedrin to betray Jesus for thirty silver coins (cf. Matt. 26:14-16; Mark 14:10-11; Luke 22:3-6). Egeria (c. 384), a fourth-century pilgrim to the Holy Land, reports that, on Wednesday night during Holy Week in Jerusalem, "a presbyter … reads the passage about Judas Iscariot going to the Jews and fixing what they must pay him to betray the Lord. The people groan and lament at this reading in a way that would make you weep to hear them."[1] Yet, preachers must be careful not to make villains of or blame either Judas or the Jews. We all are Jesus' betrayers. Worship on this day might include confession and forgiveness or prepare the community for the confession and absolution that is part of the Maundy Thursday liturgy.

First Reading
Isaiah 50:4-9a (RCL, LFM)

Rather than repeat the exegetical commentary on this pericope, which is provided for Palm/Passion Sunday, I offer a meditative commentary here. On Wednesday of Holy Week, I cannot help but hear these words from the prophet Isaiah as *Jesus' faithful response* to God's call.

"Morning by morning GOD wakens—wakens my ear to listen as those who are taught. The Lord GOD has opened my ear" (vv. 4-5). What do you suppose Jesus is hearing this week? Perhaps Jesus heard Mary sobbing as she "took a pound of costly perfume made of pure nard, anointed Jesus' feet, and wiped them with her hair"

(John 12:3). We know that Jesus heard Judas protest. And we know what Jesus made of what he heard. "Jesus said, ... 'She bought it so that she might keep it for the day of my burial'" (John 12:7). We know that Jesus heard Philip and Andrew tell him that some Greeks wanted to see him. And we know what Jesus made of what he heard. "Jesus answered them, 'The hour has come for the Son of Humanity to be glorified. Very truly, I tell you, unless a grain of wheat falls into the earth and dies, it remains just a single grain; but if it dies, it bears much fruit'" (John 12:23-24).

And when, at table, "Jesus was troubled in spirit, and declared, 'Very truly, I tell you, one of you will betray me'" (John 13:21), Jesus heard the stunned silence of his disciples. Then Jesus heard footsteps as one disciple walked away. And we know what Jesus made of what he heard. "When [Judas] had gone out, Jesus said, 'Now the Son of Humanity has been glorified, and God has been glorified in him'" (John 13:31). And we know that Jesus heard taunting and mocking and deriding as he hung on the cross.

Hearing that the day of his burial was approaching, that his hour had come, that now God was to be glorified, hearing the passersby, the chief priests, and the bandits, Jesus "was not rebellious, [Jesus] did not turn backward" (Isa. 50:5). Jesus "gave [his] back to those who struck [him], and [his] cheeks to those who pulled out the beard. [Jesus] did not hide [his] face from insult and spitting" (50:6). In response to God's call, Jesus breathed his last.

Jesus did not close his ear. And Jesus did not rebel. And Jesus did not turn backward. Jesus trusted beyond trust that "the Lord God helps"; that he "will not be put to shame" (50:7); that the One who vindicates is near (50:8). And Jesus sustained the weary with a word (50:4). That word is life. So who will contend with us? With Jesus, we can stand up together (cf. 50:8). We can dare to try to be faithful. Like Jesus, we can open our ear.

Psalmody
Psalm 70 (RCL)

For centuries, the church has prayed Psalm 70 on Wednesday of Holy Week as both Jesus' prayer in his passion and the church's prayer in its neediness. The scornful "Aha!" and gloating (v. 3) are picked up explicitly in Mark's account of the passion (15:29), while the psalm's reference to "those who seek my life" (v. 2) echoes the theme of this day.

Psalm 69:8-10, 21-22, 31, 33-34 (LFM)

The selected verses from Psalm 69 correspond to and provide theological reflection on the life of Jesus and, in fact, are used throughout the New Testament. Jesus is the ultimate example of the kind of person for whom the psalm was composed. Jesus endured reproach for God's sake and by the vindication of the resurrection, gives hope in God's promise of salvation.

Second Reading
Hebrews 12:1-3 (RCL)

The theme of these verses is Jesus as an example of *endurance*—the cross is something Jesus endured (v. 2). In perhaps the most familiar image in this book—"a cloud of witnesses" (v. 1)—the writer of Hebrews gathers the ancient ones whose faithfulness God has confirmed, discussed in chapter 11, to bolster those still running the race of faith. The hearers are exhorted toward self-discipline in an effort to endure in the struggle of faith, whether facing difficult choices, hostility, or even martyrdom.

Yet, more important than the witnesses who surround and bolster us and our own spiritual training, we run the race of faith "looking to Jesus" (v. 2). In fact, we are to look away from everyone and everything else and concentrate singularly on Jesus. Jesus is more than the example on which we focus. Jesus is the One we "look to" for guidance and aid. For Jesus is "the pioneer and perfecter of our faith" (v. 2). Jesus endured the cross and attained faith's goal—to be "seated at the right hand of the throne of God" (v. 2)—and Jesus makes it possible for others to have access to God's presence.

"Therefore, since we are surrounded by so great a cloud of witnesses, …" (v. 1). Whenever I hear these words, I look around the room. When I hear these words on Wednesday of Holy Week, I imagine Jesus looking around the room at those who will witness what he is about to do. And I imagine that Jesus is disappointed by what he sees. Jesus is troubled in spirit. "Very truly, I tell you," Jesus declares, "one of you will betray me" (John 13:21). Now we could play the disciples' game. We could look at each other uncertain of whom Jesus is speaking. But the author of Hebrews invites us to look elsewhere. On this day when we might focus on Judas or be tempted to focus on ourselves, the writer of Hebrews calls us back to "consider" (v. 3)—to reflect seriously upon—Jesus' passion. Jesus endured the hostility of sinners, of which the event of the cross is the culmination. Jesus experienced opposition, abuse, shame, and humiliation. Jesus experienced the suffering that comes from being faithful. Yet, Jesus remained faithful, enduring the cross and disregarding its shame. Jesus achieved the joy set before him—to sit at the right hand of the throne of God—for himself and for us. By "looking to Jesus" (v. 2) and "consider[ing] him who endured" (v. 3), we will not grow weary and faint.

Gospel
John 13:21-32 (RCL)

In the intimacy of the supper, after washing the disciples' feet and teaching them about community, Jesus is "troubled in spirit" (v. 21). Jesus is angry because one of those to whom Jesus offered himself in the foot washing will hand him over. The disciples are uncertain of whom Jesus is speaking (v. 22). In fact, they cannot comprehend what Jesus said (cf. vv. 28-29). We are introduced to "the disciple whom Jesus loved" (v. 23), who plays a significant role in Jesus' passion (cf. John 19:26-27; 20:2-10; 21:7, 20-23). Here the beloved disciple asks Jesus who will betray him.

I find it interesting the way Jesus points out his betrayer. I might have said, "It is the one to whom I extend my anger." But Jesus says, "It is the one to whom I give this piece of bread" (v. 26). Jesus gives his betrayer a piece of bread, a gesture of friendship and hospitality. It would be amazing enough if Judas betrayed Jesus and then repented, and Jesus responded by giving him the piece of bread. But Jesus gives Judas bread from Jesus' own table, knowing that Judas will get up from that table and go out and betray him. "Jesus gives the morsel to the most despised character in the Johannine narrative: Judas."[2] After receiving bread from Jesus' hand, Satan enters Judas and he leaves the light of Jesus' presence to enter the darkness of night.

This sounds to me like the eucharist. This sounds to me like what Jesus does for his betrayers whenever we gather around word and table. Jesus gives us who will betray him not merely the bread of his table. Jesus gives us the bread that is Jesus' own body and the wine that is Jesus' own blood. And Jesus gives us Jesus' very self, knowing that we will get up from the table and go out and betray him. And when we come back the next time and say, "We confess that we have sinned," we tell Jesus that Jesus was right. And no matter how many times we admit that we are betrayers, Jesus extends the bread and the cup, given and shed for you.

Perhaps we can manage, even risk, coming to Jesus' table knowing that we are Jesus' betrayers. Rather than being repentant for what we have done, we can be mindful of what we will do. After receiving the bread, we—like Judas—will go out and betray Jesus. And our betrayal will lead Jesus to the cross, where Jesus offers up his body. Knowing the betrayal we are about to do, Jesus still extends his body to us in that piece of bread. In that piece of bread Jesus extends God's life and love to us who will betray him. And all we can do is receive it.

Notes

1. Egeria, *Travels*, 34, trans. John Wilkinson (London: SPCK, 1971), 134.
2. Francis J. Moloney and Daniel J. Harrington, *The Gospel of John*, Sacra Pagina (Collegeville, Minn.: Liturgical, 1998), 384.

April 21, 2011
Maundy Thursday / Holy Thursday

Revised Common Lectionary (RCL)
Exodus 12:1-4 (5-10) 11-14
Psalm 116:1-2, 12-19
1 Corinthians 11:23-26
John 13:1-17, 31b-35

Lectionary for Mass (LFM)
Exodus 12:1-8, 11-14
Psalm 116:12-13, 15-16bc, 17-18
1 Corinthians 11:23-26
John 13:1-15

The title *Maundy*, from the Latin *mandatum novum* or "a new commandment" (cf. John 13:34), leads many preachers to emphasize what Jesus *commands* his disciples—and us—to do. Jesus gives us a new commandment, to love one another. Since the Second Vatican Council, this emphasis on the new commandment has led to the renewal of priestly vows on Maundy Thursday, a practice embraced by some Lutherans and Anglicans. But Jesus says, "Just as I have loved you, you also should love one another." *"As I have loved you …"* (John 13:34). On Maundy Thursday and the days that follow, we do not run too quickly into the doing. We pause to savor Jesus' love for us. "As I have loved you," Jesus says. On Maundy Thursday, when we remember Jesus' last meal with his disciples, we celebrate Jesus' love feast in four courses. The Maundy Thursday sermon might proclaim the liturgical action that is each course of this love feast as an experience and expression of Jesus' love for us.

In the first course of this meal, confession and forgiveness, Jesus takes away our hunger pangs. Originally the public reconciliation of penitents prior to their readmission to the Eucharist at Easter, this liturgical act might be used effectively to reconcile to the assembly those whose sin is known, are estranged from the Christian community, or have fallen away from the church. Confession and absolution on Maundy Thursday is more commonly understood as the conclusion or completion of the confession the faithful made on Ash Wednesday and lived throughout Lent. The preacher might recall how we have hungered for God's love throughout Lent's forty days. Return to Ash Wednesday, and bring to the congregation's mind how we confessed that, without the nourishment of God's love, our destiny is death. On that day we acknowledged the ways both our world and we are cloaked in death. Throughout Lent we struggled to allow God to breathe us full of new life. Friends gathered to pray; buying groceries became a ministry with the poor; secrets were named and somehow lost their power; and still-grieving people entered into another's grief. Throughout Lent, we owned, we confessed our need of God's love. We also became more mindful of how hungry the people around us are for God's love, of how hungry the people around the world are for God's love, and how we really don't deserve to be filled with God's love because we haven't always been willing to share it. After forty days of living this confession, we bring the confession that we made on that first Wednesday of Lent to a close, offering up the struggles of our Lent. Then we come forward and receive the good news that we are forgiven, which is nothing other than the nourishment of God's love. With our hunger pangs satisfied, we are free to turn and to look not on ourselves but upon our host.

On Maundy Thursday, we look upon our host, Jesus Christ. Towel and basin in hand, Jesus washes the disciples' feet. In the second course of Jesus' love feast, the church washes feet. Ambrose of Milan indicates that washing feet, which was part of the early Milanese baptismal liturgy, was originally understood as part of a symbolic, even sacramental, cleansing. John 13 was read; then the bishop and presbyters washed the feet of the newly baptized. While recognizing that Jesus sets an example of humble service, Ambrose emphasizes Jesus' words to Peter, "Unless I wash you, you have no share with me" (John 13:8). Ambrose explains that, though Peter was clean, Jesus needed to wash Peter's feet to remove hereditary sin or the sin of Adam, "when the serpent tripped him and led him into trespass."[1] The feet are washed to remove the tendency to sin, since our own sins are removed by baptism.

Over time, the church embraced foot washing as a commandment to imitate the humility of Christ, rather than in a more sacramental sense. Today, this meaning of foot washing is artificial and even forced in a culture in which hosts do not have servants wash their guests' feet and guests do not even wash their own feet upon arrival. We need to recover what Ambrose calls the "mystical meaning" in this ministry of humility.[2] Rather than focusing on what we ought to do, overwhelm the hearers with the reality that *Jesus*, our Teacher and Lord—and the author of salvation—washes our feet, and that this is but Jesus' first act of humiliation for us. Jesus redeems us through humble obedience to the will of God. Only after the congregation has grappled with this reality ought the preacher move on to example, instruction, and our obedience, as Jesus teaches that strength and growth in the life of the reign of God do not come by power or authority. They come by humble service. And so we remove footwear and wash feet this day, mindful that our Master is our Servant, and that what is done for us is also to be done by us.

Then we see our host, taking his place at table. In the third course of this love feast, Jesus breaks the bread and shares the cup. Jesus gave us this meal when he was about to die and commanded that we celebrate it as the new and eternal covenant. And so we break the bread and share the cup in remembrance of him. This meal that we share with Jesus in this world is a foretaste of the meal we hope to share with Jesus in the world to come. Even more, it is the remembering of Jesus' body broken and blood outpoured, God's way of preaching the good news that nothing, not even death, will keep God from loving us. But still it is more. It is Christ present among us, here and now. Freeing us from all those things that would separate us from him, binding us together with him as a force to change the world, and pouring into our hearts and lives the power of God to change it.

And in case we want to know how to change the world, we see Jesus, no longer at the table as host. Jesus passes through the garden on his way to the slaughterhouse. Stripped like a dining-room table after the guests have gone, Jesus suffers in freedom and Jesus suffers alone. Jesus suffers apart and Jesus suffers in shame. Jesus suffers in body and Jesus suffers in spirit. Jesus suffers for and with every Christian, for and with everyone, for and with everything that suffers. And so, in the fourth course of Jesus' love feast, we strip our altar once the supper is done.

When it's over, this feast won't feel finished. It won't leave us satisfied. And it shouldn't, because we have two more days. But, after this feast, our hunger will be different. No longer about us, our hunger is to look upon our host, to see Jesus as he dies on the cross and rises from the tomb and celebrates with us the great Easter feast. But we have a long way to go before we get there. And I can feel our spirits growling. So let the feasting begin!

First Reading
Exodus 12:1-4 (5-10) 11-14 (RCL)
Exodus 12:1-8, 11-14 (LFM)

For the writers of the New Testament, the Passover provides a framework for understanding both the death of Jesus and the meal that Jesus shared with his disciples on the night before he died. In the synoptic gospels, the Last Supper is a Passover meal. In the fourth gospel, the Last Supper, as well as Jesus' arrest, trial, and crucifixion, occurs on the Day of Preparation. As the true Passover lamb, Jesus dies on the day that lambs for Passover are slaughtered (cf. John 19:36).

The appointed verses from Exodus 12, which prescribe the liturgical practice for remembering and reenacting the saving events of the exodus, make the connection that Jesus is the true Passover lamb that frees us from the plague of death. Yet, preachers must exercise care in how they make this connection. The Passover celebration remains the way each generation of Israelites both commemorates and participates in the once-for-all event of God freeing them and creating them as a people. Christian proclamation, therefore, avoids both reducing the Passover to a prefiguring of Jesus' death on the cross or implying that the new covenant in Jesus' blood, celebrated in the Lord's Supper, somehow negates or renders obsolete God's covenant celebrated at Passover.

The passage is a divine command, divided into a description of concrete liturgical practices (vv. 1-10) and an interpretation of those practices (vv. 11-13). Verse 14 makes clear that this festival is to be observed perpetually, from generation to generation. In Exodus, the Passover celebration precedes the Passover event (vv. 1, 12).

As an instructional manual for celebrating the Passover, verses 1-10 center on the lamb, which provides both the blood that the people put on their houses and the food (together with unleavened bread and bitter herbs) that the people eat. The instructions indicate the kind of lamb to be used, the way these lambs are to be distributed among the people, and how they are to be used. Most important is that every family unit, and therefore every member of the community, has access to a lamb and can participate in the celebration.

In verses 11-13 eating the lamb and putting lamb's blood on doorposts and lintels are interpreted. Those who eat the lamb do so hurriedly. Their bags are packed; they have shoes on their feet and staffs in their hands. So confident in God's promise, they are ready to leave Egypt with a moment's notice. Eating hurriedly in traveling clothes also lends the festival a sense of danger and anxiety. The blood on the doorposts is a sign that publicly marks the people as saved from destruction, protected by God, and participating in God's promise of freedom and life.

Rather than "explain" the Passover, preachers might assist their hearers in imaginatively entering into the celebration. The preacher might describe how a family carefully selects the lamb and reverently slaughters it. Each member of the family takes a turn painting the doorposts as they discuss God freeing them from oppression and abuse, protecting them from death, and making them participants in God's promise of new life. How does it feel to eat in a hurry, as if, at any moment, someone is going to order you to hop in the car or head for the train? How does it unsettle us in our lives and in the world, as we remain ready to respond to God's saving activity in our midst?

Turning from Passover to Last Supper, what must it have been like for the disciples at that last meal, when Jesus called their unleavened bread his body and the wine they drank his blood? Did the disciples connect Jesus and the Passover lamb, at least for an instant, even if they immediately banished that terrible thought from their minds? When the early church contemplated Jesus' blood painted on the wood of the cross, it saw God's promise of freedom, protection, and deliverance from death. What does it mean in your community and generation to call Jesus our Passover lamb? Surely, it means that we can rely on God's promise in Jesus Christ.

Psalmody
Psalm 116:1-2, 12-19 (RCL)
Psalm 116:12-13, 15-16bc, 17-18 (LFM)

Psalm 116 is a song of thanksgiving from one whose prayer has been answered. In verses 1-2, 5-9, and 15-16, the psalmist acknowledges God as rescuer; in verses 12-14 and 17-19, the psalmist promises to keep the vows the psalmist made. That the one who prays this psalm "will lift the cup of salvation" (v. 13) and "offer to you the sacrifice of thanksgiving" (v. 17) led to Psalm 116 being included in the Passover liturgy as the prayer of anyone saved by God's action in the exodus. As the church came to understand Jesus as Passover lamb and the Lord's Supper as the Christian Passover feast, Psalm 116 was included in the eucharistic liturgy. The psalm becomes the song of Jesus and the church. Jesus provides the cup and sacrifice; they unite the church with Jesus in his death and resurrection.

Second Reading
1 Corinthians 11:23-26 (RCL, LFM)

Paul explains the meaning of the Lord's Supper—and why the individual meals the Corinthian congregation celebrates are not the Lord's Supper (11:20)—by handing on (again) an early Christian tradition. While the tensions in the Corinthian community, made manifest in the way people dine, dress, and speak to each other, might be relevant to many a congregation, this pericope is appointed for Maundy Thursday because it is the oldest literary account of the Last Supper.

Paul's introduction (11:23) reminds the Corinthians that what he previously "handed on" to them, presumably as part of his visit during the first century C.E., is even older than that, since Paul "received" this tradition himself and faithfully passed it on to them. "The tradition that Paul recalls in 11:23-26 is similar to but older than the narrative versions that appear in the synoptic gospels (Matt 26:26-28; Mark 14:22-24; Luke 22:19-20)."[3] Paul says that he received this tradition "from the Lord" (v. 23); Paul indicates that Jesus himself established the tradition of eating the bread as a sign of his death and drinking the cup as a sign of the new covenant. Like the Passover tradition, the teaching about the eucharist that Paul received and handed over was faithfully and authoritatively handed on from one generation to the next. The Lord's Supper, and Paul's teaching about it, is firmly rooted in the memory of the earliest Christians and fully applicable to the lives and community of those to whom it is "handed on." On Maundy Thursday, Paul's teaching is applicable to every Christian community in which Paul's words about the eucharist are read and heard and bread and wine are shared in remembrance of Jesus.

This brief account of the Lord's Supper highlights the beginning and end of a meal, presumably Jesus' Last Supper with the disciples. Verse 23 is translated "on the night when he was betrayed," because the Greek word means "handed over" and is thought to refer to Judas handing over Jesus to the authorities. Yet, Paul's use of the same verb elsewhere suggests that Jesus was handed over *by God* "for our trespasses" (Rom. 4:25). These words might be translated, "on the night when God handed over the Lord Jesus to death for our sake, he took a loaf of bread ..."[4] Paul proclaims Jesus' death as an act of obedience to God's will—as foreshadowed in Isaiah 53—and as God's action by which the world is saved.

The disciples are identified as "you." This pronoun allows the Corinthians—and all who hear these words—to participate in this event. At the beginning of the meal, Jesus performed a thanksgiving ritual—the Jewish *běrăkâ*—over the bread (vv. 23-24). Jesus' words over the cup at the conclusion of the meal recall the "new covenant" announced by Jeremiah (31:31), and suggest that this is a covenantal meal. This supper joins people together and connects them to their God. As the "new covenant," this meal anticipates and is a foretaste of the eschaton.

A key to this tradition is eating and drinking "in remembrance of me" (vv. 24-25). To remember God's saving events in the past is to remember who God is. Even more, remembering whom God is implies reminding God of who God has promised to be. The annual celebration of the Passover was to be "a day of remembrance for you" (Exod. 12:14). As those who celebrate Passover participate in the exodus by remembering and reminding God of God's saving event, so those who eat the bread and drink the cup participate in the saving effects of the death and resurrection of Jesus Christ.

Paul's interpretative contribution to this tradition may be identifying Jesus as "Lord" (v. 26). Paul reminds the Corinthians that, after the night when Jesus was betrayed, after Jesus' death, Jesus was raised as Lord. Jesus is coming as Lord; participation in this meal anticipates, proclaims, and is a participation in Jesus' death, resurrection, and return. By participating in the Lord's Supper, we announce the good news, the revelatory significance, of Jesus' death and resurrection.

A challenge in preaching on this passage is not to produce a catechetical lecture on the meaning of the Lord's Supper. This passage clearly indicates that the story of the events of Jesus' passion and resurrection stood at the center of Paul's—and the early church's—preaching and teaching (cf. 1 Cor. 15:3-5; Gal. 3:1). Rather than providing information, bring to mind the central story that we remember and repeat every time the church gathers at table, and proclaim the good news that through this meal we participate in and proclaim the saving event of Jesus' death and resurrection.

Gospel
John 13:1-17, 31b-35 (RCL)
John 13:1-15 (LFM)

The hour has finally come for Jesus to love us to the end. Throughout John's gospel and Jesus' ministry, we hear repeatedly that the hour had not yet come (cf. John 2:4; 7:30; 8:20). Now, as the third and final Passover in this gospel draws near, Jesus knows that the hour has come for him to turn toward death, "to depart from this world and go to the Father" (v. 1). And so Jesus announces that the hour has come (vv. 31-32). As the betrayer leaves Jesus' table, Jesus proclaims that *now* the Son of Humanity will be glorified, the glory of God will be seen in Jesus' death on the cross (vv. 31-32), and that this will happen "at once" (v. 32). Recalling that moment when the chief priests and the Pharisees sent temple police to arrest Jesus (John 7:32-35), Jesus now says to his disciples what he said then: "I am with you only a little longer. You will look for me; and … now I say to you, 'Where I am going, you cannot come'" (13:33). The hour has come when Jesus is lifted up on the cross, glorifies God and draws all people to himself, and returns to the Father.

The hour will be an ultimate expression of Jesus' love for those whom Jesus called "his own" (v. 1; cf. John 1:11-12; 10:3, 4, 12). Jesus will love them "to the end" (v. 1), both to the end of his life and with a depth of love that, when we reflect upon it, is incomprehensible, even unimaginable. Jesus' death makes the depth of his love for his own known, and this makes God known. Jesus' self-giving love introduces both the foot washing and everything else that is to come.

Knowing that his hour has come, Jesus moves into action (vv. 3-4). He rises from the table, prepares himself to act as a servant, and begins to wash the disciples' feet (vv. 4-5). "Jesus' knowledge (v. 1), even of his betrayer (vv. 2-3), and his love for his own (v. 1), are expressed through actions (vv. 4-5)."[5]

Jesus comes to Simon Peter, who objects to Jesus washing his feet (v. 6). Peter's protestations indicate that his understanding of Jesus' actions conflicts with Jesus' purpose in performing them. Peter cannot comprehend God's revelation in Jesus' words and actions, so Peter refuses to allow Jesus to wash his feet (v. 8). Peter understands that Jesus is overthrowing established practice, but he fails to grasp Jesus' unconditional love for the disciples. Jesus warns Peter that what is at stake is having a share with Jesus (v. 8), an illusion to the relationship with Jesus established in baptism. Jesus has more in mind than giving Peter an example to follow. "To 'have part with Jesus' through washing means to be part of the self-giving love that will bring Jesus' life to an end (cf. v. 1), symbolically anticipated by the footwashing (v. 8)."[6] Peter continues to cling to his own misunderstanding by insisting that Jesus wash his hands and his head as well as his feet. Jesus describes the disciples, save one, as those who have bathed and have no further need to wash, except for the feet. Jesus' knowledge, which comes from his union with "the Father" and acceptance of the divine will, includes knowing who will betray him (vv. 10-11). Here is the depth of Jesus' love. More than the teacher becoming the servant, Jesus loves his own to the end, even though his own misunderstand, protest, resist his love, and even betray him.

As Jesus dresses and resumes his place at table, he asks his own whether they understand what he has done to them (v. 12). Jesus then answers his own question (vv. 13-14). First and most important, the disciples and we need to understand what it means that Jesus is our Teacher and Lord. More than the humility with which Jesus embraces his role, the self-giving love that our Lord and Teacher has for us is limitless. More than redefining status and providing an example of humble service, Jesus provides the example of the self-giving, limitless love with which God loves us and we are to love one another. The disciples are to repeat in their lives Jesus' self-giving love, symbolized in the foot washing (vv. 14-15). More than humble service, more than reordering societal roles, Jesus' example urges disciples to limitless, self-giving love, even for those who misunderstand, protest, resist, and even betray. Loving to the end, loving without limit, loving even to death is the norm of life and conduct for the believing community. Washing feet, humble service, and reordered social roles are simply indications of this love, and are not themselves the goals for which we strive.

The lectionary hammers this point home by adding the new commandment to love one another (vv. 33-35) to the narrative of the foot washing. But before Jesus gives the disciples a new commandment, he calls them "little children" (v. 33). Jesus' limitless love for his failing followers is obvious in the way he lovingly addresses them. Though they misunderstand, fail, and even betray Jesus, the disciples remain his infinitely loved "little children."

Only now do we come to the "new commandment" (vv. 34-35), which too often mistakenly becomes the focus of Maundy Thursday preaching. Jesus commands the disciples to *love* one another. Jesus' new commandment is bigger than *humbly serving* one another or overthrowing the social order. Jesus' command to love matches his own example of loving his own to the end. In John's gospel, in the foot washing, Jesus gives an example (v. 15). The "new commandment" follows Jesus giving the morsel of bread to the one who will betray him (see commentary on the gospel for Wednesday in Holy Week, above). Yet, in both his example and his new commandment, Jesus calls his disciple—and us—to follow him in love so deep that it leads to self-giving death. Jesus makes this explicit when he commands the disciples to love one another "as I have loved you" (v. 34). Inspired by Jesus' love for them, the disciples' limitless, self-giving love, even for those who misunderstand, resist, protest, and even betray, will make Jesus' disciples obvious to everyone (v. 35).

Notes

1. Ambrose, "On the Mysteries," 6.32, in T. Thompson, *On the Sacraments and On the Mysteries,* rev. ed. (London: S.P.C.K, 1950), 136.
2. Ambrose, "On the Mysteries," 6.33, in ibid., 137.
3. Raymond F. Collins and Daniel J. Harrington, *First Corinthians,* Sacra Pagina (Collegeville, Minn.: Liturgical, 1999), 426.
4. Richard B. Hays, *First Corinthians,* Interpretation: A Bible Commentary for Preaching and Teaching (Louisville: John Knox, 1997), 198.
5. Francis J. Moloney and Daniel J. Harrington, *The Gospel of John,* Sacra Pagina (Collegeville, Minn.: Liturgical, 1998), 374.
6. Ibid., 375.

April 22, 2011
Good Friday

Revised Common Lectionary (RCL)
Isaiah 52:13—53:12
Psalm 22
Hebrews 10:16-25 or
  Hebrews 4:14-16; 5:7-9
John 18:1—19:42

Lectionary for Mass (LFM)
Isaiah 52:13—53:12
Psalm 31:2, 6, 12-13, 15-16, 17, 25
Hebrews 4:14-16; 5:7-9

John 18:1—19:42

The Service of the Word in the classical Western liturgy for Good Friday consists of Isaiah's fourth servant song, a selection from Hebrews, and the Johannine passion narrative. Provision is made for preaching following the reading of the Passion. For the Fourth Evangelist, Jesus' passion is the hour of Jesus' glorification and his coronation as king. Jesus, who willingly and completely controls the situation, is enthroned on the cross, where he completes his work of defeating the forces of evil and drawing all people to himself. Isaiah and Hebrews help the church to consider the significance of Jesus' death. Isaiah emphasizes the wrongfulness, humiliation, and suffering of Jesus' death. Hebrews celebrates the access to God that Jesus' death gives us. Preachers need to be careful not to blend or conflate passion accounts, a temptation in services based on Jesus' seven last words from the cross, and inadvertently present either an account of Christ's passion not found in Scripture or an interpretation of Christ's passion unfamiliar to the church.

First Reading
Isaiah 52:13—53:12 (RCL, LFM)

God declares, "The righteous one, my servant, shall make many righteous, and he shall bear their iniquities" (Isa. 53:11). Isaiah's fourth servant song proclaims the suffering of God's servant for many. Isaiah's suffering servant is the suffering community of exiles, whose distress atones for all Israel and brings God's salvation to the nations. Yet, on Good Friday, Christians understand that Isaiah's suffering servant can only be Jesus, who was lifted up from the earth and drew all people to himself (cf. John 12:32). Isaiah provides a way of understanding and proclaiming the significance of Jesus' death on the cross.

Since the servant is *God's* servant, we understand that the pericope both begins and ends with the voice of God, who speaks of "my servant" (52:13). In both 52:13-15 and 53:10-12, which frame the account of the servant's passion, the Lord God declares the servant's glorification. In Isaiah 52:13-15, God announces in public, formal terms the servant's ultimate destiny; the servant will be exalted and glorified. The servant will be exalted before rulers and nations.

Jesus' suffering as God's glorification is a theme found in the readings from John's gospel appointed for Holy Week (John 12:23-24, 28-29, 31-33; 13:31-33). John indicates that Jesus is glorified before rulers and nations when Jesus was crucified and the inscription that Pilate orders to be put on the cross—"Jesus of Nazareth, the King of the Jews"—is written in Hebrew, Latin, and Greek (see John 19:19-20). In 53:10-12, God makes sense of the servant's suffering by revealing that the servant suffers according to God's plan: "it was the will of the LORD to crush him with pain" (v. 10). God will exalt the servant because the servant fulfills God's purposes—obediently pouring out himself unto death, identifying with transgressors, interceding for sinners, and taking on the affliction and death that bear sin away.

We might understand Isaiah 53:1-10 as the confession of the church, which sees Jesus' death bringing God's plan for salvation to completion. Verses 1-3 and 7-9 treat the servant's rejection; verses 4-6 stress the significance of the servant's suffering. This confession is poetic rather than historical or theological, and preachers do best to approach it as such. On Good Friday, we who recall—and in so doing witness— Christ's crucifixion see and comprehend its significance and proclaim the meaning of Christ's passion. The rhetorical question—"Who has believed what we have heard?" (53:1)—makes clear that what followers see in and confess about the servant's suffering is not obvious.

In 53:3-5, the contrast between what those making the confession witness and what they come to understand about what they see is striking. The one whom we accounted stricken, struck down by God, and afflicted, because his appearance was marred beyond human semblance, bears our infirmities and is crushed for our iniquities. The one who was despised and rejected by others, the one from whom others hid their faces endured the punishment that made us whole. His bruises healed us. So the witness declares, "Who has believed what we have heard?" As an answer, the witness declares that the arm of the Lord has been revealed. More than revealing God's own self in the servant's suffering, God reveals a new understanding of the servant's suffering.

To use these verses from Isaiah to proclaim the significance of Jesus' suffering, the preacher might approach them as a poetic retelling of Jesus' suffering and death by lifting up the allusions to Christ's passion. Sermon preparation includes reading the appointed readings from Isaiah and John together and noting connections. For example, the language of verse 5—*wounded, crushed, punishment*—directly suggests that the servant was actively and physically assaulted (see John 19:1-3). That iniquities are laid upon him suggests the servant's innocence (see John 18:38; 19:12). We are told that the servant "did not open his mouth," which recalls Synoptic accounts of Jesus before the high priest. Some versions translate 53:5 as "he was pierced for our transgressions," bringing to mind that "one of the soldiers pierced his side with a spear, and at once blood and water came out" (John 19:34). The declaration that "the LORD has laid upon him the iniquity of us all" (53:6) suggests the cross laid on Jesus and, in fact, is Christian *kerygma* for God's handing over the Son to death (see John 18:30, 35). Verse 6 declares that we are the beneficiaries of the servant's suffering even as we fail to understand what the servant does.

Verses 7-9 provide a straightforward account of the servant's final days. Their mood accentuates the wrongfulness of the servant's death. The comparison to a lamb that is led to the slaughter (53:7) is Passover language, so important in John. Jesus is the "Lamb of God who takes away the sin of the world" (John 1:29). Though the servant is innocent and remains silent, he is violently and aggressively mistreated. "By a perversion of justice he was taken away" (53:8) is a fitting description of Jesus' trial. The declaration that "rulers shall shut their mouths because of him" (52:15) points to Jesus before Pilate (John 18:37-38). "They made his grave with the wicked" (53:9) suggests the place of crucifixion and the criminals crucified on either side of Jesus. That "his tomb [was] with the rich" (53:9) points to Joseph from Arimathea, a rich man who took the body of Jesus, wrapped it in a clean linen cloth, and laid it a new tomb (John 19:38-42).

Psalmody
Psalm 22 (RCL)
Psalm 31:2, 6, 12-13, 15-16, 17, 25 (LFM)

The Revised Common Lectionary and Lectionary for Mass switch the psalms appointed for Palm/Passion Sunday. Therefore, brief commentary was previously provided for both these psalms (see above, p. 198). When we read or sing these psalms on the Sunday of the Passion or Good Friday, we are not to identify, either individually or as an assembly, with the psalmist who prays to or praises God, because that role belongs to Jesus alone on these days. Instead, we are to listen to the words of the psalm as the words of Jesus as a way of experiencing and understanding his passion.

Second Reading
Hebrews 10:16-25 (RCL)
Hebrews 4:14-16; 5:7-9 (RCL ALT., LFM)

Both readings from Hebrews consider the implications of Christ's death on the cross for us. Both readings exhort the people to approach the throne of grace with boldness, to approach with a true heart and with the full assurance of faith. Yet, on

Good Friday, the reason that we can do this is more important than the exhortation, and that reason is Jesus Christ. "Since we have confidence to enter the very presence of God through the new way that Christ opened for us," the author of Hebrews says. "Since we have a great high priest who has passed into God's very presence, …" (cf. Heb. 10:19-20; 4:14). Especially on Good Friday, the preacher so emphasizes "since" that the preacher does not have to say "let us," because the people of God are so moved by Christ's passion that they boldly approach the throne of grace, symbolized today by the cross, which the church adores on this day, with a true heart and the full assurance of forgiveness.

In the reading from chapter 4, Jesus is presented as our great high priest. The writer names him as both "Jesus" and "Son of God" (v. 14). By joining these two names, the author joins the two qualifications of a priest. "Jesus" is one of us. The title "Son of God" indicates that God appoints Jesus. As the One who both shares our humanity and has a special relationship with God, Jesus assures that, when we approach God, we will be met with sympathy and understanding, because Jesus has been tested as we are tested (v. 15). A Good Friday message that arises from this passage is that Jesus experienced completely the human condition.

Jesus, who has been as we are in every respect, "has passed through the heavens" (v. 14) and entered the very presence of God. Jesus opened access to God for us and is in God's presence interceding on our behalf. "That our high priest 'has passed through the heavens' (v. 14) evokes the image of the Jewish high priest on the Day of Atonement, passing through the veil of the Temple and entering the holy of holies, the place of God's presence as symbolized by the ark of the covenant, which rested in the inner chamber of the tabernacle."[1]

Jesus' sympathy with our "weakness" (v. 15) refers to our lack of faithfulness and propensity to turn away from God, since Jesus, who was "without sin," was unwavering in his faithfulness to God. Jesus is not sympathetic because he sinned as we do, but because he was tested in every way that we are.

Hebrews 5:7-9 illustrates both that Jesus was tested in every that we are and that he remained faithful and obedient to God. The author provides a vivid description of Jesus "in the days of his flesh" (v. 7). Like all of us, Jesus cries out to God in the face of imminent death. On Good Friday, the portrait of Jesus in fervent prayer, appealing to the One who is able to save him from death with loud cries and tears, recalls Jesus in Gethsemane (see Matt. 26:36-46; Mark 14:32-42; Luke 22:40-46). Yet, we can also imagine Jesus' entire passion, especially as the church has viewed it through the lens of Isaiah and the Psalms. Verse 8 reveals that, although Jesus is "Son of God," Jesus so identified with us that he was not exempt from learning that obedience to God can lead to suffering.

Having completed his preparation as our high priest (v. 9), Jesus becomes our source of salvation. Since Jesus is our high priest, we can get a firm grip on our confession and prayerfully approach the throne of grace. We can be confident that Jesus will give us both forgiveness and help.

In Hebrews 10:16-18 the Lord describes the "covenant that I will make with them after those days" (v. 10). The verse quotes Jeremiah 31:33: "But this is the covenant that I will make with the house of Israel after those days, says the LORD: I will put my law within them, and I will write it on their hearts; and I will be their God, and they shall be my people." Adapting Jeremiah 31:34, the author adds God declaring, "I will remember their sins and their lawless deeds no more" (v. 17). In Jesus Christ we are forgiven!

The author then summarizes the implications of Christ's death: since we have forgiveness, we do not need to make offering for sin (v. 18). The positive implications of Christ's death begin in verse 19 with "therefore." Yet the christological grounds for the admonition (vv. 19-21), rather than the admonition itself (vv. 22-25), ought to be stressed in a Good Friday sermon. Since we are forgiven through the blood of Jesus Christ, we have boldness or confidence to enter God's presence. Christ's self-giving love does not leave us outside God's presence, waiting on the ministry of our high priest. Jesus removes all obstacles to our access to God and opens for us a new and living way through his flesh. By referring to Jesus' flesh as "the curtain," the author of Hebrews brings to mind the Synoptic Gospel accounts of the curtain of the Temple being torn in two, from top to bottom, at the moment of Jesus' death (see, for example, Matt. 27:51). The way that Jesus opens through his flesh, therefore, is access to God because of Christ's self-offering, Christ's blood, and Christ's death. The commentary above on 4:4-16 will help us to understand the second christological ground for the admonition: "we have a great priest over the house of God" (v. 21).

Joined to Christ when our hearts were sprinkled clean and our bodies were washed with pure water in baptism, we can approach God with sincerity, integrity, and abundant faith (v. 22). We can "hold fast to the confession of our hope without wavering" (v. 23), even as the final results of Christ's work are not complete and we continue to face enemies. We can pester one another in ways that produce love and good works (v. 24).

Gospel
John 18:1—19:42 (RCL, LFM)

For John, Jesus' death is not a tragedy. We hear no cries of agony and no, "My God! My God! Why have you forsaken me?" There is no earthquake, no darkness over all the face of the earth, no curtain of the Temple torn in two. For John the crucifixion is when Jesus is "lifted up" so that those who believe in him may have eternal life, so that Jesus might reveal himself as the Son of Humanity, so the ruler of this world will be driven out and Jesus will draw all people to himself (cf. John 3:14; 8:28; 12:32-33). It is the "hour" (cf. John 2:4; 7:6, 30; 8:20; 12:23; 13:1; 17:1) of Jesus' "glorification" (cf. John 11:4; 12:23, 28), the occasion of his departure to the One from whom he came. For John the cross is the moment when the One by whom the world was made lofted himself to the place of power and light, which he had in the beginning with God. If we are preaching from John, we need to preach Jesus' passion as God's plan, Christ's victory, and the hour when salvation is complete.

Our reading begins with an encounter between Jesus and his enemies in a garden (18:1-11). The scene shows that Jesus completely controls his fate. While we traditionally think of this episode as the betrayal and arrest, in the hands of the Fourth Evangelist, Jesus dominates the events of the garden and completely controls what occurs there. In an unnamed garden, two opposing forces converge. On the one side stand Jesus and his disciples; on the other, Judas, a cohort of Roman soldiers, and some police from the chief priests and Pharisees, who approach Jesus, carrying lanterns, torches, and weapons (18:1-3). The stage is set for violence.

But Jesus, knowing all that will happen to him, steps forward and asks who they are looking for. When they ask for "Jesus of Nazareth," Jesus bowls his enemies over, knocking them to the ground, when he identifies himself as I AM, *ego eimi*, the name for God. I can imagine Jesus helping his enemies to their feet and asking them a second time whom they are looking for. Jesus identifies himself as I AM a second time, and then states the conditions under which his enemies can arrest him—they must allow the disciples to go free. Jesus fulfills what he had prayed at the final supper (cf. John 17:12). It seems that even Judas is allowed to get away.

In typical fashion, Peter misunderstands and draws his sword in an attempt to change the course of events, even if it takes violence to do so. Jesus tells Peter to put his sword away because Jesus is determined to drink the cup the Father has given him— as opposed to asking the Father to take this cup away, if it is possible. The passion is underway because Jesus, who is completely in control, allows it to begin.

Jesus is then seized by his enemies (v. 12) and led to the house of Annas, the father-in-law of Caiaphas, the high priest (v. 13). In a twist of irony the narrator recalls Caiaphas's words to express the purpose of Jesus' death—to gather the scattered children of God to himself. Peter and another disciple follow Jesus and gain access to the court of the high priest along with Jesus (v. 15). The scene contrasts Jesus' faithfulness with Peter's—and our—cowardice. The maid who keeps the door asks Peter if he is Jesus' disciple. Whereas Jesus responded, "I AM" in the garden, Peter lies and answers, "I am not." Peter then joins the very ones who came to the garden to seize Jesus around a charcoal fire (vv. 17-18).

The scene shifts to Jesus' interrogation by the high priest (vv. 19-24). Jesus' answer to Annas's question about Jesus' disciples and his teaching highlights the devastating effects of Peter's denial. Jesus answers that he spoke openly in the world, taught in synagogues and in the Temple, and said nothing in secret. Knowing all that is to happen, Jesus knows that his time of teaching is over. If people want to know the words of Jesus, they must ask those who heard them and know what Jesus said. The teaching of Jesus now rests in the hands of his disciples. One of the temple police slaps Jesus. In response to being slapped, Jesus says that, if he has spoken blasphemy, bring witnesses to testify to that fact. If Jesus spoke truthfully, he should not have been slapped. Here we see that Jesus is not guilty, a fact to be confirmed in Jesus' trial before Pilate (cf. John 18:38; 19:4, 6). More than not guilty, Jesus speaks the truth, unlike Peter who lied.

The scene returns to Peter, a disciple who has heard Jesus' teaching. Still standing by the fire with those who came to seize Jesus, Peter is asked a second time if he is Jesus' disciple. Peter denies Jesus a second time, saying, "I am not" (v. 25). Then, to make it impossible for Peter to deny his relationship with Jesus, a relative of the man whose ear Peter cut off asks whether he saw Peter in the garden with Jesus. Peter denies a third time. In this instance, Peter not only denies being Jesus' disciple; Peter denies being in the garden, his relationship with Jesus, and all links to the disciples. Peter denies what even Judas acknowledges (cf. John 18:2). "And at that moment the cock crowed," and Jesus' words to Peter come true (John 18:27; cf. 13:38). Jesus knows all that is to befall him; what Jesus said would happen does happen. So, when Jesus tells the high priest, "Ask those who heard what I said to them" (John 18:21), Jesus knows that the time will come when betraying, denying disciples will speak Jesus' teaching. Even more, failing disciples will be able to speak of Jesus' unconditional love for them, and how Jesus made God known in that love.

While Peter denies, Annas sends Jesus bound to Caiaphas, and then they take Jesus from Caiaphas to Pilate's headquarters on the eve of Passover (cf. John 18:24, 28). The religious leaders remain outside the headquarters to maintain their ritual purity as they seek the death of the Lamb of God. Interrogated by Pilate (18:28—19:16), Jesus is revealed to be a king. In actuality, two trials take place. Inside Pilate's headquarters, Jesus stands trial before Pilate; outside Pilate's headquarters, Pilate stands trial before the Judeans.

When they arrive with Jesus, Pilate goes out to the religious leaders (18:29-32) and the trial of Pilate begins. He asks what accusation they bring against Jesus. Rather than state the charges, the religious leaders respond that they have already determined that Jesus is a criminal. Pilate answers that, if the religious leaders found Jesus guilty, they should also punish him. The leaders indicate that Jesus must die at Roman hands. Jesus must be lifted up from the earth in order to draw people to himself, just as he said (cf. John 12:32).

If Jesus is to die a Roman death, he must be a revolutionary. Pilate must go in and question Jesus (18:33-38). "Are you the King of the Jews?" Pilate asks, "What have you done that the chief priests handed you over to me?" Jesus answers that his kingdom is not of this world; it is not political, violent, or revolutionary. Jesus' kingdom rests on making God known in the world, bearing witness to the truth, and gathering those who listen to the truth to his kingdom (cf. John 18:36-37). Though Pilate asks Jesus whether he is a king, Jesus speaks of a "kingdom"—a place where God reigns, a community of those who are of God. Rather than threatening Rome, Jesus subtly invites Pilate to enter this place, but Pilate dismisses Jesus' offer with his question, "What is truth?"

Though Pilate cannot enter Jesus' kingdom of truth, he does not find Jesus to be a political revolutionary. So Pilate goes out to Jesus' accusers and declares Jesus innocent (18:38-40). Pilate has found a legal loophole to release Jesus—the custom of setting someone free at Passover. But Jesus' accusers ask for Barabbas, a violent revolutionary. Not ready to crucify Jesus, Pilate has him flogged (19:1). In the process of torturing Jesus, the soldiers ironically coronate him king. They crown Jesus with thorns and dress him in a purple robe. Then the soldiers mockingly but truthfully hail Jesus as "the King of the Jews" (19:3). Jesus is crowned, clothed, and proclaimed king by Roman soldiers.

Pilate goes out to Jesus' accusers again (19:4-7) and declares Jesus innocent a second time. Jesus comes out under his own power, still in control, dressed as a king. Unlike the Synoptic Gospels, Jesus remains dressed in purple robe and crown. He goes to the cross, his glorification, as a king. Pilate calls Jesus "the man," as in Son of Man. The chief priests and police demand that Pilate crucify Jesus. Presented with their coroneted king, "the innocent Son-of-Man,"[2] Jesus' accusers fulfill his words: "When you have lifted up the Son of Man, then you will realize that I am he" (8:28). They finally bring their charge against Jesus to Pilate: Jesus claims to be the Son of God (19:7). Jesus' accusers cannot or will not see that Jesus is.

Pilate is "more frightened than ever" (19:8) by the possibility that Jesus might be "the Son of God." He enters the headquarters again and asks Jesus the foundational question of John's Gospel: "Where are you from?" (19:9). But Jesus gives no answer to what we understand to be this foundational christological question. In his previous encounter with Pilate, Jesus tried to invite the Roman governor into God's kingdom and was rejected. Now, Jesus remains silent. Pilate threatens Jesus with his political power over life and death, but Jesus is not impressed. Jesus points to the One "from above," who has ultimate power over life and death, and in so doing answers Pilate's question of where Jesus comes from. Could it be that Jesus cannot help himself, but gives even Pilate one more chance to enter Jesus' kingdom of truth?

Though Pilate is still not ready to enter Jesus' kingdom of truth, he does, at least, seek to release Jesus. But now, Jesus' accusers put Pilate on trial. They cry, "If you release this man, you are no friend of the emperor. Everyone who claims to be a king sets himself against the emperor" (19:12). On the Day of Preparation for Passover, Pilate brings Jesus out, declares him king, and expresses surprise that Jesus' accusers would crucify their king. Then, at noon—the precise hour when the Passover lambs are sacrificed—as the chief priests declare themselves to be better friends of the emperor than Pilate (19:15), Pilate capitulates to their demands and hands Jesus over to be crucified, to be lifted up. The chief priests, who insisted that Jesus be put to death for claiming to be the Son of God, have claimed first Barabbas and now the emperor as their king. Yet, on the cross, Jesus, who has been coroneted, will be enthroned and glorified.

They take Jesus to be crucified (19:16-37). Still in control, Jesus carries the cross himself to Golgotha. Jesus is "lifted up" between two others, already gathering people to himself. The author of John does not dwell on the bloody details of crucifixion (19:18), and neither ought the preacher of John's passion narrative. The author of this gospel moves immediately to the inscription on the cross, another instance of Rome's ironic proclamation of Jesus as king, written in the cultured languages of the empire. That Jesus is king is universally proclaimed and can be read by all who pass by, one more indication that Jesus is drawing all people to himself. Even though Jesus' accusers protest, Pilate will not change the inscription. Once again, Pilate unwittingly proclaims the truth.

Roman soldiers divide Jesus' clothes into four parts and cast lots for the seamless inner garment so that it is not torn (19:23-24). The soldiers fulfill Psalm 22:18. The church fathers interpret this garment as the community of disciples who have heard Jesus' teaching and cannot be torn apart, even when they fall into the hands of crucifiers.

Jesus then speaks to his mother and the beloved disciple (19:25-27). "Woman, behold your son! ... Behold your mother!" And from that hour, or because of Jesus' hour, Jesus' mother and the beloved disciple become family. The cross is not there, Jesus does not die, to redeem us one by one. It's not just "me and sweet Jesus." Jesus is suffering to set all poor, ornery creatures into families. Jesus suffers so that we can belong to each other. Jesus gives himself away to us so that we might give ourselves to each other. Jesus unites all people as he gathers us to himself. In the language of John's Gospel, Jesus makes us all someone's mother and someone's son.

Then "Jesus, knowing that all was now finished" (19:28), knowing that his hour had come, knowing that the Father had given everything into his hand, knowing that everything that God had in mind for heaven and earth was brought to completion in this death, cries, "I thirst!" "I want to drink the cup that the Father gave me!" (cf. John 18:11). "I want to see it through!" The scriptural reference is to Psalm 69:21. By water, vinegar, or anything else Jesus will stay awake, because this is his "hour," and he will taste every blessed second of it till it is all ticked away. "I thirst." "I am in control."

When Jesus received the wine, he said, "It is finished" (19:30). "It is complete." There is no cry of failure, no "My God, why?" There is no bedtime prayer, "Father, into thy hands," and no last gasp, "I'm finished, done in, ruined." "It is finished!" In that shout Jesus turns his death into a triumph: "I've won; I've beaten darkness and death at their own game, on their own turf. I've brought the light, the glory, and the life of God for everyone to see, and now I'm off to the Father, taking all humanity with me."

"Then he bowed his head and gave up his spirit" (19:30). Jesus hung his head, handed over *the* (not his) Spirit, and died. Jesus deliberately chose the moment of his death. After Jesus spoke at the Festival of Booths, the narrator of John's gospel reports that now Jesus spoke "about the Spirit, which believers in him were to receive; for as yet there was no Spirit, because Jesus was not yet glorified" (7:39). Now, in the hour of his glorification, Jesus hands over or delivers the Spirit. Whether represented by the seamless community of disciples or the new relationships that Jesus creates, Jesus entrusts the Spirit to the new family gathered at the foot of the cross.

After Jesus dies (19:31-37), Jesus' accusers, who would not enter Pilate's headquarters, so that they would not be ritually defiled and unable to eat the Passover (cf. John 18:28), want the crucified removed from their places of execution as part of preparation for the festival. The legs of the two crucified with Jesus are broken. Since Jesus is already dead, his legs are not. Jesus' side is pierced with a lance, and blood and water flow from his pierced side. Scripture is fulfilled because the Passover Lamb is killed without a bone being broken (cf. Ps. 34:20-21; Exod. 12:10, 46; Num. 9:12). The narrator invokes a witness to these events, whose testimony the narrator vouches for as true, "so that you also may believe" (19:35). The patristic church saw Eucharist and baptism in the blood and water. Having entrusted the Spirit, Jesus now gives the community baptism and Eucharist. Jesus is present as the worshiping community baptizes and celebrates Eucharist.

John's account of Jesus' passion ends where it began—in a garden—as Jesus is buried by friends (19:38-42). Two secret disciples become public. Joseph of Arimathea secures the body of Jesus from Pilate and Nicodemus brings a very large amount of myrrh and aloes. Together, they anoint Jesus' body with the spices and wrap it in linen cloths. Then they place Jesus in a new tomb. Jesus is buried as a king. In the garden that began this passion account, Jesus was surrounded by enemies, betrayed by Judas, and misunderstood by Peter. In this garden, Jesus is surrounded by friends, who publicly witness to their relationship with him by attending to his body in a royal manner.

Notes

1. Fred B. Craddock, "The Letter to the Hebrews," in *The New Interpreter's Bible* (Nashville: Abingdon, 1998), 12:58.
2. Francis J. Moloney and Daniel J. Harrington, *The Gospel of John*, Sacra Pagina (Collegeville, Minn.: Liturgical, 1998), 495.

April 23, 2011
Holy Saturday

Revised Common Lectionary (RCL)
Job 14:1-14 or Lamentations 3:1-9, 19-24
Psalm 31:1-4, 15-16
1 Peter 4:1-8
Matthew 27:57-66 or John 19:38-42

Holy Saturday, as opposed to the Easter Vigil, is a time of waiting between Jesus' death on the cross and his glorious resurrection. The gospel reading presents Jesus lovingly laid to rest by Joseph of Arimathea. First Peter portrays Jesus proclaiming the gospel to the dead, so that they might live in the spirit as God does (4:6). Lamentations seems to put words of an unanswered individual lament into the mouth of Jesus. Like Scripture's teaching on death itself, these lections provide different, even conflicting, perspectives on what happened to Jesus during the time that he lay bound by death in the tomb. Should the preacher have occasion to preach on Holy Saturday, the reason for and purpose of the service, as well as the needs of the faith community, may well determine which portrait of Jesus' time in the tomb provides the basis for the good news.

First Reading
Job 14:1-14

"If mortals die, will they live again?" (v. 14). Our only hope is in God. Using images of the flower and the shadow, Job names the fleeting nature of human life and that human beings are bound by time (vv. 1-2, 5). Human life is so insignificant that it seems strange for God to judge it. Job then imaginatively considers what grounds might give human beings hope for life beyond death. Job finds momentary hope in the tree, which sprouts again after it is cut down. Yet, human beings are not like trees. Human beings are like rivers that dry up and lakes that evaporate; they vanish and do not reappear. They lie down and do not arise again; they will not awaken or be roused from their sleep. Since hope cannot be found in nature, Job turns to God and asks that God hide him until God's wrath is past and, at an appointed time, remember him. In this hope, death or Sheol becomes a place of hopeful waiting (some commentators add hard service) until God brings release. On Holy Saturday, we join Job in hopeful waiting for God to do the impossible and bring new life out of death.

Lamentations 3:1-9, 19-24

On Holy Saturday, we can almost hear Jesus say, "God has made me sit in darkness like the dead of long ago. God has walled me about so that I cannot escape" (3:6-7). Yet, this is surprising since the speaker in Lamentations offers a first-person description of his own horrendous suffering and a litany of God's deliberate destructive actions, specifically against this man himself. The speaker's suffering is intimate, personal, and anguished. If we imagine the speaker to be Jesus, the good news is that Jesus knows what it is to be so isolated, abandoned, and encircled that there is no way out except by being set free. Even more, the speaker knows what it is to suffer at the hands of a God who lashes out, besieges with bitterness, isolates and imprisons, and refuses to hear prayer. This is a God that too many too often encounter and experience. Imprisoned by death in the tomb, the speaker nonetheless dares to hope in this God, expecting this God to save him. This Jesus, who knows personal affliction and experiences God as his enemy, hopes in God's promise, which is sometimes all that we have.

Psalmody
Psalm 31:1-4, 15-16

In the verses from Psalm 31, we hear the speaker, who during Holy Week is Jesus, plead to the Lord for help in his plight. God is the psalmist's rock and refuge. Since the psalmist's times are in God's hand, the psalmist pleads for deliverance from the hand of the assailant. That the psalmist is Jesus is appropriate since the speaker is innocent, unjustly persecuted, and accused. Even more, the psalmist puts his trust in the Lord.

Second Reading
1 Peter 4:1-8

Almost as an answer to Job's question—"If mortals die, will they live again?"—the reading from 1 Peter proclaims the good news that not even the dead are beyond salvation in Jesus Christ. Paraphrasing John's gospel, the dead are among those Jesus draws to himself when he is lifted up from the earth on the cross. According to 1 Peter, the gospel was proclaimed even to the dead, "so that ... they might live in the spirit as God does" (4:6). While scholars may debate what 1 Peter really means by "the dead," the good news on Holy Saturday is the hope that, in Christ, those who have died will receive new life through the gospel. The gospel is Christ's suffering, death, resurrection, and ascension as the motivation for the lives of faithful Christians. As is true for the rest of Holy Week, the emphasis here is on "since ... Christ suffered in the flesh" (v. 1), rather than "arm yourselves … to live" (vv. 1-2). More than suffering physically, Christ suffered in the world dominated by human desire, in order to triumph over human desire, live by the will of God, and battle against the forces of human desire. "The end of all things is near" (v. 7), for the dead as well as the living.

Gospel
Matthew 27:57-66 OR John 19:38-42

Both gospel readings appointed for Holy Saturday narrate Jesus' burial by Joseph of Arimathea. The Matthean account was read on Passion Sunday and the Johannine account on Good Friday. On those days, Jesus' burial is rightly overshadowed by the crucifixion. Or, with hints of Jesus' resurrection included in both accounts, Jesus' burial might be reduced to a necessary stop on the journey from cross to empty tomb. Holy Saturday invites the church to consider the significance of Jesus' burial.

Joseph of Arimathea makes an important declaration by requesting Jesus' body from Pilate, preparing it for burial, and laying it in a new tomb. Jesus had just been condemned and executed as an enemy of both God and the empire. Joseph's gesture might be interpreted as both blasphemy and treason. Joseph buries Jesus honorably, lavishly, royally. In Matthew's account, a "rich" disciple wraps Jesus in a "clean" linen cloth and lays it "in his own new tomb" that is sealed with a "large" stone. In John's account, Jesus is buried as a king. Joseph of Arimathea and Nicodemus anoint Jesus' body with a very large amount of myrrh and aloes, wrap it in linen cloths, and place Jesus in a new tomb. The manner in which Jesus is buried points beyond shame and humiliation to Jesus' glorification and victory on the cross.

April 23/24, 2011
Resurrection of Our Lord
The Great Vigil of Easter

Revised Common Lectionary (RCL)

Genesis 1:1—2:4a
Psalm 136:1-9, 23-36
Genesis 7:1-5, 11-18; 8:6-18; 9:8-13
Psalm 46
Genesis 22:1-18
Psalm 16
Exodus 14:10-31; 15:20-21
Exodus 15:1b-13, 17-18
Isaiah 55:1-11
Isaiah 12:2-6
Proverbs 8:1-8, 19-21; 9:4b-6 or
   Baruch 3:9-15, 32—4:4
Psalm 19
Ezekiel 36:24-28
Psalm 42 and Psalm 43
Ezekiel 37:1-14
Psalm 143
Zephaniah 3:14-20
Psalm 98

Romans 6:3-11
Psalm 114 (not used in *ELW*)
Matthew 28:1-10 or John 20:1-18 (*ELW*)

ELW adds: Jonah 1:1—2:1
   (*Jonah 2:2-3 [4-6] 7-9*)
Isaiah 61:1-4, 9-11
   (*Deuteronomy 32:1-4, 7, 36a, 43a*)
Daniel 3:1-29 (*Song of the Three 35-65*)

Lectionary for Mass (LFM)

Genesis 1:1-2:2 or 1:1, 26-31a
Psalm 104:1-2, 5-6, 10, 12, 13-14, 24, 35 or
Psalm 33:4-5, 6-7, 12-13, 20-22
Genesis 22:1-18 or 22:1-2, 9a, 10-13,
   15-18
Psalm 16:5, 8, 9-10, 11
Exodus 14:15—15:1
Exodus 15:1-2, 3-4, 5-6, 17-18
Isaiah 54:5-14
Psalm 30:2, 4, 5-6, 11-12a, 13b
Isaiah 55:1-11
Isaiah 12:2-3, 4, 5-6
Baruch 3:9-15, 32—4:4
Psalms 19:8, 9, 10, 11
Ezekiel 36:16-17a, 18-28
Psalms 42:3, 5; 43:3, 4 or 51:12-13,
   14-15, 18-19

Romans 6:3-11
Psalm 118:1-2, 16-17, 22-23
Matthew 28:1-10

The Easter Vigil, also called the Paschal Vigil and the Great Vigil of Easter, is held in the hours of darkness between sunset on Holy Saturday and sunrise on Easter Day, most commonly in the evening of Holy Saturday. As a vigil, it is a rather lengthy affair, consisting of four services—Light, Readings, Baptism, and Eucharist. Historically, people (especially adults) are baptized and received into full communion with the church during this service. The Easter Vigil is the church's oldest worship service, with the exception of the Saturday-Sunday vigil that was celebrated in New Testament times, like the one that Paul and his companions observed at Troas (Acts 20:5-8), from which the Easter Vigil is derived. The Easter Vigil is considered to be the first celebration of Easter Day and includes both the first celebration of the eucharist during the Easter season and the first use of the acclamatory word *Alleluia*, a distinctive feature of the liturgy of the Easter season, which has been eliminated since the beginning of Lent.

The Service of Readings includes twelve Old Testament narratives: creation, the flood, the testing of Abraham, Israel's deliverance at the Red Sea, salvation offered freely to all, the wisdom of God, a new heart and a new spirit, the valley of dry bones, the gathering of God's people, the call of Jonah, the Song of Moses, and deliverance from the fiery furnace. Together, these readings span salvation history and declare that God always brings order our of chaos, freedom out of captivity, speech out of silence, light out of darkness, hope out of despair, and life out of death. In this context, the resurrection of Jesus becomes God's ultimate act of salvation, to which the Old Testament points, and not an isolated event. As Jesus said to the disciples after the resurrection:

> "These are my words that I spoke to you while I was still with you—that everything written about me in the law of Moses, the prophets, and the psalms must be fulfilled." Then [Jesus] opened their minds to understand the scriptures, and he said to them, "Thus it is written, that the Messiah is to suffer and to rise from the dead on the third day, and that repentance and forgiveness of sins is to be proclaimed in his name to all nations, beginning from Jerusalem." (Luke 24:44-47)

While the Vigil does not require a sermon, many assemblies appreciate a homily that helps them to both reflect upon their experience of the Vigil and "connect the dots" of this beautiful and complex liturgy. Since congregations frequently do not read all twelve Old Testament readings, the intention behind the readings chosen can provide a direction for the homily. For example, readings might be selected to proclaim that God uses water to call forth life (creation), drown evil and make a new beginning (flood), set captives free (Red Sea), offer salvation to all, and sprinkle us clean. The preacher might then use these themes to celebrate that we are joined to Christ's death and resurrection in baptism (Rom. 6:3-6). Alternatively, readings might be selected to show that God brings hope out of despair: Abraham sacrificing Isaac,

Israel pursued by the Egyptian army, God's promise to gather God's people, mercy shown to Nineveh, a fourth man walking in the fiery furnace, and Mary weeping at the tomb.

The reading from Romans and the gospel account of Christ's resurrection provided in the lectionary make clear that the brief Easter Vigil homily is, first and foremost, the proclamation of Christ's resurrection. This is not the night for exegesis or explanation. At its best, the homily helps the assembly to reflect upon the Great Vigil as an experience of Christ risen and present in their midst. The hermeneutic key for this preaching is that "the life and history of Israel, the saving work of Jesus, and the mission of the early church as these events are proclaimed in Scripture to be connected to one another and to the church's worship … as the single, continuing story of God's saving activity in Jesus Christ."[1] The preacher might bring scriptural stories and allusions; words, images, and actions from the Vigil; and the proclamation of Christ risen into conversation with each other and the assembly using one of the primary motifs of the service—Light, Word, Baptism, and Eucharist. To facilitate the kind of reflection I suggest, I provide brief reflections on most of the readings appointed for the Easter Vigil. Space limitations prohibit commentary on each one. Yet, it is often more beneficial to show than to tell how an Easter Vigil sermon takes shape. I therefore begin by providing an example of an Easter Vigil homily, the theme of which is light.

An Easter Vigil Homily

"When … the earth was a formless void and darkness covered the face of the deep, God said, 'Let there be light.' And there was light'" [Gen. 1:1-3]. On this Most Holy Night, the church declares, "The light of Christ, rising in glory, dispel the darkness of our hearts and minds" [Easter Vigil liturgy]. We lit the paschal candle, symbolizing Christ rising in glory and triumphing over sin and death. We passed the light so that, with hand candles, we received and shared the light of Christ's resurrection. We followed the paschal candle from there to here, singing a lengthy, archaic, Christian chant that proclaims Passover and Israel crossing the Red Sea [Exod. 14:10-31], as foreshadowing Christ's cross and resurrection, his passover from death to new life that rescues us from evil and the gloom of sin, renews us in grace, and restores us to holiness. And we plunged the paschal candle into the stony, watery grave of the baptismal font to suggest that in baptism we share in Christ's death, and in the light and life of Christ's resurrection.

As Paul says, "Do you not know that all of us who have been baptized into Christ Jesus were baptized into his death? Therefore we have been buried with him by baptism into death, so that, just as Christ was raised from the dead by the glory of the Father, so we too might walk in newness of life. For if we have been united with him in a death like his, we will certainly be united with him in a resurrection like his" [Rom. 6:3-5]. We share the light of Christ.

239

And here is light [the preacher points to those baptized at the Vigil]. Here is Christ's own light. Here is the light of resurrection dawn shining into the church, shining into our lives, shining into the world. We see it in these new brothers and sisters. Tonight we heard that "early on the first day of the week, while it was still dark, Mary Magdalene came to the tomb and saw that the stone had been removed from the tomb" [John 20:1]. We heard that Jesus called Mary by name, she saw the risen Lord, and the light of faith dawned in her. Tonight, on the first day of the week, while it was still dark, we went to the stone tomb that is our baptismal font, where our old life is drowned and buried, and we heard Jesus call our new sisters and brothers by name and name them "child of God." We saw Christ truly risen in these, Jesus' own newly born ones. And the light of faith dawned in us anew. We remembered that Jesus named us when our old selves drowned. God gave us a new heart and a new spirit [Ezek. 36:24-28]. And we rose, are rising, will rise with Christ. Best of all, we saw that the glory of Christ's resurrection is not diminished, even when its light is divided and shared [from the Easter Vigil liturgy]. In fact, Christ's light grows brighter as we share it! Salvation, it seems, is intended for all [Isa. 55:1-11].

Renewed in baptism and enlightened by Christ, tonight we celebrate that the light of Christ, rising in glory, always creates order and calls forth life [Gen. 1:1—2:4]. The light of Christ, rising in glory, always brings new beginning and God's covenantal love [Gen. 7:1-5, 11-18; 8:6-18; 9:8-13]. The light of Christ, rising in glory, provides for us in times of terrible testing [Gen. 22:1-18], makes a way to safety where there is none [Exod. 14:10-31], enlivens us when our bones are dry and our life is gone [Ezek. 37:1-14], and delivers us from the furnace of death [Dan. 3:1-29].

Tonight we see the light of Christ shining in our newly baptized sisters and brothers, and we know that it shines in us, in the church, and in the world. Tonight, the light of faith dawns anew. The light of Christ, rising in glory, dispels the darkness of our hearts and minds. For Christ is risen! He is risen indeed!

Old Testament Readings
Creation
Genesis 1:1—2:4a (RCL)
Genesis 1:1—2:2 or 1:1, 26-31a (LFM)

Word, light, and water all figure predominantly in God's work of creation. God says "Let" fourteen times and it is so. God says, "Let there be light" as God's first act of creation. Once the lights are on everything else follows. God places lights in the heavens. God gathers the waters and calls them to bring forth life. God calls the earth to do the same. Then God creates humankind. The light of Christ's resurrection dawns in the darkness of the first day of the week, the darkness of the tomb, the darkness of the church building on this night. God speaks and calls the baptismal waters to bring forth new life in those who the church baptizes. The creation account sets the stories that follow in a cosmic and transcendent context and declares a sovereign God who creates order, light, and life.

The verses from *Psalm 136* (RCL) are a thanksgiving to God for creating the heavens and the earth, and for providing for and redeeming us. In the verses from *Psalm 104* (LFM), we who are God's creatures retell the creation story as praise to our Creator. The verses of *Psalm 33* (LFM alt.) celebrate God's creative word and that the earth is full of the goodness of the Lord.

The Flood
Genesis 7:1-5, 11-18; 8:6-18; 9:8-13 (RCL)

God makes with Noah a covenant between God and all creation and promises security. God changes from destroying a creation that refuses to be faithful and obedient to resolving to stay with, endure, and sustain creation, even though creation grieves God. The rainbow, reminiscent of a warrior's bow but pointed away from the earth and a thing of beauty, serves as a reminder of peace with God. By changing in this way, God makes a new beginning for creation possible. First Peter interprets the flood as a figure of the cleansing waters of baptism and the church has made this connection ever since (1 Pet. 3:20-21). Joined to Christ in the cleansing waters of baptism, God promises to never abandon us. We have peace with God and a new beginning. More than a flood, baptism is our rainbow, a sign that God remembers God's promise.

As a response to God's promise, *Psalm 46* declares that God is on our side and our refuge. Our security rests in God's sovereignty. The earth removed, the mountains carried into the sea, and the oceans roaring and troubled all provide powerful allusions to the flood.

The Testing of Abraham
Genesis 22:1-18 (RCL, LFM)
Genesis 22:22:1-2, 9a, 10-13, 15-18 (LFM ALT.)

"It is God who will provide the lamb for the sacrifice" (v. 8), the central message of this reading, is a declaration of complete trust and confidence that is, at the same time, open-ended. God does indeed provide Abraham with a ram and the world with the Lamb of God who takes away the sin of the world. In fact, the early church read this story typologically; the ordeal of Abraham's son Isaac foreshadowed the ordeal of God's Son Jesus. As Isaac carried the wood on which he was to be offered up to the place of sacrifice, so Jesus carried his own cross.[2] Though we may have difficulty with this interpretative approach, one truth remains. As it was for Abraham, God's way is often unexpected and beyond our understanding. Yet, God is utterly reliable. God alone is the source of life. Christ's resurrection is the unexpected way that God provides new life when and where only death is expected.

As a response to the testing of Abraham, *Psalm 16* is an intense, joyful, loving confession of trust. The psalmist personally and intensely asks God to protect his life.

Israel's Deliverance at the Red Sea
Exodus 14:10-31; 15:20-21 (RCL)
Exodus 14:15—15:1 (LFM)

Inasmuch as the early church understood Jesus as the Paschal Lamb and his death and resurrection in terms of the Passover, it is not surprising that the church came to see Israel passing through the sea as a figure of baptism—our sharing in Christ's death and resurrection. Paul writes, "I do not want you to be unaware, brothers and sisters, that our ancestors were all under the cloud, and all passed through the sea, and all were baptized into Moses in the cloud and in the sea" (1 Cor. 10:1-2). Cyril of Jerusalem teaches that, just as Pharaoh was submerged in the sea, so the devil disappears in the waters of salvation. Ambrose of Milan teaches that those who pass through the waters of the font pass from sin to life, from guilt to grace, from vileness to holiness. They do not die but rise again. The emphasis in this figure of baptism is the enemies that Christ drowns in the waters of baptism.

Exodus 15:1b-13, 17-18 is Miriam's song of victory. God is praised as a majestic and glorious warrior who triumphed over a real, powerful, and threatening enemy. The song then turns to the promises of what God will yet do for the people.

Salvation Offered Freely to All
Isaiah 55:1-11 (RCL, LFM)

God's promises of an everlasting covenant with David are enlarged to include all God's people everywhere. All who hunger and thirst are invited, not to an event but to a relationship of salvation. On this night of vigil, the church understands that all are invited to the relationship of salvation accomplished by Christ and given by God in water, bread, and wine, and God's word of promise—images found in the reading (vv. 1-3). Though God accomplishes this relationship of salvation in ways we could not imagine—since God's ways are not our ways and our thoughts are not God's thoughts (v. 8)—God's word accomplishes what God planned (v. 11).

We respond to God's offer of salvation with a song of thanksgiving. *Isaiah 12:2-6* is an expression of thanksgiving, trust, and praise, followed by the reasons for this response. "With joy you will draw water from the wells of salvation" (v. 3). Then, all are called to give God thanks and praise.

The Wisdom of God
Proverbs 8:1-8, 19-21; 9:4b-6 (RCL)
Baruch 3:9-15, 32—4:4 (RCL ALT., LFM)

Both Proverbs and Baruch proclaim God's wisdom, which on this night we recall is Christ crucified and risen (cf. 1 Cor. 1:21-30). Though Lady Wisdom in Proverbs is an attribute of God and the agent of divine action in creation, rather than being equal with God, the church has long contemplated the parallel between Wisdom and the preincarnate Christ (cf. John 1:1-14; Col. 1:15-18). Wisdom seeks out the unlearned and invites them to study her teaching (8:1-3). The invitation is to eat bread and drink wine (9:5), and walk in the way of insight. At the Easter Vigil, we cannot help but think of the Eucharist, where the risen Christ nourishes and teaches us the way of new life.

Baruch's exhortation to hear the commandments and wisdom echoes Lady Wisdom's invitation to the people to learn from her (cf. Prov. 8:1-5). Here, wisdom is found in the commandments. Since God's people have not walked in God's way, they are in the land of their enemies, defiled with the dead, and among those bound for Hades. Yet, human beings cannot find wisdom themselves; only the Creator can. And God gives wisdom in the promise of light (vv. 14, 33)—on this night the risen Christ—that brings life, strength, and peace in God.

Psalm 19 proclaims the incomparable values of the law of the Lord (vv. 7-10). The Lord's teaching revives the soul. The statutes of the Lord rejoice the heart. The commandment of the Lord gives light to the eyes.

A New Heart and a New Spirit
Ezekiel 36:24-28 (RCL)
Ezekiel 36:16-17a, 18-28 (LFM)

In this oracle, the power and promise of Christ's resurrection reaches into our very being. God taking God's people from the nations and gathering them from the nations recalls Jesus drawing all people to himself from the cross (cf. John 12:32). God will remove our heart of stone and give us a new heart, a heart made of flesh. God will give us a new spirit, God's own spirit. That God "will sprinkle clean water upon you, and you shall be clean from all your uncleannesses, and from all your idols I will cleanse you" (36:25) alludes to baptism, by which God raises us to new life with Christ. Cleansed and transformed, we will obey God and live in the land that I "gave to your ancestors" (v. 28)—the promised land, resurrection. God will be our God and we will be God's people.

In response to God's promise of a new heart and a new spirit in Christ, the church uses *Psalms 42 and 43* to profess its thirst for the living God, as a deer longs for flowing streams, and ask God to bring it to God's holy hill and sanctuary.

The Valley of the Dry Bones
Ezekiel 37:1-14 (RCL)

Matthew describes signs, including the resurrection of the saints in Jerusalem, which point to the significance of Jesus' death (27:52-53). Matthew's description is based on Ezekiel 37:1-14—Ezekiel's vision of the dry bones returning to life (see the commentary on the gospel for Palm/Passion Sunday, above). It includes an earthquake, the opening of graves, and the saints being raised and coming out of their graves. By using this passage, Matthew shows that Jesus' death marks a turning point in God's relationship with humanity because it makes the resurrection of human beings possible. The tombs of the saints are opened and they are raised. After

Jesus' resurrection, the raised saints come out of their tombs and appear to many in Jerusalem. According to Ezekiel's vision, the resurrection of the dead signifies the restoration of Israel. Even more, the revived people will know and acknowledge God.

In response to Ezekiel's vision, the people sing, "Revive me, O LORD, for your name's sake" (*Psalm 143*, my trans.). While the NRSV translates the requests "preserve," the word revive, together with references to the ground, those long dead, and those who go down to the pit (vv. 3, 7), connect this psalm to Ezekiel's vision.

The Gathering of God's People
Zephaniah 3:14-20 (RCL)

Jerusalem is called to sing, shout, rejoice, and exult because its sentence of destruction is lifted and none other than God, the Sovereign of Israel, is in its midst. God then speaks, promising to remove disaster, deal with oppressors, change shame into praise, and bring the people home. We can hear this oracle proclaiming that, in Christ, God lifts our death sentence and brings us home to God's very presence.

Psalm 98 is likewise a call to sing and to shout because the Lord has made Israel victorious before all the ends of the earth and will judge the world with righteousness and the people with equity.

The Call of Jonah
Jonah 1:1—2:1 (ELW)

"But the LORD provided a large fish to swallow up Jonah; and Jonah was in the belly of the fish three days and three nights" (1:17). Augustine compares Jonah to Christ and observes that, as Jonah passed from the ship to the belly of the fish, so Christ passed from the cross to the tomb, or into the abyss of death. As Jonah suffered this for the sake of those who were endangered by the storm, so Christ suffered for the sake of those who are tossed on the waves of this world.[2] The resurrection is anticipated as Jonah was in the belly of the fish and Jesus lay in the tomb for three days.

The response to this reading, *Jonah 2:1-3 (4-6) 7-9*, can be heard as the prayer of Jonah, Jesus, and us.

An Everlasting Covenant
Isaiah 61:1-4, 9-11 (ELW)

"The spirit of the Lord GOD is upon me, because the LORD has anointed me ..." (61:1). Christians cannot hear these words without thinking of Jesus' sermon at the synagogue in Nazareth (cf. Luke 4:16-19). As Isaiah makes clear, God works through a human agent who will undertake and enact God's intentions. By God's spirit and anointing, God authorizes this human agent to carry out God's work of restoration and transformation. As the result of this one's ministry, the community will rebuild, repair, and raise up (v. 4). On this night, being "clothed ... with the garments of salvation" and "covered ... with the robe of righteousness" (v. 10) are baptismal allusions.

Deuteronomy 32:1-4, 7, 36a, 43a is from the Song of Moses. As a congregational response, it proclaims that the Lord will give God's people justice.

Deliverance from the Fiery Furnace
Daniel 3:1-29 (ELW)

This story is best read in ways that reflect its humor and delight, which are evident in the use of redundancy and repetition, as well as details such as the orchestra giving the signal for obedience by court flunkies and the exaggerated heat of the furnace. The faithfulness of God's servants is being tested, as well as God's ability to save those who put their trust in God. Nebuchadnezzar asks, "Who is the god that will deliver you out of my hands?" (v. 15). The answer is clear: God is able to deliver those who put their trust in God. Some see in this story allusions to Christ's resurrection: the furnace is a kind of tomb; the fourth man has the appearance of a god (angel), and God's faithful servants return from sure death to life. Resurrection may be especially appropriate if we understand Jesus' resurrection as God reversing the imperial authority's attempt to impose its will on God's servant. Others see in this story the vindication of martyrs before the whole world. Whatever else we see, that God can and will save God's servants from death is obvious.

Epistle Reading
Romans 6:3-11 (RCL, ELW)

On this night, the reading from Romans functions as an explanation of baptism as our participation in Christ's death and resurrection. In baptism we share in Christ's death; therefore, sin no longer has absolute control over us because Christ conquered sin by dying. Christ also triumphed over death by rising. In baptism, we also triumph over death by rising with Christ. Notice that, while our dying is past tense, our rising is future tense. We will be raised as part of the final resurrection. Until then, the life we have is because of Christ. We are "alive to God in Christ Jesus" (v. 11). In Christ we are destined for resurrection.

Psalmody
Psalm 114 (RCL)
Psalm 118:1-2, 16-17, 22-23 (LFM)

Psalm 114 recalls God delivering Israel from slavery in Egypt and calls the whole earth to tremble at God's presence. It unites story and presence, which is what the church has been about in this Service of Readings. Psalm 118 is a call to give thanks for God's enduring mercy, by which the right hand of the Lord has acted so that we will not die. The church understands the rejected stone becoming the chef cornerstone (v. 22) as an allusion to Christ.

Gospel

Matthew 28:1-10 (RCL, LFM)

Matthew's account of the empty tomb is the most exciting and unambiguous. This is truly the main event that we have waited for, alluded to, and hinted at all evening. The preacher might retell the story in a way that highlights the big, bold, and unambiguous strokes with which Matthew paints his portrait of Jesus' resurrection. The preacher might recall mighty events of God painted with big, bold strokes in the readings and the big, bold strokes with which the congregation kept the Great Vigil, particularly baptism.

Mary Magdalene and the other Mary, the two women who witnessed Jesus die and saw him buried (Matt. 27:56, 61), discover the empty tomb. The earthquake recalls the valley of dry bones and the resurrection of the saints, and underscores Jesus' resurrection as an apocalyptic event. To drive the point home, an angel, whose appearance is like lightning and clothes are white as snow, descends from heaven, rolls away the stone, tells the women that Jesus has been raised, invites them to see the place where Jesus lay, and instructs them to go and tell the disciples that Jesus is risen and where they can find him—in Galilee, as Jesus promised (Matt. 26:32). The angel tells the women—and the church—how to interpret the empty tomb and recalls that Jesus had predicted this (Matt. 16:21-23; 17:22-23; 20:18-19).

Twice the angel tells the women, "he has been raised" (vv. 6-7). The angel does not say that Jesus has risen. The passive voice indicates that the One whom Jesus called Father acts: God raised Jesus up. The same God who created the universe, set a bow in the clouds, provided Abraham with a ram, brought Israel through the sea, and saved three servants from a fiery furnace raised Jesus from the dead. God shows eschatological power in raising Jesus. The reign of God is among us.

The women leave the tomb quickly and, filled with great joy, run to tell the disciples. If this is not amazing enough, they run into Jesus. Recognizing Jesus as the risen Christ, the women worship him. Then Jesus sends them off to Galilee, where they will see him again. And so will we! As we make our way to font and table, we—like the women—approach, take hold of, and worship the risen Christ.

John 20:1-18 (ELW)

In John's account of the resurrection, the empty tomb is a minor player. It provides no message, only a mystery. Mary Magdalene, who lacks any official role in the early church but keeps surfacing at critical moments, is the first one up on "the first day of the week." She makes her way to the tomb, prepared to express her love and devotion to dead Jesus. It is then that she comes upon the mystery—the stone has been removed from the tomb.

Mary doesn't know what to make of it. She is dismayed. Jesus isn't there. He's been misplaced, probably dishonored. And so Mary runs, finds Simon Peter and the other disciple, the one whom Jesus loved, and tells them, "They've taken the Lord out of the tomb, and we don't know where they've laid him." Mary makes no mention of God acting or of the possibility of resurrection.

Peter and the beloved disciple run back. They see the empty tomb. They even see the linen cloths and the cloth that had been on Jesus' head. It's been carefully folded and laid in a place by itself. Sounds a bit like someone climbing out of a sleeping bag, not like a grave robbery. But Peter and Mary see only emptiness and absence. But somehow, "the other disciple, the one whom Jesus loved," "saw and believed." That the beloved disciple believed but Peter and Mary didn't understand suggests that Easter is not about collecting clues or getting enough evidence. Resurrection is something more than seeing an empty tomb.

So what do we tell our hearers? How about that Easter isn't about Jesus? After all, John's story of Jesus came to a wonderful conclusion on the cross, where Jesus perfected the task given to him by the Father. "It is complete," Jesus said. Jesus was exulted and the glory of God was revealed not in an empty tomb but on the cross. So if Easter isn't about an empty tomb, or even about Jesus, what is Easter about?

Easter is about us. Easter is the story of disciples like us, who languish in misunderstanding and doubt. These are disciples who betray Jesus, resort to violence, stand with Jesus' enemies, and deny that they know him. These are disciples who fail or refuse to grasp that God's glory is to be found on the cross. These disciples were there on that first Easter. They are with us even in us as we celebrate Easter. Left to ourselves, Mary and Peter, and you and I, will not survive in the hostile world. And so the God of Jesus does something to look after us and make us holy. God raises Jesus from the dead.

The other disciple, the one who represents us, Christians who live not by evidence but by the faith witness of the church, is the first one to come to faith in the resurrection. The beloved disciple was able to believe far beyond what Mary and Peter saw. Where they saw only emptiness, the beloved disciple saw destruction of death and believed in new life. In the face of dismay, alienation, and defeat, and without any concrete evidence, faith is born.

We could spend a lot of time considering why the beloved disciple believed and Peter and Mary did not. Truth be told, that's simply the way it is. Some disciples look into tombs of ambiguity and see God overcoming death. Some of us cannot penetrate the tomb or make sense of the grave cloths. For us there is more. We are told that the disciples did not yet understand the Scripture. But we have the Scripture. We know the story—from creation to Noah to exodus to empty tomb. Jesus must rise from the dead.

For still other disciples, even the story isn't enough. Mary Magdalene cannot see Jesus through her tears. And Jesus' question, "Why are you weeping?," is meant to make a point and not to provide a model of pastoral care. Jesus knew all along that he was supposed to die, and that he must rise. There is no reason to weep, especially not now. But some disciples just cannot see that. Mary sees Jesus, but not really. But when

Jesus calls Mary by name, everything changes. Being called by name makes all the difference. More than not crying, Mary "turns" (v. 16) from confusion to clarity, from fear to faith, from death to life. Mary can rejoice. Mary can be sent. Mary becomes an apostle. She can say, "I have seen the Lord" (v. 18).

In the waters of baptism Jesus, arisen, calls us by name and we turn from confusion to clarity, from fear to faith, from death to life. We rejoice and Jesus sends us to announce what we have seen—our risen Lord. As we gather as church, we hear the story. Jesus must rise from the dead. Faith comes only when we encounter the risen Lord, which we did this night of vigil. An encounter with the risen Lord is what we have to offer.

Easter is about God giving us disciples what we need—Jesus, arisen from the dead. So that, when the world is so hostile that we fail or refuse to grasp that God's glory is found on a cross, when the world is so hostile that we betray Jesus, resort to violence, stand with Jesus' enemies, and deny that we know him, still we can look into tombs and look upon grave cloths and trust that God is vanquishing the power of death, bringing new life, and drawing all people—all creation—to himself.

Notes

1. Craig A. Satterlee and Lester Ruth, *Creative Preaching on the Sacraments* (Nashville: Discipleship Resources, 2001), 17.
2. Augustine, *Epistola* 102, *Epistulae* 31-123, trans. A. Goldbacher, *Corpus Scriptorum Ecclesiasticorum Latinorum* 34, no. 2 (Vindobonae: F. Tempsky, 1898), 570-78; Augustine, *City of God* 18:30, trans. Marcus Dodd (Edinburgh: T&T Clark, 1871), 2:250.